T5-AGC-613

Printed and bound in Canada by Art Bookbindery
www.artbookbindery.com

ISBN 978-0-9794458-0-4

GET INTO THE STORY VOLUME II

ACKNOWLEDGEMENTS

I would like to thank the pastoral staff members of Covenant Fellowship Church for their commitment to our families by releasing me for weeks and weeks to write both the God's Story curriculum and this companion devotional. They graciously took up the work of pastoral care when I was away writing. Also, the publishing of this devotional simply would not be possible if not for the faithful service of all those who participated in the editing and production of the manuscript. I am indebted to Bill Patton for his careful theological review, and Sarajane Orlando and Janel Feldman for their help in reading and correcting each week's devotional. I would also like to thank Charity Campbell for her administrative and formatting skills, Doug Nottage for the graphics, and Paul Schwarz for reviewing the completed draft in whole.

DEDICATION

I would like to dedicate this volume to my loving wife, Lois, and my six children — Emma, Nathan, Martha, Noah, Anna, and Amelia. They graciously did without their husband and father over the many weeks I spent away writing.

INTRODUCTION

Dear Parent,

Welcome to *Get Into the Story*. I hope this series of New Testament family devotions serves you in caring for your children. As a father of six, I found I needed help in leading my children through the Bible. And as a pastor responsible to oversee our churches ministry to children, I wanted to help all the parents in our church stay consistent in their family devotions. *Get Into the Story* is the result of trying to meet those desires. It was created to work in conjunction with our church's God's Story Sunday-school curriculum. By using this family devotional outline along with the God's Story curriculum, you will be reviewing the same lesson your child (or children) heard on Sunday morning. Like God's Story, the *Get Into the Story* program follows the Bible from Genesis to Revelation, with a special emphasis on God's redemptive plan for His people.

Fifteen minutes a day is all you need. Try gathering the family together in the morning or just after you have finished your evening meal. With *Get Into the Story*, we have sought to make it easy for you to lead your family through the Bible. Simply read the assigned passage with them, read the discussion notes, and ask your family the questions provided. There are five devotions for each week, so if you miss a day you can still stay on track.

Every Monday, Tuesday, and Thursday you will cover a discussion point from the main passage. On Wednesdays, to keep every Scripture passage connected to God's story of redemption, you will explore "Where Is the Gospel?" Finally, each Friday you will journey on "The Road to Emmaus." Soon after His resurrection, while on the road to Emmaus, Jesus showed two disciples how the Psalms and Prophets pointed to Himself and all that had recently taken place. Following in their footsteps, you will investigate a passage from the Psalms or Prophets to discover how it points to our Savior.

Bible study as a family has never been easier. So "Get Into the Story" with your family — starting today! There are few labors that bring a parent a greater sense of the joy than leading your family in a faithful daily Bible study. May the Lord reward your labors with a harvest of good fruit in the lives of your children.

Marty Machowski

THE BIRTH OF JESUS FORETOLD

God announced the coming of His Son in fulfillment of the Prophets.

MONDAY

THE STORY: LUKE 1:1-38

Luke begins his Gospel account by explaining to us the careful, orderly way he researched and retold the story of Jesus. After a short introduction, Luke tells us of the angle Gabriel who announced the coming of John the Baptist and Jesus Christ the Messiah. Two women, Elizabeth and Mary, are to miraculously conceive. Elizabeth was barren, much like Sarah (Abraham's wife) was barren. Once again God promised to fill a barren womb with life, demonstrating His magnificent power to accomplish His plan. Mary's pregnancy was to be even more amazing. God Himself would cause Mary, a virgin, to conceive a child by the Holy Spirit, before she was even married! Her son, Jesus, would fulfill the Old Testament prophecy of an everlasting king on David's throne. The angel further announced that the child would be called "holy – the Son of God."

TALK ABOUT IT:

How was the announcement of Jesus' coming an answer to God's promise to Abraham? (God promised Abraham that all nations would be blessed through his descendants. We learn in Matthew 1:1, 2 that Jesus was descended from Abraham. All the nations will be blessed through Jesus, who is bringing salvation.)

Why did Zechariah lose his voice? (Zechariah lost his voice because he didn't believe the angel's words to him.)

PRAY:
Thank God for keeping His promise to send an eternal king to be on the throne forever. Ask God to help you believe and trust in God's amazing plan.

TUESDAY

THE STORY: LUKE 1:39-45
Mary sang a song of praise. After the angel told Mary about God's plan, Mary went with haste to see Elizabeth. Upon Mary's arrival, Elizabeth's baby jumped inside her. Elizabeth was filled with the Holy Spirit and then said some amazing things. She said that Mary's baby would be her Lord! She knew that Mary had believed the angel Gabriel's words and had faith that what he said would come to pass.

TALK ABOUT IT:
What was amazing about Elizabeth's greeting? (She knew what happened to Mary even though Mary didn't tell her!)

What did Elizabeth's baby do when she heard Mary had arrived? (Elizabeth's baby, the infant John the Baptist, leaped inside of her.)

Why should we be joyful about the comming of Jesus? (The baby Jesus grew up to live a perfect life and then die on the cross to take our sins away.)

PRAY:

Ask God to help each person in your family rejoice over the comming of our Savior.

WEDNESDAY
WHERE IS THE GOSPEL?

THE STORY: LUKE 1:46-55

When Mary saw Elizabeth with child, she realized that what the angel Gabriel told her was true. Then she heard Elizabeth's prophetic blessing. Filled with wonder and joy, she worshipped God with a song.

Mary was a sinner just like us. She needed a Savior and she knew that with the birth of the baby inside of her, God's promise would be fulfilled. She knew that God's plan of salvation would somehow be about her son. Her words are a song of praise to God for His incredible mercy promised to Abraham and his descendants. The fulfillment of God's promise to Abraham was going to come through Jesus. But Mary could not have understood that her son would be sacrificed on the cross in order to fulfill that promise. It is through Jesus that people from every nation would be blessed.

The Gospel is also found in Zechariah's prophecy when he talks about God redeeming His people (Luke 1:68) and how Jesus will give knowledge of God's salvation (Luke 1:71-77).

TALK ABOUT IT :

Why did Mary call God her Savior? (Mary called God her Savior because she knew that she was a sinner and that only God could save her from her sin.)

Do we also need a Savior? Why? (Yes, we also need a Savior. Our sin separates us from God. As sinners we can never save ourselves. It is only by God's mercy in sending Jesus that we can be saved.)

PRAY:

Ask the children what we would want to say if we were going to sing a song of praise to God for Jesus. Take their answers and help them form their words into a prayer. If you know a worship chorus that contains some of what they suggest, sing it with them.

THURSDAY

THE STORY: LUKE 1:57-80

John the Baptist is born. Just as the angel of the Lord prophesied, Elizabeth gave birth to a son. The people were surprised when Elizabeth decided to call him John, because there was no one with that name in their family. When Zechariah confirmed that the baby should be called John, he demonstrated faith in God's plan and he immediately regained his speech. The Holy Spirit filled Zechariah, and he prophesied that God had raised up a "horn of salvation." This was a reference to Jesus.

TALK ABOUT IT:

What do we learn about Jesus from this prophetic word? (We learn that through Him, God would redeem His people. We also learn that Jesus will be a "horn of salvation" who saves us from our enemies and brings us peace. Jesus would come as promised by the prophets and make Israel able to serve God in righteousness.)

What does having all this detail in Zechariah's prophecy tell us about God? (God is a sovereign God in control of all details. He is powerfully bringing His plan of salvation to pass.)

PRAY:

Thank God for being all-powerful. Thank Him that He is able to bring salvation to all of us. Praise God that nothing can stop His awesome plan!

FRIDAY
ON THE ROAD TO EMMAUS

THE STORY: ISAIAH 4:2,3

Jesus is the righteous branch spoken of in Isaiah's prophecy. His death on the cross and His righteous life enable us to live in righteousness and holiness. When Jesus, the Branch of the Lord, returns again, He will defeat sin and death forever. Jeremiah 23:5, 6 connects the Branch of the Lord with Jesus by using the name "the Lord our Righteousness."

TALK ABOUT IT:

What verse of Zechariah's prophecy (Luke 2) speaks of the holiness and righteousness we will demonstrate as a result of God's salvation? (Luke 2:75 speaks of us serving Jesus in righteousness and holiness all our days. This righteous living is not just a single act, but a completely changed life.)

Until Jesus comes again and sin is taken away, what can we do when we sin? (We can confess our sin to God and to others and ask Jesus to forgive us of our sin.)

PRAY:

Have your children share ways in which they see sin in their lives, and then have each one pray and ask God to forgive them and help them live for God until He returns.

THE BIRTH OF JESUS

In the fullness of time God sent forth His Son.

MONDAY

THE STORY: LUKE 2:1-7 & MATTHEW 2:1-6

Mary and Joseph Return to Bethlehem. God ordained the census to bring Mary to Bethlehem, where the Savior was to be born. At first glance it may appear to happen by chance. But that is not the case. Matthew records the words of Micah 5:2: "But you, O Bethlehem Ephrathah, who are too little to be among the clans of Judah, from you shall come forth for me one who is to be ruler in Israel, whose origin is from of old from ancient days." Paul tells us that Jesus was born at just the exact moment according to a predetermined plan. In Galatians 4:4 we read, "When the fullness of time had come, God sent forth His Son, born of a woman, born under the law."

TALK ABOUT IT:

How do we know that Jesus came according to God's plan? (Paul tells us in Galatians 4:4 that God sent forth His Son when the fullness of time had come. That is just another way to say "according to His plan." Just like we might set an alarm clock and plan to get up at a certain time, God set a time to send His Son Jesus. When God's planned time came, Jesus was born.)

How should God's ability to plan all things encourage us? (Not only was Jesus born at the perfect time, so were we! Read Acts 17:26. We are all a part of God's perfect plan!)

PRAY:

Thank God for His wonderful plan, for making us all a part of it, and for allowing us to know and believe the Gospel.

TUESDAY

THE STORY: LUKE 2:8-21

The angels announced the birth of Jesus to the shepherds. And there were a lot of shepherds in Israel. Not only did the people use the animals for food and clothing, they also used them as sacrifices. It is interesting to note that the perfect sacrifice, Jesus the Lamb of God, would be first publicly announced to shepherds!

After the heavenly concert from the angels, the shepherds traveled to see the baby Jesus. When they arrived to see Jesus, the shepherds told those gathered there about what they had seen and heard. Mary treasured these things in her heart. Though she knew from her encounter with the angel Gabriel that this was going to be a special birth, Mary didn't know exactly how it would unfold. How wonderfully blessed she must have felt as the shepherds recounted their story!

TALK ABOUT IT

Who did the angels say God's peace would come to? (The angels proclaimed peace to those with whom God is pleased.)

Is it possible for us to earn God's favor in order to find His peace? Can we force God to like us? (No. We cannot earn God's favor. No matter how hard we try, we could never please God by our works. This is because we are sinful. That is why Jesus had to be born. Jesus took the penalty for our sin on the cross. When God saves us and gives us peace, He does so because of Jesus' work, not ours. Here the angels were praising God for His plan to bring peace to those He loves through His Son Jesus.)

PRAY:

Pray that God would open your eyes to the gospel, bringing His peace to your heart and life through Jesus.

WEDNESDAY
WHERE IS THE GOSPEL?

THE STORY: LUKE 2:11-14

If a person is drowning in a pool, a lifeguard who rescues the person would be their savior. A lifeguard would be savior a with lower case "s." Jesus is Savior with an upper-case "S" because He is God and is the Savior of the world. All other saving from danger is a reflection of God's image in man.

Though Jesus was King, He did not come in full display of His glory, might and power. Instead he came in humility that He might become a servant of all, dying on the cross for our sins. This humility was evident from His birth, where He was born in a stable and placed in a manger. Jesus gave up His glory to come to earth because He loved us. Later He would die for our sins so we could be saved from the penalty of sin. Isn't it amazing that God Himself came as a baby?

TALK ABOUT IT:

What happened in the heavens after one angel announced the coming of Jesus? (A great many angels suddenly appeared and began to praise God.)

How should we be like the angels? (Once we understand why God sent Jesus, and how Jesus came in humility to save us, we should show our gratitude for God's saving plan by proclaiming his glory in worship and praise. God is worthy of our praise!)

PRAY:
Pray that God would place the truth of His Word richly in our hearts and pray that He would place a love for worshipping Him there as well.

THURSDAY

THE STORY: MATTHEW 2:7-21
God's plan is unstoppable. It was not long after Jesus was born that King Herod sought to destroy Him. Herod did not want another king. So he tried to discover where Jesus was so that he could kill the baby king. God's plan to bring a Savior to His people would not be stopped even by a powerful king. God warned the wise men to travel home by a different route, warning Joseph to take his family to Egypt until Herod was dead.

Herod was so determined to destroy Jesus that he had all the baby boys ages 2 and under killed. After a time, Herod died, and then an angel directed Joseph to bring Jesus back to Israel. In Hosea 11:1, the prophet foretold this: "Out of Egypt I called my son..." God was not surprised by Herod's threats. For even those threats were a part of God's predetermined, invincible plan.

TALK ABOUT IT:
Can anyone stop God's plan? (No, nobody can stop or thwart the plan of God.) Why do you think Matthew 2:15 cited Hosea's prophecy? (Matthew tells us that these events happened on purpose according to God's plan. One might be tempted to wonder if God was really in control when reading about Herod's threats. Instead - we see that God is greater than any threat to His plan. God always knew what would happen and worked everything as part of His plan.)

PRAY:
Thank God that He is powerful and can work all things together for our good.

FRIDAY
ON THE ROAD TO EMMAUS

THE STORY: HOSEA 11:1,2

Sometimes when we read an Old Testament passage, we would not see its connection to Jesus if it were not for the Bible itself making the connection. Hosea 11:1, 2 is such a passage. Matthew applies Hosea as a typological picture of Jesus. Just as Israel went down to Egpyt, so did baby Jesus. And as Israel was led by God out of Egypt, so was Jesus. God called Jesus out of Egypt, and Jesus followed His Heavenly Father perfectly (see John 5:19).

TALK ABOUT IT:

When did God call Israel out of Egypt? (God used Moses to bring Israel out of the slavery of Egypt.)

What slavery did Jesus conquer and leave behind? (Jesus was not a slave, but conquered sin by living a perfect life and taking our punishment for sin by His death on the cross. Jesus extends His righteousness to us so that we can be free from the bondage and slavery of sin.)

PRAY:

Thank Jesus for conquering sin and releasing us from the control of sin so that we might be free to worship and obey God.

JESUS PRESENTED IN THE TEMPLE

From the time of His dedication at the temple,
Jesus increased in favor with God and man.

MONDAY

THE STORY: LUKE 2:22-24

Jesus fulfilled the law. From the very beginning of His life, Jesus fulfilled the law.
Mary and Joseph brought Jesus to be circumcised according to the everlasting
covenant God made with Abraham (see Genesis 17:12). In Deuteronomy 16:6
God tells the people they must celebrate the Passover in Jerusalem (the place
He chose as a dwelling for his Name). Many Jews could not travel there due to
distance, but those who were able to honor God's command traveled in caravans
for safety and companionship. Jesus kept the law perfectly, including these
annual visits to Jerusalem. Luke 2:41 confirms that Mary and Joseph made this
pilgrimage every year.

TALK ABOUT IT:

Why was it important for Jesus to fulfill the Law? (Jesus stood in our place and
perfectly fulfilled the Law for us. The Law was set up as the measuring rod against
which sinners could see their sinfulness and transgressions before God. Because of

sin in our hearts, it is impossible for any of us to keep the Law. We are all law-breakers and therefore we should all receive the penalty of death. But Jesus, as both Son of God and Son of man, did what no other man could do - He kept the Law fully and completely!)

How do you break God's law? (Review the commandments in Exodus 20 if the children are struggling to figure out which ways they have broken God's law.)

PRAY:

Thank God for Jesus, who kept all of the Law. Thank Him for extending His salvation to you.

TUESDAY

THE STORY: LUKE 2:36-40

Jesus had a welcome party. Even though Jesus humbly came to earth, was born in a stable and laid in a manger, God made sure there was praise. When Christ was born, God brought angels to sing, and wise men and shepherds to worship. And God made sure there was praise when Jesus came to the temple to be dedicated. Anna, a devout woman, worshipped and prayed day and night in the temple waiting for Israel's Redeemer. As a prophetess, Anna recognized that Jesus was that Redeemer. She worshipped God and explained the significance of Jesus to those who were also waiting for redemption.

TALK ABOUT IT:

Why is worship the proper way to respond to Jesus? (In Exodus 20:3-6, God commanded that we worship Him alone. Since Jesus is God, it is right and proper that He should be worshipped.)

How do we worship Jesus today? (We worship Jesus with our praise and by living for His glory.)

PRAY:
Ask God to help you worship Him with both your words and actions.

WEDNESDAY
WHERE IS THE GOSPEL?

THE STORY: LUKE 2:29-35
Simeon's prayer is filled with the gospel. When Simeon looked upon Jesus he saw God's salvation. This salvation would not just be for the Jews but for the Gentiles as well. Simeon also revealed that there would be grief for Mary as her soul would be pierced by a sword. Mary would indeed suffer as she watched Jesus crucified.

TALK ABOUT IT:
Why is the mention of Gentiles significant? (God's promise to Abraham was that through him all the nations of the earth would be blessed. Now, through Jesus, both Jew and Gentile can be saved.)

What do we know that Simeon also knew? (We can know that Jesus is the Savior. Simeon knew that Jesus was the Savior because the Holy Spirit revealed it to him. Many in Simeon's day did not know who Jesus was. Because we have the written Word of God, which clearly tells us who Jesus is, we know that Simeon was right!)

PRAY:
Pray that the Holy Spirit would help you see and believe in Jesus the Savior, like Simeon did.

THURSDAY

THE STORY: LUKE 2:41-52

Jesus was drawn to the temple. It was common for families to travel in caravans for fellowship and protection. It is likely that Mary and Joseph had other younger children by this time. At age 12, Jesus was close to manhood, and his parents assumed he was with another family in their caravan. It took Mary and Joseph three days to find Jesus. All along, Jesus was at the temple sitting among the teachers and asking questions. When asked about His whereabouts, Jesus simply said, "Did you not know that I must be in My Father's house?" Already, Jesus was aware of His calling. He amazed those who met Him, and He grew in favor with God and men.

TALK ABOUT IT

Was Mary angry with Jesus? (Mary was certainly upset about losing her child. If she was angry, she didn't hold onto her anger. Instead, Luke tells us that she "treasured up all these things in her heart." At some point Mary would transition from training Jesus to being trained by Him. Her son would become her Savior.)

Why did Jesus call the temple His Father's house? (The temple was the place where God's presence dwelt. It was God's house. Since God was Jesus' Father, the temple was His Father's house on earth. Now, God dwells in the hearts of believers by His Spirit.)

PRAY

Pray that God would make His home in the heart of every member of your family.

FRIDAY
ON THE ROAD TO EMMAUS

THE STORY: PSALM 98:1-9

Christ is the one who will judge the world in righteousness. It is through Jesus that God made His salvation and righteousness known to the nations. One prime example of this is Simeon's reaction when he said, "For my eyes have seen your salvation." Simeon was excited to see the Savior!

TALK ABOUT IT

Why can we assume the psalmist is referring to Jesus when we read about the salvation of the Lord? (There is no salvation from God apart from the cross. Whether Israel is being saved from an immediate enemy or from sin, all salvation is ultimately found in the work of Jesus Christ.)

How should we respond to God's salvation? What does the Psalmist suggest? (We should worship the Lord with shouts of joy, clap our hands, sing, and make music with all types of instruments.)

PRAY

Pray that God would help you see the glory of His salvation and that He would give you the same kind of joy the Psalmist and Simeon knew.

THE MINISTRY OF JOHN THE BAPTIST

John announced the ministry of Jesus with a call to repent.

MONDAY

THE STORY: MATTHEW 3:1-3

Isaiah foretold John's ministry. In Isaiah 40:3 we read, "A voice cries in the wilderness, prepare the way of the Lord." Isaiah was speaking of a day when a voice would cry out in the wilderness to the people. John the Baptist was that voice. John ministered outside of the city, and his voice cried out to a people hopelessly lost apart from the grace of God through Jesus. John spoke of the coming of the kingdom of God - the very theme of Jesus' ministry. Soon the King was revealed. Jesus once spoke to the crowd about John the Baptist. He said that John was a prophet, but more than a prophet. Jesus said that among those born of women there was no one greater than John. He also said that from the days of John the Baptist, the kingdom of heaven is forcefully advancing (see Matthew 11:7-12).

TALK ABOUT IT:

Who was the King of the kingdom spoken of by John? (Jesus is the King of God's kingdom.)

The people who live in the kingdom of a king are called to obey the king's laws. What are we commanded to do as people who are ruled by King Jesus? (We are commanded to love God and each other. This is only possible if God causes us to be born again and places His Spirit in our hearts.)

PRAY:

Ask God to help you love Him and one another by pouring out His grace on your life.

TUESDAY

THE STORY: MATTHEW 3:4-11

John's baptism was one of repentance. John called the Jews to repent of their sins and be baptized. John brought them a prophetic message of repentance. The fact that they could trace their lineage back to Abraham was no guarantee of faith or obedience in their hearts. John told the religious leaders that God could raise up children of Abraham from the rocks. No one can receive salvation simply by virtue of being born a Jew or by being born into a Christian family. Salvation comes to each person by God's grace, through individual faith and repentance.

Malachi 4:5, 6 had prophesied the return of Elijah, who would turn the hearts of the fathers and children back to one another. This was first attributed to John by the angel who visited John's father Zechariah (see Luke 1:17). Jesus confirmed that John the Baptist was the return of Elijah (Matthew 11:14), for he came in the spirit and power of Elijah. Finally, after about 400 years without a prophet (from the days of Malachi), God had sent another prophet to Israel.

TALK ABOUT IT:

What did John tell the people they must do? (John told the people to repent of their sins.)

What does it mean to repent? (Repent means to turn back. In the case of sin, repentance is to turn away from sin and back to the Lord. We are also called to repent and turn away from our sin and idols to worship and serve the Lord.)

PRAY:

Have each of the children ask God to help them repent. You may want to invite them to mention specific ways they have sinned against God. Remind them of the gospel, which promises we can receive forgiveness for our sins.

WEDNESDAY
WHERE IS THE GOSPEL?

THE STORY: LUKE 3:1-6

John the Baptist was very clear to indicate that men were sinful, in need of a Savior. In the Gospel of Luke we learn that John the Baptist quoted a larger portion of Isaiah than is indicated in Matthew. Luke 3:6 includes Isaiah 40:5b: "And all flesh shall see the salvation of God." John was not merely introducing a great prophet; he was introducing the Lord Himself, who would bring salvation to all people. This would come through the life, ministry, death and resurrection of Jesus.

TALK ABOUT IT:

What does Luke 3:6 mean when it says all flesh (mankind) shall see the salvation of God? (This is an announcement of the fulfillment of the promise to Abraham that all the different peoples of the earth would be blessed through him. There will be people from every language, tribe and nation in heaven.)

People look different on the outside. What is the one thing they all have in common? (All men, no matter their skin color, are made in the image of God and reflect the glory of God in spite of their sin. And all men need God's savlation.)

PRAY:
Thank God for bringing people from every nation to salvation.

THURSDAY

THE STORY: LUKE 3:10-18

John prophesied that Jesus would also baptize. John's teaching came with authority. Many thought he might be the Messiah himself. John was quick to correct them, saying he was unfit to even untie the sandal of the Messiah soon to come. John said that he baptized in water, but the Messiah to come would baptize with the Holy Spirit. Jesus did indeed pour out the Holy Spirit upon men. John's baptism could not change hearts. When Jesus pours out the Holy Spirit on a person's heart, that person is made alive again, transformed and changed. And God's law is written upon the person's heart.

TALK ABOUT IT:

What is different about Jesus' baptism? (Jesus would not just baptize with water, he would baptize with the Holy Spirit.)

Are people baptized in God's Spirit today? (Yes, Jesus fills us with the Holy Spirit when we repent and place our trust in Jesus. For many people, this experience of the Spirit is quite overwhelming and dramatic. Then we also experience fresh infillings of the Spirit, punctuating the Christian life. The filling of the Spirit is something the Bible tells us to pursue continually [see Acts 2:4 and 4:31, and Ephesians 5:18]. The Holy Spirit is to be an experienced reality in the life of the believer from conversion on.)

PRAY:

Pray that God would pour out His Spirit on you that you might be filled with His presence and power to spread the gospel message.

FRIDAY
ON THE ROAD TO EMMAUS

THE STORY: ISAIAH 40:1-5

Matthew attributes this section of Isaiah 40 to the ministry of John the Baptist.
John was the one whose voice called out in the wilderness to announce the coming
of the Lord. When you make a road, you need to level the ground, cutting the
high hills and filling in the valleys. John's message was designed to announce
Jesus, figuratively making a road on which Jesus would travel. John did so by
introducing Jesus as the one who would pour out His Spirit and gather up His
people to Himself.

TAKE IT HOME:

What does it mean that the glory of the Lord will be revealed? (Because of Jesus,
a day is coming when the full glory of the Lord will be revealed. God's glory
is His marvelous splendor, purity and unapproachable light. This glory will be
unveiled at the second coming of Christ. With new bodies in heaven, all believers
will see God's glory.)

How should this prophecy encourage us? (The prophecy shows God's amazing
control over all things and His careful unfolding of a detailed plan. We are all a
part of God's plan.)

PRAY:

Thank God for His amazing control over all things. Ask God to pour out His
Spirit on your family.

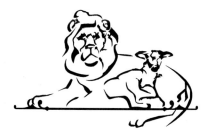

THE BAPTISM OF JESUS

The baptism of Jesus marks the beginning of His road to the cross.

MONDAY

THE STORY: MATTHEW 3:13-15

Jesus was baptized. Jesus had no need of baptism because He had no sin. He humbled Himself for our sake and was baptized by John. Jesus identified with us. He walked with man, ate with man, and was baptized by a man. At first, John refused to baptize Jesus. He knew that he was the sinner, not Jesus. Jesus, however, insisted that He must be baptized to fulfill all righteousness. Paul tells us that though Jesus had no sin, God made him to be sin for us (2 Corinthians 5:21). Jesus' baptism was not for His sake but for ours.

TALK ABOUT IT:

Why didn't Jesus need John's baptism? (John's baptism was a baptism of repentance, or turning away, from sins. Jesus was sinless and did not need to repent.)So why was Jesus baptized if He had no sin? (Jesus came as a man and would take upon Himself the wrath of God for our sin. Jesus began His ministry by receiving John's baptism.)

PRAY:

Thank Jesus for His willingness to take our sinful humanity upon Himself and die for our sins.

TUESDAY

THE STORY: MATTHEW 3:16,17

God revealed Himself in the trinity. Each person in the Godhead (Father, Son and Holy Spirit) made His presence known at the baptism of Jesus. The doctrine of the Trinity teaches what is evident in Scripture: God is three persons with one essence. This is a concept we cannot fully understand. We know that God is one (Malachi 2:10), and yet we know that the Godhead has three persons. All three persons of the Trinity made themselves known at Jesus' baptism.

TALK ABOUT IT

Where do we see the three persons of the Trinity in this passage of Scripture? (Jesus the Son of God was present, the Holy Spirit descended upon Jesus as a dove, and God the Father spoke from heaven.)

Can we fully understand how three can be one? (No, some things about God are just too big for our little minds to understand. In our pride we would want to completely comprehend God, but we will never be able to fully know all there is to know about Him. We have the distinct joy and honor of learning more and more about Him forever.)

PRAY

Thank God for His infinite and wonderful greatness. Thank Him that He is greater than we are and cannot be figured out.

WEDNESDAY
WHERE IS THE GOSPEL?

THE STORY: JOHN 1:29-34

John called Jesus the Lamb of God. Given that Mary, Jesus' mother, was related to Elizabeth (John's mother) it is likely John had met Jesus or at least knew about Jesus growing up. John gives us a clue when he says, "I myself did not know Him." At some point when John saw Jesus, he realized that Jesus was the promised Messiah. John proclaims that Jesus is the Lamb of God, the one who will take away the sin of the world. Long before John's ministry, Abraham told his son Isaac that God Himself would provide a lamb for the sacrifice. That day, God did not allow Abraham to sacrifice his son but provided a ram. Here John tells us God has provided a sacrifice for sins - Jesus, the Lamb of God. Abraham's ram was a foreshadowing of Jesus, the Lamb of God.

By His baptism, Jesus instituted a new sacrament for believers. Our baptism is a symbol of Christ's burial in the tomb (when we go under the water) and a symbol of the resurrection (when we come up out of the water).

Paul teaches us in Romans 6:4: We were buried therefore with him by baptism into death in order that, just as Christ was raised from the dead by the glory of the Father, we too might walk in newness of life.

Jesus identified with sinful man when He was baptized. We identify with Jesus, His death and His resurrection when we are baptized.

TALK ABOUT IT:

How did God use the lamb in the Old Testament to point forward to Jesus? (Lambs were sacrificed to atone for man's sin. They point to Jesus the Lamb of God sacrificed for our sin).

Should we remember Jesus and his sacrifice when confessing sin? (Help your children see that each time we confess or repent we should remember Jesus - not just think about those people we sinned against.)

PRAY:
Thank the Lord for sending the Lamb of God to die for us to take away our sin.

THURSDAY

THE STORY: MARK 6:14-29
John the Baptist gave his life for truth. God called John to a ministry of truth. John's words set the stage for men to realize they needed a Savior. His ministry paved the way for Jesus. John spoke against Herod's marriage to Herodias because Herod stole his brother's wife. Though Herod was attracted to the message of John, to please Herodias he threw John in prison. Then, manipulated again by his wife, he had John beheaded.

The prophet who announced the ministry of our Savior paid the ultimate price for proclaiming the truth. John went straight to heaven rejoicing because his ministry was complete. John had introduced a greater prophet, Jesus, who would also be killed for what He proclaimed. But this prophet, the Son of God, would conquer death!

TALK ABOUT IT:
Why did Herod kill John? (Herod wanted to please his wife more than God. Herod was very aware of what people thought of him. He did not want to be known as a man who was afraid to exercise his power. Herod struggled with the fear of man – he wanted to please people instead of God.)

Draw out your children to see if they can think of a time when they have struggled with the fear of man.

PRAY:
Confess your own fear of man and ask God to give you courage like John to follow God no matter what people think of you.

FRIDAY
ON THE ROAD TO EMMAUS

THE STORY: ISAIAH 11:1-5
In an amazing display of prophetic accuracy, Isaiah tells us that the Spirit of the Lord will rest upon a descendant of David, a righteous king who will care for the poor and needy and judge the earth. No one can fit that description but Jesus.

TALK ABOUT IT:
Where do you see similarities to Jesus' baptism in this passage? (Isaiah 11:2 says the Spirit of the Lord will rest on him, and at Jesus' baptism the Spirit of the Lord came upon Him like a dove. Matthew 3:15 says Jesus was baptized to fulfill all righteousness. Isaiah 11:4 says that with righteousness He will judge the needy and Isaiah 11:5 says righteousness will be His belt.)

What does Isaiah mean when he says that He will "strike the earth with the rod of His mouth"? (The rod is the implement of judgment. Just like parents give their children the rod of correction, so Jesus will one day bring judgment upon the earth.)

PRAY:
Knowing that Jesus will one day come to judge the earth and that we will all be judged by Him, pray that God would pour out His Spirit on you that you might be saved.

THE TEMPTATION OF JESUS

Christ overcame temptation and defeated Satan.

MONDAY

THE STORY: LUKE 4:1-4

"Man does not live by bread alone." Jesus quoted from Deuteronomy 8:3 to rebuff Satan. Moses first spoke those words to Israel to remind them of their wanderings in the desert, where God provided manna. God did this, it says, to teach them that man does not live on bread alone but on every word that comes from the mouth of the Lord. Israel's wandering in the desert was meant to humble them and to test them to see if they would obey God's commands. Jesus quotes from Deuteronomy to rebuke Satan and to signal that He would succeed where Israel failed. Jesus passed the test on our behalf.

TALK ABOUT IT:

Did Jesus experience the same suffering and hunger we would if we didn't eat for 40 days? (Yes, Luke is careful to mention that Jesus was hungry. When Satan came to tempt Jesus with earthly bread, Jesus was hungry for the food of the earth, but he answered Satan with a word from heaven!)

How are we easily tempted when we are hungry? (We can become angry when we don't get food, or impatient and ungrateful if it doesn't come as fast as we want it to come.)

PRAY:

Thank God for resisting temptation and defeating Satan on our behalf.

TUESDAY

THE STORY: LUKE 4:5-8

In Luke 4:8, Jesus said, "You shall worship the Lord your God, and Him only shall you serve," quoting from Deuteronomy 6:13. Satan actually asked Jesus to worship him. Israel failed to worship God alone, but Jesus refused Satan's temptation, rebuking him firmly.

TALK ABOUT IT:

Why was Satan's temptation so powerful? (Satan was trying to offer Jesus a shortcut to a kingdom. Instead of paying the price on the cross for the redemption of men, the tempter claimed He could give Jesus an earthly kingdom if he worshipped Satan. Jesus was no ordinary man; He was also God. No ordinary man would have withstood Satan's temptations, but Jesus stood the test.)

Ask your children if they can think of a time when they were strongly tempted.

PRAY:

Thank God for resisting temptation and making a way for us to have power to resist temptation too.

WEDNESDAY
WHERE IS THE GOSPEL?

THE STORY: HEBREWS 4:15,16

Jesus was tempted in the wilderness and passed the test so that we who have failed could receive His righteousness. Now He stands before the Father as our high priest making intercession for us. This He does, full of grace and mercy, knowing the difficulty we face in our battle against sin and temptation. The passages from Luke 4 He quoted in His defense against Satan, are from the account of Israel's wandering in the desert. They wandered for 40 years – grumbling and complaining and ultimately failing. Jesus accomplished in 40 days what they could not in 40 years!

TALK ABOUT IT

What does the word "temptation" mean? (To be tempted is to be enticed or to be drawn to sin. In temptation, either Satan or our sinful nature brings close to us the possibility that we could sin.)

Why should Jesus' experience of temptation be encouraging to us? (Jesus can understand what we are going through when we are tempted, and through the Spirit of God, we, too, can say no to temptation.)

PRAY

Thank Jesus for being willing to be tempted for us. Ask God to help you overcome temptation.

THURSDAY

THE STORY: LUKE 4:9-13

Satan saved his most devious trick for last. First, he tempted Christ with food and immediate pleasure. Second, he tempted Christ with a shortcut to power. And finally, he tempted Christ with the Word of God. Satan quotes from Psalm 91:11, 12. In short, he told Jesus, If your word is true, prove it. Jesus saw right through Satan's scheme and rebukes him a third time. Jesus does so by quoting Deuteronomy 6:16. Defeated, the devil left Jesus until an opportune time. That time would come when Satan entered Judas' heart, and Judas betrayed Jesus. What Satan did not know was that God is always in control and was even using Satan's manipulations to accomplish His predetermined plan.

TALK ABOUT IT :

Was Satan correct in quoting Scripture? (Yes, Satan was correct. Psalm 91:10-12 was true. God could have called down legions of angels. In Matthew 26:53 Jesus said so Himself when Peter cut off the servant of the high priest's ear. Jesus also said that He would not call down legions of angels, so that the Scriptures could be fulfilled. Isaiah 53:7 tells us that he was led like a lamb to the slaughter and did not open his mouth.)

Can we use the Word of God to overcome temptation? (Yes. Quoting Scripture is a great way for us to fight the lies of Satan and defeat temptation.)

PRAY:

Pray that God would help you study His Word that you might be able to withstand the temptations of sin and the enemy.

FRIDAY
ON THE ROAD TO EMMAUS

THE STORY: ISAIAH 61:1-3

After His temptation in the wilderness, Jesus read this passage of Scripture. Jesus attributed the words of Isaiah to Himself, saying, "Today this Scripture has been fulfilled in your hearing." Jesus had been in the synagogue when other teachers read, but that day Jesus read the scroll. The Spirit descended upon Jesus at His baptism. Now Jesus had passed the test of Satan's temptations. With the reading of Isaiah, Jesus uttered a kind of battle cry. The kingdom of God was advancing, and the defeat of Satan and the releasing of his prisoners was drawing nigh.

TALK ABOUT IT

What does this passage say Jesus will do for us? (Jesus will bind up the brokenhearted, free us from captivity, release us from darkness, provide for us, give us a crown of beauty and give us gladness and a garment of praise. In addition we will be called righteous because of the Lord's work.)

What was holding us captive? (Sin holds unbelievers captive. Romans 6:17, 18 says that when we trust Christ we are freed from the bondage of sin and we become slaves of righteousness.)

PRAY

Pray that God would release you from slavery to sin and make you a willing slave of Christ.

THE WEDDING FEAST

Jesus is the Creator.

MONDAY

THE STORY: JOHN 2:1-5

Mary called to Jesus. Mary's faith and confidence in Jesus was displayed in the way she approached her son for help. Weddings in Jesus' day lasted seven days. It would be a terrible embarrassment to run out of wine. Jesus initially objected. But Mary, persistent and full of faith, simply directed the servants to do whatever Jesus said. Mary didn't tell Jesus what to do; she simply entrusted the problem to Him. In a similar way, God honors our faith in Him and our persistent prayers. Jesus honored His mother's request; by doing so He begins His supernatural ministry and reveals that He is no ordinary man.

TALK ABOUT IT:

How did Mary demonstrate faith in Jesus? (First, she came to Jesus with her need. Second, she was confident Jesus could help her. Third, she shared her confidence with others.)

How can we follow Mary's example? (Both Psalm 55:22 and 1 Peter 5:7 tell us that we can cast our cares upon the Lord. In Philippians 4:6 Paul tells us not to be anxious but to present our requests to God in prayer.)

PRAY:

Ask each family member for prayer requests, and then in faith, as a family, present those requests to God.

TUESDAY

THE STORY: JOHN 2:6-11

Jesus creates wine from water. Though Jesus initially told His mother that His time had not yet come, He decided to step out in power to honor the host, honor His mother, and give a powerful picture of His divinity. The host would not run out of wine again. Jesus created about 150 gallons of wine. Colossians 1:16 tells us that Jesus is the creator of the world, and that in Him all things were made. Jesus demonstrated His power to create by changing the water into wine. When the master of the feast tasted the wine, he was quite impressed with the quality. Wine normally takes weeks and months to be aged to perfection - that is, unless it is perfectly made!

TALK ABOUT IT :

How did Jesus turn the water into wine? (The Bible does not tell us how Jesus did it. Whether it was by a creative word or His creative will, we do not know. But we do know that it was by His power.)

How did this sign - turning the water into wine - affect the disciples? (God used this miraculous sign to touch the life of the disciples and cause them to believe that Jesus was more than an ordinary man.)

PRAY:

Thank God for His creative power that made all things and for His willingness to help us to believe.

WEDNESDAY
WHERE IS THE GOSPEL?

THE STORY: JOHN 12:23-32

In response to the need for wine, Jesus told His mother, "My hour has not yet come." Jesus understood the hour was approaching when He would miraculously provide the wine of the new covenant, in His blood, on the cross. Jesus was already planning to offer men the wine they could not provide for themselves. But that hour had not yet come.

With a demonstration of His power, in turning the water to wine, Jesus' ministry was about to begin. And once started, it would move ever closer to the cross. It is no accident that Jesus' first miracle speaks powerfully of the cross and the gospel. He wanted it that way. Jesus came to offer mankind the wine of His blood for the forgiveness of sins. He came for their participation in the great wedding yet to come. The new wine was for their great joy. Mary's talk of the need for wine, at a wedding, reminded Jesus of the wine of the new covenant. It reminded Him of His mission to call to Himself a bride without spot or blemish. Jesus knew that the hour was coming when His blood would be shed and the greater miracle of salvation would be accomplished.

TALK ABOUT IT :

What did Jesus mean by "my hour has not yet come"? (Jesus meant the hour of his death. It would be in that hour, when his blood was poured out like wine, that the Father would turn His face away and pour out His justified wrath for the sins of man upon His Son.)

Why do you think adults receive wine (or red juice) when they share communion, or the Lord's Supper, at meetings? (The wine reminds them that Jesus provides forgiveness of sins through his blood shed on the cross. It also reminds them that they need to personally receive the cleansing that his blood alone can provide. Jesus also commanded that this be done in remembrance of him.)

PRAY:
Ask God to help you to personally receive the gift of His salvation, which Jesus miraculously provides.

THURSDAY

THE STORY: JOHN 2:12
Jesus had a family. Mary and Joseph had other children after Jesus was born. Jesus had younger brothers and sisters! One of Jesus' brothers, James, became a leader in the early church in Jerusalem. Most people attribute the Book of James to him. Joseph is notably absent in the life of Jesus at the wedding. It is likely that Joseph died at some point, leaving Mary a widow with children. Jesus, as the eldest son, would have had a special sense of care for His mother. He carried this responsibility all the way to the cross, where He charged the disciple John to care for Mary as his own mother (John 19:27).

TALK ABOUT IT:
What do you think it would have been like to be one of Jesus' brothers?

Did Jesus' brothers and mother believe in Him? (Mary, Jesus' mother, seems to have believed from the beginning. Jesus' brothers, however, at one point thought Jesus was out of His mind (Mark 3:21). After the Resurrection, Jesus' mother and brothers are found waiting along with the disciples, in constant prayer, for the promised Holy Spirit.)

PRAY:
Ask the Lord to save your whole family and fill them with His Spirit.

FRIDAY
ON THE ROAD TO EMMAUS

THE STORY: ISAIAH 62:11,12

Isaiah proclaimed the Savior is coming! Isaiah refers to Jesus. When He comes, the people He saves will be called "Holy People" and "Redeemed of the Lord". It is through Jesus' sacrifice on the cross that we are redeemed and are made holy.

TALK ABOUT IT:

How can we, a sinful people, be called holy? (Jesus lived a sinless life. We can be holy because Jesus extends His holiness and righteousness to us. We are holy only in Christ!)

Given what Jesus did for us, how should we live? (We don't do good works to try to save ourselves, but we should do good works so as to walk in the salvation God purchased for us through His Son. When we do good works, we walk in the blessing of our righteousness in Christ.)

PRAY:

Pray and ask God that we would be as excited knowing Christ as Isaiah was in his prophecy.

JESUS CLEANSES THE TEMPLE

God desires people who worship from their hearts.

MONDAY

THE STORY: JOHN 2:13-17

God's house is for worship alone. The Passover was at hand, and many Israelites needed to purchase animals for sacrifices. Those with foreign currency needed to change their money. The moneychangers and merchants set up shop right in the temple. The temple was the center of Jewish life. It was the place where God's presence lived among the people. These shopkeepers were more interested in making money than worshipping God. When Jesus arrived at the temple, He became righteously angry and drove the shopkeepers out. He overturned the tables of the moneychangers. Though Jesus was clearing them out, He had respect for their property. The coins could be gathered and a whip of cords would not hurt the sheep and oxen. Jesus didn't smash or open the cages of the pigeons to let them out. He was trying to help them to see that God's house was not a marketplace.

TALK ABOUT IT:

Jesus chased the animal sellers and the moneychangers out of the Temple. Who didn't Jesus chase out of the temple? (Jesus did not chase out those who came to worship. In John 6:37 Jesus says, "All that the Father gives me will come to me, and whoever comes to me I will never drive away." God does not cast out those who come to worship!)

How should this passage affect the way we view church when we gather on Sunday for worship? (We should be careful to come to worship the Lord. Worship includes singing and listening to the preaching, but it also involves servce and fellowship. If we are not paying attention to the preaching, or if we are distracted in worship, or if we can't wait until the service is over, we might want to check our hearts.)

PRAY:

Ask God to place a love for the church in your heart and cause it to grow.

TUESDAY

THE STORY: JOHN 2:18-22

The Jews demanded a sign from Jesus for clearing out the temple. Jesus answered them by saying that if they destroyed the temple, He would raise it up in three days. It had taken 46 years to build the temple, and it wasn't yet finished! It wasn't until after the Resurrection that the disciples realized Jesus was talking about the temple of His body.

TALK ABOUT IT :

Jesus said that He was God's temple. How is Jesus a temple? (In heaven there will not be a temple building. The Lord God Almighty and the Lamb are its temple. See Revelation 21:22.)

Why did the Jews demand a sign? (People who do not believe by faith demand proof they can see or touch. When the Pharisees demanded a sign in Mark 8:11, Jesus told them that no sign would be given.)

PRAY:
Ask Jesus to help you believe. Faith is a gift from God. Pray and ask God to increase your faith in Him.

WEDNESDAY
WHERE IS THE GOSPEL?

THE STORY: MATTHEW 27:39-43
The disciples didn't know what Jesus was talking about when He told the Jews that He could rebuild the Temple in three days. Jesus was referring to His resurrection. But after Jesus rose from the dead, they remembered (see John 2:22). People hurled insults at Jesus during His crucifixion, mocking what He said about the Temple (see Matthew 27:39, 40).

Jesus' resurrection validates His ministry claims. His resurrection ultimately proves He is Lord over all, including life and death. The Resurrection proves that His sacrificial death on the cross triumphs for us all. (See Romans 6:4 and Romans 8:11.)

TALK ABOUT IT :
What temple was Jesus referring to when He said He would rebuild it in three days? (The temple he spoke about was His body, see John 2:21).

Why is the Resurrection important? (The Resurrection shows us that Jesus was God and that He had victory over death. Now we can trust His promise that those who believe and trust in Him will also have eternal life).

PRAY:

Have everyone in your family take a turn honoring Christ and exalting Him in a prayer of thanksgiving for raising the temple in three days. Though He was mocked, we have the privilege of praising Him!

THURSDAY

THE STORY: JOHN 2:23-25

Jesus could see the motive of their hearts. When Jesus drove the merchants and moneychangers out of the temple, He called the temple "my Father's house." The Jews demanded a sign of His authority to do this. After cleansing the temple, Jesus remained in Jerusalem for the Passover. In Jerusalem He did perform signs, and many believed in His name, but Jesus did not entrust Himself to them because He knew their hearts. After seeing Jesus minister, they were satisfied and believed on His name - a way of saying they affirmed His character, but there is no evidence that their belief was in Jesus as their Savior.

TALK ABOUT IT:

Can we tell what is in a man's heart by what He says? (We cannot always tell what is in a man's heart by what he says. Our words need to be backed up by our actions. It is easy to say you believe something but not live in a way that matches your words.)

Can God tell what is in our hearts? (Yes - God is not fooled by shallow words. God sees our hearts.)

PRAY:

Pray that God would give us a faith that comes from deep within our hearts. Pray that God would help us live on the outside what we believe on the inside.

FRIDAY
ON THE ROAD TO EMMAUS

THE STORY: PSALM 69:7-13

The disciples remembered this passage and attributed it to Christ, who cleared the temple of the moneychangers (John 2:17). This psalm describes a righteous servant who suffers insults on account of his love for God. Jesus was rejected and deserted by His closest friends. He was mocked and scorned, disgraced and shamed both before and upon the cross. Though written by David, likely during one of his own struggles, the Psalm points to Christ and the suffering He would endure for us.

TALK ABOUT IT:

What does it mean to have zeal for God's house? (Zeal is intense passion for something. Jesus had an intense passion for God's house and didn't want it used as a place of trade.)

Since we do not worship at the temple and don't have animal sacrifices, how does this verse about zeal for God's house apply to our lives? (God dwells in His people now. Believers are God's house, both as individuals and especially when gathered. We should have zeal for the church - the gathering of believers, which makes up God's house today.)

PRAY:

Talk about ways your family shows zeal for God's house - the church - and then pray God would help you be faithful to your commitment.

NICODEMUS

You must be born again to enter the kingdom of heaven.

MONDAY

THE STORY: JOHN 3:1-15

"Unless a man be born again he cannot see the kingdom of God." Nicodemus came to Jesus at night. In view of John's use of light and darkness (John 3:19), we may deduce that Nicodemus, though seeking, was an unbeliever fearful of being seen with Jesus in the daylight. Jesus' words, "born again," can be literally translated "born from above." Nicodemus took them literally, but upon further explanation Jesus revealed that a person needed to be born of the Spirit of God to enter into heaven. Nicodemus did not understand. We are not told how Nicodemus responded, but he is mentioned later in John 19:39 with Joseph of Arimathea caring for Jesus' dead body. One would like to believe that Nicodemus eventually understood what Jesus meant, and one day in heaven we may see Nicodemus.

TALK ABOUT IT:

What does it mean to be born again? (Rather than think of "born again," think "born of God." Before people are saved, they are, according to the Bible, spiritually dead in their sins. They do not have the ability to respond to the gospel with faith. In order for people to have saving faith in Jesus Christ, God must first touch them with His power, making them alive by His Spirit. Then they can believe. Once God causes our spirits to come alive, or be born again, our hearts respond in faith to the gospel. At that time, God gives us His Spirit and comes to live with us. God tells us that He places His Spirit in our hearts as a guarantee that we are going be with Him forever in heaven. (See 2 Corinthians 1:21, 22.)

Can anyone become a Christian without the work of the Spirit? Can anyone become a Christian by doing something themselves? (No. The Bible is clear that our faith is not brought about by our works. (See Ephesians 2:8, 9.)

PRAY:

Pray for each person in your family and ask God to pour out His Spirit upon them, cause them to be born of God, and give them faith to believe.

TUESDAY

THE STORY: JOHN 3:16-18

Apart fom Christ, man stands condemned. When Adam and Eve sinned, all mankind was condemned to die. Jesus came into the world to save the world, not to condemn it. Those who don't believe stand condemned already.

TALK ABOUT IT:

What does it mean to be condemned? (Condemnation is the judgment of eternal death and punishment that comes to all those who have been found guilty of sin by God. Since we are all sinners, we all deserve to be condemned.)

Why are those who believe in Jesus free of condemnation? (When Jesus received God's wrath for our sin on the cross, He took the condemnation of all those who believe.)

PRAY:

Thank Jesus for taking God's wrath in our place so that we can be free of condemnation.

WEDNESDAY
WHERE IS THE GOSPEL?

THE STORY: 1 JOHN 5:1-5

The third chapter of John introduces the idea that becoming a Christian is a new birth. This new birth comes to everyone who believes in Jesus. What we believe about Jesus is of primary importance. 1 John 5:5 tells us we must believe that Jesus is the Son of God.

Many people celebrate John 3:16 all by itself. But we need the whole of the Scriptures, which tell us everything we need to believe about Jesus. It is not sufficient to believe that Jesus was a good teacher or that He was a prophet. We must believe that Jesus was both man and God, that Jesus died for our sins taking the penalty we deserved, and that He rose from the dead as He said He would.

Jesus bore the wrath of God for our sin. That is why a man who trusts in Christ is "not condemned" (John 3:18). If Jesus was only a good teacher, or a remarkable prophet, or a man like any other, He would not have been able to take away our sin. When we believe in Jesus, God places His commands in our hearts and places the Holy Spirit to live within us. It is by the power of the Spirit of God that we obey God's commands and live for Him. In fact, though all believers struggle with remaining sin, they are able to overcome sin and grow in the grace of obedience.

TALK ABOUT IT:

What does John tell us we need to do in order to become a Christian? (We need to believe - see 1 John 5:5)

What evidence marks the life of those who believe? (They love God by obeying His commands.)

PRAY:

Pray that God would help you to believe and place your trust in Jesus as the one who died on the cross for your sins and then rose again. Pray that God would fill you with His Spirit and change your sinful heart so that you would desire to obey the Lord and honor Him with your life.

THURSDAY

THE STORY: JOHN 3:19-21

Wickedness hates the light. John tells us that light has come into the world and that men hate the light because their evil deeds are exposed by the light. John 8:12 records these words of Jesus: "I am the light of the world. Whoever follows me will not walk in darkness, but will have the light of life." Jesus came to expose the teachers of the law. They appeared to be righteous, but inside they were sinful. Time and time again Jesus exposed the hidden, sinful motive of men's hearts.

TALK ABOUT IT:

Why do people hide the evil they have done? (People keep the evil of their hearts hidden to appear more righteous than they really are.)

Can God see the sin that we hide? (Yes. Even if everyone else does not know our sin, God does. If we confess our sin and bring it out into the light, God promises to forgive us and cleanse us from our sin. (See 1 John 1:9.)

PRAY:

Take time to ask your children if they have any sin they are trying to keep hidden. If they do, ask them if they would like to confess and share it with you. (Offer to speak to them privately.) Then pray for them, and pray that God would help your whole family to walk in the light.

FRIDAY
ON THE ROAD TO EMMAUS

THE STORY: ISAIAH 52:13

This passage falls in a section of Isaiah that very specifically points to Jesus. Here in this verse, the servant will be raised and lifted up, and then highly exalted. John 3:14 says that Jesus will be lifted up - a reference to His crucifixion.

TALK ABOUT IT:

Read Isaiah 52:13 and Philippians 2:7-10. How does Paul's description of Jesus match Isaiah's description? (Paul tells us in Philippians 2:7-10 that because Jesus took on the nature of a servant, God exalted him.)

What are the three key ideas that match? (Jesus was a servant, was lifted up on the cross and is highly exalted.)

PRAY:

Thank Jesus for taking the nature of a servant and dying in our place on the cross.

JESUS HEALED MANY

Jesus proclaims the good news with the Spirit's power.

MONDAY

THE STORY: LUKE 4:14-21

The "good news" is announced. Jesus arrived at the synagogue on the Sabbath, stood, and read from the prophet Isaiah. When he finished, all eyes were fixed on the carpenter's son. Having captured their attention with a stunning reading, Jesus announced that the Scripture He read was fulfilled. The Spirit of the Lord was upon Him indeed. The one whom Isaiah had prophesied about was in their midst. Jesus did, in fact, go forth with the good news. He did set the captives free, pushing back the curse of sin and the work of the enemy. Jesus also freed people from oppression and sickness.

TALK ABOUT IT:

What is the "good news"? (The "good news" is the gospel. In Acts 10:34-43 Peter tells us that the "good news" is the message that there is peace through Jesus Christ, Lord of all. Peter went on to explain the ministry of Christ, starting with His baptism, then His crucifixion, and finally His resurrection.

Can you point out the four major components of the gospel (good news)? (The four components are the ministry of Jesus in life, Jesus' substitutionary death, the resurrection of Jesus, and the forgiveness of sins for those who believe.)

PRAY:
Thank God for sending us Jesus to release us from our captivity to sin.

TUESDAY

THE STORY: LUKE 4:22-30
Upon hearing Jesus read the scroll of Isaiah and comment with authority, the people who knew Him as the carpenter's son marveled. But their amazement did not move them to faith. They only thought Jesus spoke graciously until He spoke of God's mercy to people outside Israel. The Israelites had come to believe they had God's exclusive favor simply by virtue of their heritage as children of Abraham. When Jesus reminded them that God sent Elisha to a Sidonian widow and a Syrian leper, rather than the widows and lepers of Israel, they were filled with wrath. They drove Jesus out of town to kill him, intending to throw him down a cliff. But Jesus simply passed through them and escaped easily.

TALK ABOUT IT:
Why didn't Jesus just allow them to kill him there? (Jesus didn't just need to die in order for sins to be atoned for; He needed to be cursed by God and receive His justified wrath for our sin. The cross was a symbol of God's curse. In addition, God Himself would determine the time and method of His sacrifice; that time had not come.)

How was Jesus like Elijah? (Both Jesus and Elijah were prophets. Both were rejected by Israel and ministered to people who were outside Israel.)

PRAY:
Praise God that the message of the gospel is for all men - Jews and Gentiles alike!

WEDNESDAY
WHERE IS THE GOSPEL?

THE STORY: LUKE 4:31-37

Through the mocking voices of the demons we discover Jesus' true identity. Jesus is no mere man; He is the Son of God, the Holy One of God, the Christ. Jesus was anointed by God as the next king - the last in the Davidic line. The demons mocked Jesus, but by going to the cross, Jesus gained the victory over all the powers of Satan. On the cross, the curse and wrath of God fell upon Jesus, yet brought freedom to the captives and released the chains of sin. Those who were demonized, like the man in the synagogue, were easily set free by Jesus. This demonstrated Jesus' power over Satan.

TALK ABOUT IT:

What two things caused the people of Capernaum to be amazed? (According to Luke 4:32, 36, the people of Capernaum were amazed by Jesus' authority in word and deed.)

Ask your children to tell you what most amazes them about Jesus.

PRAY

Have everyone praise the Lord and thank Jesus for those things that most amaze them about Him.

THURSDAY

THE STORY: LUKE 4:38-44

Jesus went on from the synagogue to Simon's house and healed Simon's mother-in-law. Later in the day He brought healing to everyone who was brought to

Him. Some demons cried out, "You are the Son of God," but Jesus rebuked them and would not let them continue speaking. The next day Jesus was followed by the crowd, who wanted keep Him there, but Jesus objected, saying He must preach the "good news" to other towns also.

TALK ABOUT IT:

How is Jesus' refusal to remain in Capernaum an example for us? (As Christians we are not to keep Jesus to ourselves but to follow His example by taking the "good news" of the kingdom to everyone.)

When is a person old enough to preach the good news to others? (There is no age when a person is old enough. Even a three-year-old can share the "good news." We should remember to first preach the Gospel to ourselves. There is no need to preach to others until we have believed ourselves. It is not until we believe that we can receive the Holy Spirit to empower our witness.)

PRAY:

Ask God to help you believe the gospel and then have the courage to take the message of God's "good news" to others.

FRIDAY
ON THE ROAD TO EMMAUS

THE STORY: EZEKIEL 37:25-29

Jesus is a king, in the line of David, who will reign forever. So Jesus is the prince forever Ezekiel refers to in Ezekiel 37:25. The everlasting covenant referred to in Ezekiel 37:26 is Jesus' covenant in His blood. Because the penalty of our sin is paid for by Jesus, our fellowship with God is restored. God places His Spirit in our hearts. This means that God's presence no longer dwells in a temple built by human hands. Now God's people are His temple. Because God gives us eternal life, He will live in us forever.

TALK ABOUT IT:

Why can't this passage be referring to David? (David died and gave up his throne to his son, Solomon.)

Which part of this prophecy are you most grateful for? (There is much in this prophecy to be grateful for so there is no single correct answer.)

PRAY:

Pray a prayer of thanks for the part of this prophecy you are most grateful for.

NEW TESTAMENT · LESSON 11

THE CALLING OF THE FIRST DISCIPLES

Jesus called the disciples with power; they responded in faith.

MONDAY

THE STORY: LUKE 5:1-8

We learn from John 1:35-42 that Jesus had already met Simon and renamed him Peter. Jesus got into Peter's boat and asked him to put out from shore so He could teach the crowds. He had already healed many, and the crowds followed Him. Putting away from the shore allowed people to gather along the shoreline, making it easier for them to see and hear Jesus. After Jesus finished speaking, He asked Peter to go out into the deep waters and put down his nets. They caught so many fish that two boats almost sank under the weight. Peter, suddenly aware that Jesus was Lord, fell down to his knees in fear, and in awareness of his sinfulness.

TALK ABOUT IT:

Why did Peter fall to his knees? (Peter realized he was in the presence of God and he was afraid because of his sin. The holiness of God exposes our sinfulness.)

Why did Jesus tell Peter not to be afraid? (Though Peter should have been afraid because of his sin, Jesus was Peter's Savior. Jesus would die to take Peter's penalty. It was Jesus' substitutionary death on the cross that enabled Him to forgive rather than to judge Peter. So Peter did not need to fear.)

PRAY:

Thank God for the cross, which makes it possible for us to confess our sin and be forgiven.

TUESDAY

THE STORY: LUKE 5:9,10

Jesus called Peter into His service. Between Peter's call and Jesus' death, resurrection and ascension into heaven, He would train Peter. It would be Peter, on the day of Pentecost, who would preach to the multitude and see 3,000 people repent and believe in Jesus. That catch of people would match this catch of fish and validate Jesus' words (see Acts 2:41)

TALK ABOUT IT:

What did Jesus mean by "catch men"? (Jesus meant that Peter and the other disciples would spread the gospel message to those who had not heard it and that those people would be added to the church.)

Are we called to be "fishers of men"? (Yes, we are called to proclaim Jesus and help gather people into the church. Think of the gospel as the net we use to haul people into the boat - the church.)

PRAY:

Pray for help and courage to not be afraid to preach the gospel to neighbors. Pray that God would give you an opportunity to share the gospel with your unbelieving neighbors and family members.

WEDNESDAY
WHERE IS THE GOSPEL?

THE STORY: JOHN 1:40-51

Luke 19:10 says that Jesus came to seek and to save the lost. In this story we see the calling of the first disciples. They were to be more than Jesus' companions; they were to join Him in the mission to "catch men" (see Luke 5:10). This catching of men would only be possible through the grace of God available through the Cross and the Resurrection.

Right from the beginning Jesus demonstrated His power to the disciples, and they responded with statements of faith and truth. When Jesus told Nathanael that He knew him before they actually met, and went on to describe the setting, Nathanael was amazed. He instantly believed and praised Jesus, saying, "You are the Son of God! You are the King of Israel!" (see John 1:49). In Luke 5:8, after the miraculous catch of fish, Peter responded, "Depart from me, for I am a sinful man."

TALK ABOUT IT:

What are the two responses Jesus evoked from the first disciples? (Jesus evoked both awe and guilt. Awe as illustrated in Nathanael's declaration of faith, and guilt as illustrated by Peter's response.)

What do the disciples' responses teach us? (The disciples' responses demonstrate that God is holy, unlike any other. They also teach us that man is sinful in relationship to God. It is only through the sacrifice of Jesus on the cross, which takes our sins away, that we can stand before a holy God without shame and fear.)

PRAY

Praise God for His holiness and thank Him for sending Jesus to take our guilt away so that one day we will be able to stand in the presence of God free of condemnation, fear and shame.

THURSDAY

THE STORY: LUKE 5:11

The disciples left everything. After Jesus and the disciples brought their boats to shore, Peter, James and John left everything to follow Jesus. Imagine leaving the biggest catch you have ever seen in your life to follow a wandering teacher? Of course, Jesus was more than a wandering teacher; He was King! They would see Jesus multiply fishes and loaves, heal the sick, and walk on water. They made the right choice.

TALK ABOUT IT:

Do you think it was easy for the disciples to leave everything they had? (No, it was not easy. Sometimes we can read stories like this too romantically, thinking the disciples made a quick decision without effort and went merrily along with Jesus. The truth is that they had to count the cost. Later, in Luke 18:28, Peter would say, "We have left our homes and followed you." Jesus in turn assured Peter that anyone who has "given up" for Jesus will be rewarded.)

What are we called to give up for Jesus? (There is no list of things a person must give up to follow Jesus. The important thing is not what we give up, but our willingness to give up all. Led by the Spirit of God, we will all be called upon to make real sacrifices for the advance of the gospel. We may be called to sacrifice time, money, friends, jobs, homes or other things we love, in obedience to God's will.)

PRAY:

Ask God for a willing heart to give up whatever God requires for the sake of the Kingdom and the advance of the gospel.

FRIDAY
ON THE ROAD TO EMMAUS

THE STORY: ISAIAH 35:8

Isaiah described a highway called the "Way of Holiness" that the unclean will not journey on. In John 14:6 Jesus said "I am the way..." Early Christians and Paul were even called followers of the Way (see Acts 24:14).

TALK ABOUT IT:

Why is it appropriate to think of Jesus as our highway to holiness? (Apart from trusting Jesus, we can not be holy by ourselves.)

Are there additional ways to travel other than Jesus? (No - according to Acts 4:12, Jesus is the only way.)

PRAY:

Thank Jesus for being our Way to heaven and making what would have been an impossible journey into a well-paved highway of salvation.

JESUS HEALS THE PARALYTIC

Forgiveness is the greater healing.

MONDAY

THE STORY: LUKE 5:17-20

Among a crowd of skeptics, men of faith were found. We often do not consider who made up the crowd in this familiar story. The word had gotten out about Jesus. His reputation for miracles and healing drew Pharisees and teachers of the law from the surrounding villages. When the men who carried the paralyzed man could find no way through the crowd of religious rulers, they decided to try lowering their friend to Jesus through the roof. The text tells us that the power of the Lord was present for healing, but we do not read about any Pharisee being healed. The rulers came to evaluate and judge Jesus. They were filled with doubt in their hearts. When Jesus saw the men lower the cripple through a hole in the roof, He commended their faith.

TALK ABOUT IT:

How many religious rulers were present? (We are not told the exact number, but in all of Israel there would have been thousands of scribes, Pharisees, and teachers of the law, We can assume reading the text that at least a large part of the crowd was made up of religious rulers.)

How did the men demonstrate their faith? (They did not give up. They persisted in their efforts to bring the crippled man to Jesus so that he might be healed. Perseverance and persistence in pursuing the Lord is one way that faith in God is demonstrated.)

Do we ever find ourselves in a situation where persistence in our pursuit of Jesus is called for? (Yes, we are called to persevere in prayer. When we pray but do not see an immediate result, we should have faith and keep praying.)

PRAY:
Ask God to help you pursue the Lord like the men of faith in this story.

TUESDAY

THE STORY: LUKE 5:20-25
Jesus knew their thoughts. When Jesus forgave the sins of the crippled man, the Pharisees questioned in their minds His authority to forgive sins. Jesus, however, knew their thoughts. We can too quickly glance over the amazing fact that God is aware of every one of our thoughts. We can fool ourselves into thinking that our sinful thoughts are somehow hidden from Him. They may be hidden from everyone else, but not from God. Rather than rebuke these men for doubting, Jesus gave them reason to believe. He healed the paralyzed man. By healing the man, Jesus demonstrated that He had the authority to forgive sins.

TALK ABOUT IT
Does God know all our thoughts? (Yes, God knows all our thoughts.)

How should this affect the way we live our lives? (We need to remember that we can't hide our sinful thoughts from His view. God knows them.)

What is the best way to keep our sinful thoughts from being hidden? (The best way to keep them from being hidden is to confess them. The Bible tells us 1 John 1:8-9 that when we confess our sins, we are bringing them out into the light. Parents, take time to invite your children to think about their thoughts and confess anything to you they have been hiding.)

PRAY:

Ask God to help you not hide your sinful thoughts. Ask Him to help you be humble, to confess your sins to Him and talk about your struggles with sin to others.

WEDNESDAY
WHERE IS THE GOSPEL?

THE STORY: MATTHEW 9:1-8

The teachers of the law, the scribes, and Pharisees knew full well that only God had the power to forgive sins. In response to their objections (remember, Jesus knew what was in their hearts), Jesus challenged them by healing the crippled man. By this He was saying they were correct. Only God could forgive sins; Jesus is God.

The teachers, scribes, and Pharisees were amazed along with everyone else. Jesus was more than a good man or teacher. He was God Himself, sent to suffer and die for our sins. Jesus could forgive the man based only on the cross. The paralyzed man placed his faith in Jesus, the Savior, and God forgave him.

TALK ABOUT IT:

Which is easier to do: heal a man, or forgive his sins? (Clearly forgiving sins is the more difficult task. Though both are acts of mercy, the forgiveness of sins would require that Jesus go to the cross.)

We don't always appreciate how special forgiveness is. How can we take forgiveness for granted? (When we sin, we sometimes are casual or glib about the way we ask Him to forgive us. We fail to stop and consider the great cost and hardship that came upon Jesus when He took the Father's wrath for our sin upon Himself.)

PRAY:
Ask Jesus to help every member of your family consider the cost of our forgiveness.

THURSDAY

THE STORY: LUKE 5:24-26
The paralytic was healed and everyone was amazed. It is interesting to see the results of Jesus' miracle. The paralytic left praising God, and everyone, which including the Pharisees, gave praise to God. Though they didn't fully see that Jesus was God, they knew that any healing was the result of God. For them, Jesus could have been a prophet, for the prophets could heal. Prophets from the Old Testament did heal, but they did not personally forgive sins. The people present were struck with such awe that they failed to realize God was among them. Had they realized that Jesus was God, their response would have been to worship Him.

TALK ABOUT IT:
What do we know about Jesus that the crowd did not? (We know that Jesus is God.)

What should our response be in reading a story like this? (Our response should be more than the crowd's reaction to the healing. We should respond like them with amazement, but then, since we know Jesus is God, our amazement should lead us to worship.)

PRAY:
Take time to offer worship and praise to the Lord for His marvelous deeds.

FRIDAY
ON THE ROAD TO EMMAUS

THE STORY: PSALM 119:97-104

Though the claim of this passage might be pursued by any man, Jesus is the only man who fulfilled the claim. Jesus is the only one who meditated on the law of the Lord all the day and kept His feet from every evil way.

TALK ABOUT IT:

How does Psalm 119:98 fit in with the passage for this week in Luke 5? (In Luke 5:21, the scribes and the Pharisees questioned Jesus, trying to trap him. Jesus, however, was wiser than the Pharisees. He even knew what they were thinking!)

How should we apply this passage to our own lives, even though we are not perfect in our obedience? (God's Word can make us wiser than our enemies, help keep our feet from evil, and give us understanding. We should try to meditate on God's Word every day.)

PRAY:

Ask God to help you follow the way of Psalm 119 in loving, meditating on, and following God's law.

THE SERMON ON THE MOUNT – THE BEATITUDES

Because of Christ, we can be salt and light to the world.

MONDAY

THE STORY: MATTHEW 5:1-12

With the opening of the Sermon on the Mount, Jesus described a meek, humble and merciful people who thirst for righteousness. These people are peacemakers; they are gracious even in the midst of persecution and suffering. This passage describes the character of genuine Christians. In Leviticus 18:3, shortly after delivering Israel from the Egyptians, God instructed Moses to tell the people to be different from the people of Canaan. Instead of walking in the statutes of the pagans, Israel was to follow God's rules and God's ways. Of course, for the most part, Israel drifted from faithfulness and obedience. Jesus spoke of another people in this passage who would be faithful to God's rules and God's ways. Though genuine Christians often fail, they progress toward becoming more and more like Christ. As Christians, we long to live righteous lives because of the new birth, and because of the Holy Spirit's power, we do. The Beatitudes are a banner under which we rally, and in this passage, Christ is holding the standard high. He fulfilled the law for us. Now we look to follow Him by living obedient lives.

TALK ABOUT IT:

How many of us would qualify as Christians if we had to live the Sermon on the Mount perfectly? (None of us would qualify.)

Since we all fail, why do we keep trying? (We are encouraged to grow in holiness because Jesus already lived a perfect life, and extends that life and its power to all those who place their hope and trust in Him. We grow in holiness not to qualify to become Christians, but because we already are Christians. Our motivation is not out of fear but out of love!)

Where do you most often fail to live according to the Sermon on the Mount? (Parents, help your children reflect on their lives. It is in seeing our sinfulness that our need for a Savior becomes evident.)

PRAY:
Thank Jesus for His perfect life and express your desire to live for Him.

TUESDAY

THE STORY: MATTHEW 5:13-16
The people of God are to stand out among the nations. We are to be salt, bringing the savor of life to the world. And we are to be light, bringing truth in the midst of darkness. Jesus is the light of the world; His Word is truth. In 1 Samuel 8:19-20 the people complained to Samuel that they wanted a king so they could be like the other nations. This people, who were called to be different from those in the land of Canaan, longed to be like the pagans around them.

As Christians we are to take up once again the charge to be a people set apart for God. No one will notice us if we live sinful lives like the rest of the world. If we live holy, joyful, humble, and merciful lives for Christ, and if we speak of Christ, we will be different from the people around us. We will be like a light shining in the darkness or flavorful salt on bland food.

TALK ABOUT IT:

Why are we called the salt of the earth? (We have the message of the gospel that gives life. Just as bland food's flavor is brought to life with salt, so does the message we carry bring the savor of life to those who receive it.)

If we are truly believers, how should we live, according to this passage? (We should be salt and light to the people of the world. If we are really Christians we will be like a light to the world by being like Jesus and by sharing the message, the gospel, of God.)

PRAY:

Ask God to so transform your heart that you are compelled to tell everyone what God has done in your life.

WEDNESDAY
WHERE IS THE GOSPEL?

THE STORY: MATTHEW 5:17-20

Jesus set a high standard of Christian attitudes and conduct that seems almost impossible to achieve.

Jesus went on to say in Matthew 5:17 that He came to fulfill the law and prophets. Jesus would be the one to fulfill the righteous life He described in the Beatitudes. We need not strive to follow the Sermon on the Mount to earn our way into God's favor. We strive to follow the Sermon on the Mount because we have already been forgiven and made righteous. Now, free of the condemnation of the law, we can follow the way of the law by following Jesus. If we should fall into sin, we need not be condemned. Instead, we confess our sin, and by the blood of Jesus our sins are covered.

Trying to live a perfectly righteous life apart from Christ is not possible. That is why the Pharisees failed. Though they kept a part of the law, they did not keep it all. To fail at just one point is to fail at keeping the whole law. Jesus gives us His righteousness - a perfect righteousness superior to the failed attempts we make on our own.

TALK ABOUT IT:

Can we live a life that matches the blessed man in Matthew 5:3-10? (Yes and no. We cannot live a life that perfectly matches the blessed man. By faith in Jesus we get credit for the life of Jesus, who lived these verses perfectly. Now we obey to follow Him and be like Him.)

How is this passage encouraging for a person who trusts in Jesus? (This passage promises heaven to the person who lives accordingly. Those who trust in Jesus receive the reward and blessing of heaven because through Jesus' life the requirements to achieve these blessings are met.)

PRAY:

Ask God to help you live according to God's direction without feeling condemnation for times of failure.

THURSDAY

THE STORY: MATTHEW 5:21-26

The Ten Commandments list God's laws and the standard of obedience for believers. Lest a person think he can fulfill the law on his own, Jesus went to the heart of the law in the Sermon on the Mount. He explained that men break the command against murder not only when they kill but also when they become angry. The law requires perfect obedience. Apart from Christ we have no hope to accomplish this. Jesus, however, fulfilled the law and lived a perfectly obedient life. He did not murder and was never sinfully angry. We obey because Jesus gave us a righteous standing, not so we can earn a righteous standing. If we had to be perfect, and then made one mistake, there would be little reason or hope to go on living for God. Jesus lived a perfect life in our place. Even when we fail and become angry at a Christian brother, we can reconcile and get help from God's Spirit to be more righteous next time.

TALK ABOUT IT:

How many of us are guilty of murdering someone in our hearts by being angry? (All of us are guilty of sinful anger.)

What hope do we have if the rules are so strict? (We have no hope to keep God's rules ourselves. Our only hope is in Jesus, who kept all of God's law in our place and gives us His perfect obedience when we believe and trust in him.)

How can we bring honor to God when we are in conflict with another? (We bring honor, worship and glory to God when we reconcile with a Christian brother or sister. True forgiveness is only possible because of what Jesus did on the cross.)

PRAY:

Ask God to help you quickly reconcile any conflicts.

FRIDAY
ON THE ROAD TO EMMAUS

THE STORY: ISAIAH 55:1-13

Jesus addressed the thirsty and hungry, telling them that the answer for their need was found in Him. Jesus, in the Sermon on the Mount, tells us that those who hunger and thirst after righteousness will be satisfied. In John 6:35 Jesus reveals that He is the bread of life that nourishes our lives. Isaiah foretells a day when all who are thirsty and hungry will be filled by one who will make an everlasting covenant with them. Jesus is the one who fulfilled Isaiah's prophecy.

TALK ABOUT IT

What is the "richest of fare," or the rich food Isaiah is speaking of? (Isaiah is not describing any normal food. The Word of God is the food that fills us. The Bible tells us in Deuteronomy 8:3 and Matthew 4:4 that "man does not live on bread alone but on every word that comes from the mouth of the Lord.")

How should knowing this affect the way we think about reading and studying the Bible? (Just as we would not want to go hungry or thirsty for food and drink, we should not want to go hungry and thirsty for God's Word. Just as we would die apart from food and water, so do our hearts need, and should desire, the nourishment of God's Word.)

PRAY
Pray God would help you love His Word and read it every day.

THE SERMON ON THE MOUNT – LOVE YOUR ENEMIES

Love your enemies.

MONDAY

THE STORY: MATTHEW 5:38-42

In this passage, Jesus cautions us against taking revenge. This passage is not meant to completely prohibit all resistance to all evil. For instance, Jesus resisted the evil of Satan and would not be forced to become Israel's king (John 6:15). This passage is not prohibiting us from defending ourselves or defending someone who is defenseless, such as a woman or child. Rather this passage is speaking to our sinful heart that desires to bring judgment on anyone who wrongs us. Here Jesus is introducing grace. The power to live a grace-filled life in this world comes when we consider eternity. If our hope lies beyond this life (into the next), we can easily give up material blessings and our violated sense of justice here and trust the Eternal Judge to vindicate our cause in his time.

TALK ABOUT IT:

What is revenge? (Revenge is when we want to return insult for insult or return harm for harm to someone who has done something against us. In our sinful hearts we want to judge them.)

Can you think of a time when you wanted to seek out revenge? (Parents, help your children think of a time when they sought revenge.)

PRAY:

Ask God to help us demonstrate love toward those who sin against us, just as Jesus demonstrated love toward us.

TUESDAY

THE STORY: MATTHEW 5:43-47

Love those who persecute you. In Leviticus 19:18, God commanded the Israelites not to bear a grudge against anyone. He said to love your neighbor as yourself. Here Jesus presents a radical clarification: Even our enemies are our neighbors, and we should love them! This would be particularly offensive to the Jew. To consider a Samaritan or Gentile as a neighbor was unthinkable. What the Jews did not know is that Jesus came to break down the barrier between Jew and Gentile. All people are created in the image of God; Jesus died for people of every race, tribe, and nation. Jesus demonstrated the ultimate example of loving His enemies when He died on the cross.

TALK ABOUT IT:

How did Jesus set the example in loving His enemies? (Jesus died on the cross as a sacrifice for the sins of those who were His enemies. He took the punishment his enemies deserved.)

How can we practically follow Jesus' example? (If we are to love our enemies, certainly we are to love our brothers and sisters. Children often fight against those who love them. The truth is, when someone sins against us, they pit themselves as enemies against us in that moment. If one child strikes another, he becomes that child's enemy. It is in these situations that God allows us to practice following Him. Should we encounter real enemies who insult us for what we believe or even if we were beaten, we can respond in love. When Jesus was on the cross, he called out, "Father, forgive them, for they do not know what they are doing" See Luke 23:34).

PRAY:
Thank the Lord for His example and ask for help to follow Jesus in loving all men.

WEDNESDAY
WHERE IS THE GOSPEL?

THE STORY: MATTHEW 5:17-20

Jesus fulfilled the law by meeting all of its requirements. Jesus also fulfilled the strict standard He presented in the sermon on the mount to love your enemies. Jesus followed his teaching to love His enemies. Paul said to the Romans: "If while we were enemies we were reconciled to God by the death of his Son, how much more, now that we are reconciled, shall we be saved by his life." (Romans 5:10)

The requirement that we should love our enemies and be perfect is an impossible task. Jesus gave us His perfect obedience in exchange for our sinfulness. Even though we cannot follow perfectly, we should strive to follow Jesus' example to love those who persecute us. By doing so, we give the Lord glory.

TALK ABOUT IT:

How did Jesus fulfill the law? (By keeping all of the law perfectly.

How does this passage fit with Mathew 5:44, which tells us to love our enemies? (Jesus provided the ultimate example of loving His enemies when He died on the cross for our sins.)

How should Jesus' love for us (when we were His enemies) encourage us to love our enemies? (We should extend the same love that has been extended to us by the Lord.)

PRAY:
Ask God to help you love your enemies.

THURSDAY

THE STORY: MATTHEW 5:21-26

Be perfect as God is perfect. With this command to be perfect, the notion that one might merit salvation by one's obedience is utterly dispelled. If perfection is the standard for obedience, who can qualify? No one qualifies for this righteousness by his or her own works. We can qualify only because Jesus lived a perfect life in our place. For those who believe and place their trust in Jesus, God imputes Christ's righteousness to their account. We are thus perfect in Christ on account of His perfection alone.

TALK ABOUT IT:

Why is Jesus' perfect obedience important for our salvation? (Perfect obedience is God's standard for righteousness. Apart from perfect obedience we could never dwell with a perfectly holy God.)

Will we ever be perfect? (Yes, when we reach heaven, remaining sin will be removed, and we will live forever with Christ without sin!)

PRAY:

Thank the Lord for fulfilling the law perfectly.

FRIDAY
ON THE ROAD TO EMMAUS

THE STORY: ISAIAH 50:5,6

Jesus, at the time of His arrest, was beaten and spat upon. Jesus received this punishment, suffered cruelly and was crucified for our sins. He did this with joy, scorning the shame of the cross for our sake. It was in doing so that Jesus exemplified his own teaching when He said in Matthew 5:39, "Do not resist the one who is evil. But if anyone slaps you on the right cheek, turn to him the other also."

TALK ABOUT IT:

Why didn't Jesus resist? (Jesus willingly took our punishment that He did not deserve. To resist would have been to reject being our substitute.)

How should Jesus' example affect the way we treat one another? (Jesus' example in suffering for us should motivate us to want to obey Matthew 5:44 and love our enemies.)

PRAY:

Thank the Lord for suffering the punishment we deserved for our sin.

THE LORD'S PRAYER

We live for the praise of God, not man.

MONDAY

THE STORY: MATTHEW 6:1-4

Give in secret. This passage seems to contradict the one that came a chapter before. In Matthew 5:16 Jesus taught we should not keep our light hidden. Now we are instructed to keep our acts of righteousness hidden in secret. What is the difference? Clearly Jesus is speaking against the way the hypocrites lived, parading their good works for all to see. They wanted to look good in front of others. Outwardly they displayed their good works, but inwardly they were full of sin.

TALK ABOUT IT:

Why might we be tempted to do our acts of righteousness before men? (If people see the good we do, they will think well of us.)

Is doing good acts for others to see wrong? (No, doing good acts that others can see is not wrong. It is the motive of the heart that is being questioned. If we give up our place in line as a true demonstration of kindness, we have not sinned. But if we call attention to giving up our place in line and draw our pleasure from the recognition that comes from our act of kindness, we are guilty of self-glory. God alone deserves the glory.)

In what ways might you be tempted toward self-glory? (Parents, help your children to see ways in which they might do good works for recognition or brag about good works for self-praise.)

PRAY:

Ask God to help us live in such a way that He receives the glory for our good works done in public or private.

TUESDAY

THE STORY: MATTHEW 6:5-13

Pray in secret. Jesus continues to warn against hypocrisy using the illustration of prayer. He is not prohibiting public prayer. Rather He is speaking against those who, when praying, draw attention to themselves. Their focus, rather than being on God, is on themselves. Their concern, rather than being communion with God, is the praise of their fellow man.

Jesus goes on to teach His disciples how to pray. The first half of the Lord's Prayer is all about giving God the glory due His name. This stands in stark contrast to the self-glorifying prayer of the hypocrite. Jesus then introduces his hearers to the amazing truth that God is our Father in heaven. God is personal. He is our Father. He has a name, a kingdom, and a will. After celebrating the glory of God and His person, the prayer moves on to requesting help from God for daily living. What an amazing truth! Jesus encourages us to ask God for help.

TALK ABOUT IT:

What are we asking for when we ask God for daily bread? (This portion of the prayer is not meant to suggest we should ask God for bread to eat every day. Daily bread represents our basic needs. We need food, clothing, water, shelter, and many other things every day. By praying to God each day for our daily bread we admit that we need God's help and cannot provide for ourselves.)

Jesus invites us to ask God to meet our daily needs. How should that encourage us in praying for the things we need? (If Jesus tells us to ask, we can expect He is prepared to act on our request. In fact, Jesus later presents God as a Father who loves to give good gifts to His children. See Matthew 7:11.)

PRAY:
Take time to pray through the Lord's Prayer, feeling the freedom to personalize "daily bread" to include what you need today. For instance, if you are sick, pray that God would heal you.

WEDNESDAY
WHERE IS THE GOSPEL?

THE STORY: MATTHEW 6:12-14
When Jesus prayed that God's kingdom would come and His will be done, He was praying for His own death to be accomplished. Prior to His crucifixion, Jesus prayed in the Garden of Gethsemane for the cup of suffering to pass, but only according to the will of His Father. Jesus came as a servant, lived a sinless life, and then gave up His life so that we could be delivered from temptation and evil. Apart from the work of Christ, the Lord's Prayer would be meaningless.

Forgiveness would not be possible if it were not for Jesus' death on the cross. God can forgive us only because the penalty for our sin has been taken by Jesus. Hebrews 9:22 tells us that without the shedding of blood, there can be no forgiveness. The Lord's Prayer would be meaningless if Jesus were not to die on the cross to make forgiveness possible.

Forgiveness marks our lives as Christians – the Lord's Prayer assumes those who seek God's forgiveness have already forgiven those who have sinned against them. Jesus concludes the Lord's Prayer by explaining that forgiving others is a requirement to receiving forgiveness. This does not mean that we can earn God's forgiveness by forgiving others. Rather, this is one of many indicators of true conversion. If we understand our sinfulness and the tremendous suffering Jesus endured to make a way for our forgiveness, we will gladly forgive others.

Our sin against God is worse than any crime that might be committed against us. If, however, we do not understand the priceless gift of God's forgiveness, we won't have a basis to forgive the debt of others against us. There is always a cost to forgiveness. Jesus endured the Father's wrath for our sin. He bore the cost of our sin in a justifying, redeeming way. Of course, we cannot do that. For us, the cost of forgiveness has to do with not seeking, demanding, or subtly exacting some kind of payment for the sin against us. The cost of forgiveness for us is in releasing the debt owed. Genuine forgiveness costs us the "right" to seek repayment for sin, or to try to somehow "get even." Such forgiving is only possible as we understand how great a debt of sin we have been forgiven in the gospel. It is simply unthinkable for ones who have been forgiven so great a debt of sin against a holy God to exact payment from others for their sins.

TALK ABOUT IT:

Why can it be hard to forgive someone who has sinned against us? (People who sin against us bring hurt upon us, and we can be unwilling to pay the cost of giving up our desire for retribution. Forgiveness releases the offender from the debt. We bear that cost ourselves. Our forgiveness is a reflection of God's forgiveness in the gospel.)

Is there anyone you don't want to forgive or find it difficult to forgive? (Parents, first be honest yourself, then draw out your children. What if a brother or sister or friend broke a favorite toy in a fit of anger? It would likely be difficult to forgive them. Sin in us might cause a desire to arise to break one of their toys. Revenge is a wicked temptation that is the opposite of forgiveness.)

PRAY:

Pray that God would give you the grace to quickly forgive others as God has forgiven you.

THURSDAY

THE STORY: MATTHEW 6:16-18

Fast in secret. Jesus continues His warning against hypocrisy by using a third illustration of fasting. In each case, with good works, prayer, and fasting, Jesus mentions a reward. Even though all we do is by God's grace, God promises to reward us for the good works He enables us to do! But if we do our good works to receive praise from men, that praise will be our only reward.

TALK ABOUT IT:

What is fasting? (Fasting is giving up eating for a short season as an act of self-denial and worship of God.)

Why would we want to fast? (It is easy to find our pleasure in the things of this world. Perhaps the food we eat gives us the most pleasure. In contrast, we can easily forget just how much we need God's Word, which is our spiritual food. Think for a minute. How long would it take for you to notice if you were not given any food? One or two meals later you would be aware of your hunger. In contrast, it is easy for us to go days, weeks, even months without taking in the Word of God. Taking away our food and putting in its place the reading of God's Word and prayer helps us keep our priorities straight. Fasting is an act of worship and devotion to God.)

PRAY:

Ask God to help you remember to keep God's Word and prayer as priorities in your life.

FRIDAY
ON THE ROAD TO EMMAUS

THE STORY: ISAIAH 53:8

Jesus was stricken for our transgressions. The wrath of God was poured out on Him instead of us. In 1 Corinthians 15:3 Paul says that Christ died for us in accordance with the Scriptures. Paul also says that this is of first importance and the heart of the Gospel.

TALK ABOUT IT:

Why is Jesus standing as our substitute so important? (We are all sinners and deserve to be punished for our sin. If Jesus did not take our place, no one would be able to go to heaven. Instead we would all be judged forever in the fires of hell.)

What does it mean that Jesus was stricken for our transgressions? (Jesus was stricken in two ways: by man and by God. Jesus - the perfect, sinless man - was persecuted and beaten by men. Secondly, Jesus was cursed by God upon the cross, and the wrath for our sin was poured out on Jesus.)

PRAY:

Thank Jesus for His sacrifice upon the cross, where He received the just penalty for our sin.

TREASURE IN HEAVEN

Where your treasure is, there will your heart be also.

MONDAY

THE STORY: MATTHEW 6:19-24

The heart is only big enough for one treasure. No one can serve two masters. We will either live for the things of this world or we will live for the God who created all things. Jesus tells us that our hearts can be filled with only one love. If we love the Lord and His kingdom, a love for money or fine things will not capture our attention. Unfortunately, the opposite is true. If our hearts are filled with a love of money or the things money can buy, there is no room for the Lord. We can't truly love both at the same time.

Our love for the Lord results in a relaxing of our hold on earthly things. We more easily give to those in need. God rewards us for these grace-motivated good works by giving us treasure in heaven.

TALK ABOUT IT:

What kinds of things tend to draw your heart away from the love that should go to Jesus? (Parents, help your children remember the things they fight over. Our selfishness often reveals our idols and sinful cravings. If we love something too much, we usually selfishly guard it so that it can't be lost or taken away.)

What kinds of things can you do to store up treasure in heaven? (All grace - motivated good works will be rewarded by God, who will judge everything we do.)

PRAY:
Ask God to help you love Him more than money or nice things.

TUESDAY

THE STORY: MATTHEW 6:25-32
There is no need to worry under the Father's care. Most people forget that God is behind the scenes, providing everything they need. We often think we provide for ourselves. It is true we work to receive wages, and with those wages we buy food and clothing. But God sustains our health and strength, and blesses the work of our hands. God provides our jobs, and even the rain to allow the food we eat to grow. God is in control of every detail of our lives! When we worry, we fall into unbelief. Then we feel pressure to strive for what we need. We have a heavenly Father who loves us more than all the animals He provides for. So, we do not need to worry, because if He loves us more than the animals, He will give us what we need.

TALK ABOUT IT:
Can you think of a time when God provided for your family in a way you did not expect, plan or work for? (Help your children by reminding them of times when God provided for you. This could be a job offer you did not seek out, an unexpected financial blessing or some great hand-me-down clothes or toys.)

Can you think of a time when you began to worry about your needs and forgot to trust God? (This one may be a bit more difficult for your children. You, however, should be able to recount a season when things were tight when you were tempted to doubt or strive apart from faith in God's provision.)

PRAY:
Thank God for providing for you. Ask the Lord to help you have faith and not doubt.

WEDNESDAY
WHERE IS THE GOSPEL?

THE STORY: 2 CORINTHIANS 4:4-7

Although it is very true that we cannot serve God and money, it is equally true that we cannot serve God alone unless God changes our hearts. Our hearts will by nature be fixed upon earthly treasure unless Jesus gives us a new nature and a love for Himself. Jesus died so that we could find our treasure in Him rather than the treasures of this world. Jesus is the treasure God has placed in our hearts. As unbelievers we were blind to see this treasure. God allowed His light to shine in our hearts that we might believe in Jesus. Now we carry this treasure in jars of clay. Jesus is our master. All other treasure will pass away. Why would we want to unseat the Lord for earthly gain?

TALK ABOUT IT:

Who is the light of the gospel? (The glory of Jesus is the light of the gospel, the wonder of all Jesus did.)

What is the treasure we have in jars of clay? (Jesus is the treasure we hold dear in our heart.)

PRAY:

Take time to pray for family or friends who remain blind to the light of the gospel.

THURSDAY

THE STORY: MATTHEW 6:33,34

Seek first the kingdom of God and the Lord will take care of you. It is kind of God to give us something to do instead of worrying. It would be much more difficult if the Lord said, "Do not worry; just be patient." We are doers by nature. Instead, God tells us to seek after His kingdom and His righteousness. We can pray as we trust God for food and ask Him for help. We can read the Bible and grow in purity and strength while we trust God to bless us with money for clothes. We can serve others while we trust that our needs will be met. When the Lord, His kingdom and His righteousness are our treasures, God our Father in heaven promises to take care of us.

TALK ABOUT IT:

What clue does this passage give us that tells us we are worrying too much? (We are worrying too much if we not only worry about today but tomorrow as well.)

What kinds of things can you do to seek the kingdom of God and His righteousness? (God's kingdom is His rule and authority. The best place to seek God's kingdom is in the Bible. The Bible tells us all about God's kingdom and what we can do to better follow God. For example, when we read about loving one another, doing so advances God's kingdom in our lives. When we do what God asks us to do, we advance God's rule in our heart. That advances His kingdom in our lives.)

PRAY:

Ask God to help you seek after His rule and His kingdom and His righteousness.

FRIDAY
ON THE ROAD TO EMMAUS

THE STORY: 2 SAMUEL 22:1-4

David sang these words in praise to God for deliverance. David's words, though they refer to God saving him from His immediate enemies, also point forward prophetically. The truth is, apart from the future saving work of Christ, there would be only judgment for David, not salvation. In fact, every time God saves His people from harm in the Old Testament accounts, God points to the work of Jesus that will come. It is because of what Jesus was going to do that salvation was extended to Israel. And salvation was extended to David so that Jesus could come. Every time David was saved from death, his lineage was preserved so that Jesus, the descendant of David, might come!

TALK ABOUT IT:

When we read David's words of praise today, who should we think of? (We should think of Jesus. He is our horn of salvation, our refuge, and our Savior.)

How does this passage complement Jesus' words in Matthew 6 about not worrying and about seeking first the kingdom, of God? (David trusted the Lord, and God provided for David. Few of us have a sinful king trying to kill us. If David could trust the Lord in his grave situation we should be able to trust God for our daily needs.)

PRAY:

Make David's prayer of praise your own. Pray to the Lord and thank Him for being your rock, fortress, deliverer, horn of salvation, stronghold, refuge and Savior.

WISE AND FOOLISH BUILDERS

Men are known by the fruit of their labors.

MONDAY

THE STORY: MATTHEW 7:15-20

The motivation of our hearts is known by our fruit. The Lord told Samuel that "man looks at the outward appearance, but the Lord looks on the heart" (1 Samuel 16:7). This truth is shown throughout Scripture. Here in this text we see that men will come to the church claiming to speak for God, yet inwardly they are corrupt. The fruit of their lives will not match the holiness God's Word calls for. We can recognize those who are false by what comes out of their lives. This applies to everyone. In fact, the fruit of our lives is a good indicator of where our heart's devotion is set. Our secret life is the part of our life that others do not often see. What goes on in secret will, in time, bear fruit, good or bad, in keeping with what is good or bad in our hearts.

TALK ABOUT IT:

What does the fruit represent in this parable? (The fruit represents our deeds. Anyone can say he is a Christian. But the fruit of one's life may suggest that perhaps he is not a true Christian at all.)

How does the fruit of our lives reveal what we love? (The choices we make when no one is watching reveal one's true self. The Pharisees did their acts of service before men, blowing trumpets to announce their deeds, but they were much different when no one was around.)

PRAY:

Pray that God would change your heart to love God and want to serve Him all the time, not just when others are looking.

TUESDAY

THE STORY: MATTHEW 7:21-23

Words alone are worthless. This passage teaches us the sober truth that people are not Christians just because they call themselves Christians. Just because a person calls Jesus Lord doesn't mean that God has changed his or her heart. James said it like this: "You believe that God is one; you do well. Even the demons believe – and shudder!" (James 2:19). We know that the demons will not go to heaven, yet they knew who Jesus was and even declared it publicly (see Mark 1:23,24). Even our good works apart from God's grace cannot earn us a place in heaven. Believing in Jesus' atoning death on the cross is the only way to salvation. Jesus knows all who are His. Knowing Jesus and being known by him is the key. Good words and even good deeds can never be valuable enough to purchase salvation. There is no salvation other than the salvation Christ alone purchased for those who are His. "And there is salvation in no one else, for there is no other name under heaven given among men by which we must be saved" (Acts 4:12).

TALK ABOUT IT:

What made the people think they were Christians in these verses? (They thought they were Christians based on what they said and did.)

What can bring us salvation? Can trusting in what we say and do save us, or must we trust in what Jesus said and did? (Trusting in what Jesus said and did is our only hope. All our good words and works, the best we have to offer, are like filthy rags to God. Isaiah 64:6 says" all our righteous deeds are like a polluted garment.")

PRAY:
Tell God that you understand you cannot save yourself by your words or deeds. Ask God to save each person in your family based on what Jesus has done, not our words or works.

WEDNESDAY
WHERE IS THE GOSPEL?

THE STORY: 1 CORINTHIANS 3:10-15
Jesus Christ is the rock - the sure foundation upon which we should build our lives. There is no other foundation upon which to build that will last. In the parable of the wise and foolish builders, the man who built his house on the rock is building his house upon Christ. When we trust Christ, the rock and the foundation, we trust the one who paid the penalty for our sin. That rock is the basis of our claim to forgiveness and life everlasting in heaven.

TALK ABOUT IT:
Who is the foundation for a Christian? (Jesus is our foundation.)

Does everyone build wisely on that foundation? (No, some do not build wisely, and when tested, what they build will burn up in the fires of judgment.)

What kinds of things does the Bible tell us are good works that will last as treasure in heaven? (Accept as correct Bible verse about serving one another, considering others better than ourselves, worshipping God, etc.)

PRAY:
Ask God to help each member of your family to trust Christ as the foundation for their lives. Then ask Him to help each one build in such a way that what is built will last forever.

THURSDAY

THE STORY: MATTHEW 7:24-27
The wise builder builds upon the rock. The foundation for all our good works is Christ and His Word. If we do good works but don't have the foundation of Christ, we are building on sand. It is interesting to note that storms come for both those who build on the sand and those whose foundation is Christ, the rock. James 1:1-3 and 1 Peter 1:6,7 explain that God uses the stormy trials of life to build our faith.

TALK ABOUT IT:
What is a foundation? (A foundation is the very bottom of a building, upon which everything else stands. If your foundation is bad, your whole house will eventually fall apart. Take your children to the foundation of your house and show them how strong it is. Most houses have stone, cement or block foundations.)

Why are Jesus and His Word compared to a foundation of rock? (Rock is the best foundation you can have. It is heavy and cannot be easily moved. If we trust in Christ, we are trusting in something that will never move! If Christ is your foundation, that foundation will last forever!)

PRAY:
Pray that God would change the heart of every member of your family and give you each the desire to build upon Him and His Word.

FRIDAY
ON THE ROAD TO EMMAUS

THE STORY: ISAIAH 51:5-8

It is only through Jesus that we will have everlasting salvation. Here, through Isaiah, God promised Israel a day when His righteousness, salvation and justice would come to the nations. God's salvation and righteousness will never fail, because the sacrifice of Jesus on the cross defeated sin and death forever. Those who trust in Christ walk in His righteousness and will live forever with Him in heaven.

TALK ABOUT IT:

How do we know the salvation Isaiah is writing about refers to our salvation in Christ? (Our salvation in Christ is the only everlasting salvation there is. Some may have been saved from disease, or saved from attack by enemy armies or saved from starvation, but they still needed to be saved from sin and death. It is only through Jesus that our complete and everlasting salvation is found.)

How can we receive this salvation? (If we believe in the gospel, that Jesus Christ died on the cross for our sin and rose again, and trust in Jesus as our only hope, the Bible tells us God will save us.)

PRAY:

Pray that God will give every member of your family grace to believe in Christ and place their complete trust in Him.

THE FOUR SOILS

The gospel is the seed that is sown and bears fruit in the lives of those who believe.

MONDAY

THE STORY: MATTHEW 13:1-11

Not all seed produces a crop. So many people came to hear Jesus teach that He got into a boat and went out from shore so that the crowds could gather along the lake to hear Him teach. Jesus told the crowd a story, or parable, about a farmer who was throwing down seed to plant. The seed hit four different places. It landed on the hard path, in the rocky areas, among the thorns and on good soil. Although three of the four soils allowed the seed to grow, only the plants sown in the good soil survived long enough to produce fruit or a crop. It is clear from what follows that Jesus did not explain what the parable meant. Later He explained it to His disciples but not to the crowd.

TALK ABOUT IT:

Do you think you could figure out what the parable meant without Jesus' explanation? (We might guess that it was good to be like the seed on the good soil, but we would likely not understand.)

Why didn't Jesus explain the parable to everyone? (We don't know all the reasons why Jesus didn't explain it to everyone, but we do know He purposefully withheld the explanation. Rather than wonder why everyone did not get the explanation, we should be thankful we have the words of Jesus preserved in the Bible. Like the disciples, we have the explanation! The question for us is: What are we going to do with it? Which of the soils are we?)

What is the secret of the kingdom? (The secret of the kingdom is that Jesus is the Messiah, and that His sacrifice on the cross was necessary to atone for sin.)

PRAY:
Thank God for giving us the secrets of the kingdom of heaven.

TUESDAY

THE STORY: MATTHEW 13:11-17
The secrets of the kingdom are hidden from those who close their eyes. Jesus further explained his use of parables to the disciples. He quoted Isaiah, who prophesied about people who would see and hear but not understand. Many people saw and heard Jesus but did not understand or believe. These were the kind of people to whom He told the parable of the sower. These people's hearts became calloused and hard, and they would not believe. The disciples' hearts were different. To them Jesus revealed the secrets of the kingdom of heaven.

TALK ABOUT IT :
Why should verse 17 both excite us? (We know who Jesus is. We know the exact path to salvation. The people of God and the prophets of old longed to see the salvation of God, but they couldn't.)

How should we respond when we realize that we know the very secrets of God's kingdom? (We should praise God for revealing the gospel to us. Even today the gospel message goes forth and still lands on four very different soils. Not everyone believes. Many reject the message of Jesus.)

PRAY:

Pray that God would soften the heart of every member of your family that the gospel might bear fruit in each of their lives.

WEDNESDAY
WHERE IS THE GOSPEL?

THE STORY: 2 TIMOTHY 1:7-10

The Gospel is the message about the kingdom of God that Jesus introduced in the parable of the sower. We are the farmers. We sow the seed of the gospel when we are not afraid to testify about our Lord. The plan of the gospel was God's plan to save us since the beginning of time. The prophets of old longed to see the Messiah and God's salvation revealed. With the coming of Christ, the message of the kingdom was revealed. All of us who receive that message are called to bear fruit by spreading the good news.

TALK ABOUT IT:

What does it mean to be a herald? (A herald passes along an important message to others. Often a herald would shout his message so that everyone could hear. We are to herald the gospel, telling people the message of the kingdom.)

What stands in our way from sharing the gospel? (Most of us struggle with the fear that people might reject us or think we are strange.)

PRAY:

Pray that God would give us both the opportunity and the courage to share the gospel.

THURSDAY

THE STORY: MATTHEW 13:18-23

Jesus explained the parable of the sower to the disciples. The seed, He explained, is the message about the kingdom of heaven. That message is the gospel message. The message that is sown is that Jesus Christ died on the cross for the forgiveness of our sins, and rose to new life on the third day so that we might also rise again. When that message goes out today, it falls upon the very same four types of soil.

TALK ABOUT IT:

Do you know someone who needs to hear the gospel? (Parents, draw out your children here. You can pray today for their salvation and the opportunity to sow the seed.)

PRAY:

Pray for those people and then set up a plan that might include an invitation to your home or church, thus providing an opportunity to share the gospel.

FRIDAY
ON THE ROAD TO EMMAUS

THE STORY: PSALM 14:1-7

Paul quotes this passage in Romans 3:10-12 when he explains the nature of man and the hopelessness of his condition. He goes on to contrast our sinfulness with a righteousness that is being revealed in Christ. David, the author of the psalm, looks forward to a day when salvation for Israel would come from Zion (Jerusalem). God restored the nation of Israel several times and preserved Israel from destruction. On this side of the cross, we understand that God's plan of salvation for Israel was so much more than just preserving a nation. God, through the sacrifice of Christ, brought an everlasting salvation from Israel to the people of all nations. Though David looked forward to that day, the fullness of it was hidden from him.

TALK ABOUT IT:
What does the Bible call the person who says that there is no God? (Psalm 14:1 calls that person a fool.)

What is the gospel? (Parents, never grow tired of asking your children to tell you what the gospel is. If there is one truth we want to be certain they fully comprehend, it is the gospel of the kingdom.)

PRAY:
Thank the Lord for the gospel and that we have the privilege of knowing what some of the godliest men in ancient history could only long to see.

THE HIDDEN TREASURE

Christ, our treasure, is worth everything we have.

MONDAY

THE STORY: MATTHEW 13:31-33

Jesus was teaching parable after parable. In the parable of the mustard seed and the yeast, we have stories of things that are very small that multiply and grow to make something much larger. The kingdom of God was introduced to men by Jesus. He called 12 disciples, who in turn spread the message of the kingdom across the land. Others like the apostle Paul were called to proclaim the gospel, and it spread mightily. Now we also are called to share the gospel to those who have not heard it. We are a part of that mustard tree growing to reach people from every tribe, language, and nation.

TALK ABOUT IT:

What is the kingdom of God? (The kingdom of God is His rule. Jesus is the king, and the message of the king is the gospel.)

How is the message of the kingdom spread? (The message of the kingdom of God is spread when we share the gospel. Those who hear the message believe and receive Jesus as their Savior, Lord, and King, becoming part of the kingdom of God. They in turn tell others, and the kingdom advances.)

PRAY:

Pray that God's kingdom would come to your whole home and be spread to others through your lives.

TUESDAY

THE STORY: MATTHEW 13:44

Imagine if you found treasure in a field. You couldn't take the treasure because it belonged to the owner of the field. Therefore you sell everything you have to buy the field so you can become the owner of the treasure. If you knew that the treasure was worth well more than you had, you would not mind exchanging everything you had to purchase it.

TALK ABOUT IT:

What is the treasure Jesus is referring to? (The kingdom of God is that treasure.)

Does that mean we can buy our way into God's kingdom? (No, we cannot purchase our way into the kingdom. Jesus alone purchased our way into the kingdom through His sacrifice on the cross.)

How do we get the treasure of the kingdom of God if we can't purchase it? (We receive the blessings of the kingdom of God at no cost when we place our trust in the gospel. Placing our trust in the gospel does cost us something in this sense: In order to truly receive Jesus as King, we must forsake any loyalty to sin and the idols of our hearts.)

PRAY:

Ask God to help you see the value of the kingdom of God so that you might desire it more than anything in this world.

WEDNESDAY
WHERE IS THE GOSPEL?

THE STORY: PSALM 78:1-4

Jesus quoted Psalm 78:2 in Matthew 13:35 to explain why He was speaking in parables. These parables reveal the secrets of the gospel that lay hidden since the creation of the world. The treasure in the field and the pearl of great price have great value because of the gospel. The gospel is an invaluable treasure because it makes a way for us to become children of God and enter His kingdom.

TALK ABOUT IT:

What was hidden since the creation of the world? (Jesus revealed many things that were hidden. The lambs of the Passover were really a foreshadowing of the coming of Jesus, the perfect lamb. It has now been revealed that Jesus died for the sins of God's people that we might be forgiven. God's kingdom would not be only national but would be much bigger. It has now been revealed that God's kingdom consists of all those who put their faith in Christ. All these things were revealed by Christ to his disciples and are now made plain for all who believe the Bible.)

What does the psalmist, Asaph, say we should do with all we know? (We need to continue to spread the good news, the deeds of the Lord, to the next generation. We need to tell our children what our Lord has done. Of course, the greatest of all God's work with man is His work of salvation.)

PRAY:

Thank Jesus for dying on the cross for our sin.

THURSDAY

THE STORY: MATTHEW 13:45,46

Directly following the parable of the hidden treasure is the parable of the pearl of great value. This time we see that the man in the parable was looking for valuable pearls. When he found this one pearl of great value, he was so caught up with that pearl that he sold everything he had so he could buy the pearl. Many people are searching for true happiness. It is only in laying hold of Jesus and the forgiveness of sins that we will ever know lasting, eternal joy. Receiving this gift of eternal joy is certainly worth forsaking all the temporary joys that sin uses to lure us into bondage and eternal doom.

TALK ABOUT IT:

What should we be willing to give up for Jesus? (Everything.)

Do we have to give up everything we own to follow Jesus? (No, but we need to love Jesus more than anything else and be willing to give it all up for him. When Jesus told the rich young ruler in Matthew 19:21 to sell all he had and give to the poor and then to follow Him, the young man went away sad. In the end he did not follow Jesus. He loved his possessions more than the Lord.)

PRAY:

Pray that God would so touch your heart with the gospel that you would be willing to give up everything you have in the world to follow Him.

FRIDAY
ON THE ROAD TO EMMAUS

THE STORY: AMOS 9:11-15

Through the prophet Amos, God declared that a day would come when he would repair David's fallen tent. This would be a unique restoration. All the nations will bear his name, and they will never be uprooted again. This restoration of Israel and the blessing of all nations is a prophetic vision of the salvation that comes to all nations through Jesus and His life, death, and resurrection. Jesus is a king in the line of David. Jesus restored David's throne forever. In Acts 15 the apostle James quoted this passage to explain why the Gentiles were receiving the gospel (see Acts 15:13-18).

TALK ABOUT IT:

How is Amos' prophecy like God's promise to Abraham? (God promised to bless all nations through Abraham. Through Amos, God repeats that all nations will bear His name. The theme of God blessing all nations is consistent throughout the whole Bible.)

Do we bear God's name? (One way we bear God's name is that we call ourselves Christians. More importantly, we are now children in God's family, and the name "Christian" properly describes our position as a part of God's heavenly family.)

PRAY:

Thank God for reaching out to all nations with the gospel.

JESUS CALMS THE STORM

Jesus has all authority.

MONDAY

THE STORY: LUKE 8:22-25

Jesus has authority over nature. While Jesus and the disciples traveled across the Sea of Galilee, a storm blew in quickly and threatened to capsize the boat. Afraid for their lives, the disciples awakened Jesus, who was sleeping. Jesus commanded the wind and waves to quiet, and immediately calm returned to the lake. In Colossians 1:16,17 Paul tells us that Jesus created all things, and that in Him all things hold together. Jesus created the earth and controls the earth. He later told His disciples, "All authority in heaven and on earth has been given to me" (Matthew 28:18).

TALK ABOUT IT:

What does it mean to have authority over something? (To have authority over someone or something means you have the power to command them, and they must follow.)

How can this story encourage us when we are afraid? (We can place our faith in Jesus in times of fear. Jesus is with all believers by His Spirit.)

PRAY:

Thank Jesus for His amazing authority over all things, including our lives.

TUESDAY

THE STORY: LUKE 8:26-33

Jesus has authority over demons. When Jesus and the disciples reached the other side of the lake, they were confronted by a demon-possessed man. (Matthew tells us in Matthew 8:28 that there were two demon-possessed men present. Luke tells the story of the more vocal of the two.) Not only did the demons know who Jesus was, they also knew they were subject to Jesus' authority. They didn't even begin to fight Jesus, instead pleading that He would not destroy them. Jesus gave the demons permission to enter a herd of pigs. Immediately they fled into the pigs, and the pigs rushed down a steep bank and were drowned.

TALK ABOUT IT:

Can demons have power over people? (Clearly the demons that possessed the men in the story had power over the people they possessed.)

Do we need to fear demons? (Jesus' power is much greater than that of the demons. The demons wanted no part of Jesus. Once Jesus allowed them to enter the pigs, the demons fled from the man, entered the pigs, and kept running. We should be sobered by the power of demons but secure in the power of Christ. Only those who reject Christ need fear demons.)

PRAY:

Thank God for His power over all, especially the forces of darkness and evil.

WEDNESDAY
WHERE IS THE GOSPEL?

THE STORY: MATTHEW 8:23-29

Why was it that the disciples could be assured of their safety in the midst of the raging storm? It was because the promised Messiah was in the boat with them. It is clear they did not yet understand who Jesus was. Jesus was no ordinary rabbi, no ordinary teacher, no ordinary prophet. Jesus was the Messiah, and He had come to save Israel from their sins.

When Jesus rebuked the wind and the water, the disciples questioned again, "Who is this?" Who is Jesus? That is the most important question anyone could ask. And getting the answer right is absolutely crucial. Jesus is the Son of God, who was fully man and fully God. As a man, He needed His rest, and so He fell asleep on the boat. As God, He held all things together by the power of His Word and was able to command the wind and the waves. It was not until after Jesus died, rose again, and then appeared to His disciples that they would begin to fully understand the answer to the question, "Who is this?"

When they reached the other side of the lake, Jesus was met by two demon-possessed men. Unlike the disciples, the demons needed no introduction to Jesus. One of the demons shouted out, calling Jesus, "Son of the Most High God" (Luke 8:28).

TALK ABOUT IT:

What do we learn about Jesus from this passage of Scripture? (We learn quite a bit about Jesus' power and authority. We learn that Jesus himself has the authority to rebuke the natural forces of the earth, and they obey. We also learn that the demons know who Jesus is - the Son of God.)

Does what we learn about Jesus suggest He is a mere prophet like those in the Old Testament, or does it suggest He is God? (Jesus' direct command of the earth and the demons' knowledge of his identity all point to Jesus' divinity, telling us He is God.)

PRAY:

Thank Jesus for humbling Himself and for coming to us as a man that He might be our sacrifice.

THURSDAY

THE STORY: LUKE 8:34-39

Jesus is God. The man who was freed from the demons wanted to travel with Jesus. But Jesus told him to return home. Imagine the delight of his family and friends when they saw him well again. There is an important exchange between Jesus and the man. Jesus told the man to tell his family how much God had done for him. Though Jesus did not directly say that He is God, He revealed it in His direction to the man. The man was not confused. He reported how much Jesus had done for him. In this passage, Jesus and God are used interchangeably because Jesus is God.

TALK ABOUT IT

Why is it important to recognize that Jesus is God? (Those who doubt Christianity or try to twist it nearly always say that Jesus is not God. Jesus was both fully God and fully man. Yet He did not boast of His deity but humbled himself, taking on the nature of a servant [see Philippians 2:6,7].)

PRAY

Pray a prayer of praise to Jesus, who is both God and man, who is creator over all, and who has authority over all.

FRIDAY
ON THE ROAD TO EMMAUS

THE STORY: PSALM 23

David calls the Lord his shepherd. Jesus is revealed to us as the Shepherd. David is satisfied in the Lord because He provides rest. Jesus said, "Come to me, all you who are weary and burdened, and I will give you rest" (Matthew 11:28). In Revelation 7:17 we read that one day the Lamb, who is Jesus, will lead us to springs of water and wipe every tear from our eyes. Although this passage does not claim to be a prophetic announcement of Jesus, it certainly points to Him. It is only because of the sacrifice of Jesus that David could walk on paths of righteousness. And it is only through Jesus that David could dwell in the house of the Lord forever.

TALK ABOUT IT:

How can this psalm of David comfort us today? (David trusted the Lord in his time of trouble. So can we. The Lord is also our shepherd.)

What advantage do we have over David? (When David wrote the psalm and trusted the Lord, he did not know how God would work salvation for him. We know the whole glorious, wonderful story of the Savior. If David could trust the Lord with the little he knew, we have no excuse for not trusting. All the mysteries of the gospel have been shown to us.)

PRAY:

Ask God to help you not take the gospel for granted. We have been entrusted with much. We need God's help to always hold the gospel dear.

JESUS FEEDS THE MULTITUDE

The life and ministry of Christ is sufficient to feed all men.

MONDAY

THE STORY: JOHN 6:1-4

Jesus and the disciples ministered to the people be healing their sicknesses. As they did, word spread among the people, and a very large crowd gathered. Luke 9:10 tells us in his account that the disciples had just returned from Jesus sending them out to preach and heal. Matthew 14:14 adds that Jesus healed sick people there as well. As a result of these miracles, people came to see or themselves. These people were more attracted by Jesus' miracles, although Jesus had compassion on them for He saw them as sheep without a shepherd (see Mark 6:34).

TALK ABOUT IT

Why do you think the people were attracted to the miracles? (They had never seen anything like that before. Blind people received sight, the lame were walking, and the deaf could hear. These people were utterly amazed, just as we would be.)

Is there a greater reason to follow Jesus than the healing of our sicknesses? (Yes, the greater work that Jesus did was the forgiving of our sins. Jesus was glad for their eagerness to follow. But he understood they needed more than miracles. They desperately needed a Savior who would cleanse them of sin and provide for them righteousness in the sight of God.)

PRAY

Ask God to help every person in your family to love the Lord Himself and not just His mighty works.

TUESDAY

THE STORY: JOHN 6:5-13

Jesus showed the crowd an even greater miracle. After healing their sicknesses, Jesus had the people sit down. He then, amazingly, demonstrated His power as Creator. Jesus offered thanks and then multiplied the fish and loaves. The details of how this was done or what it looked like are not given to us. We can be sure this was not a miracle of satisfied appetites having only eaten a small portion of the original fish. Twelve basketfuls were collected! This miraculous account is found in all four Gospels.

TALK ABOUT IT:

Why do you think the Lord wanted to test Philip's faith? (The Lord regularly tests our faith to cause it to grow [See 1 Peter 1:7].)

How can this story help build our faith? (At times we might find ourselves in what seems like impossible situations. Knowing that God is all-powerful and that He loves to help us in our time of need builds faith. In the past He has worked in power to help people. This can encourage us to pray and ask God for help.)

How should God's provision for the 5,000 encourage us as we trust God for the food we need? (This story helps us to see that God can and will provide all of our needs.)

PRAY:

Thank God for caring for us and providing for our needs.

WEDNESDAY
WHERE IS THE GOSPEL?

THE STORY: JOHN 6:25-40

In John 6:35 Jesus said, "I am the bread of life; whoever comes to me shall not hunger, and whoever believes in me shall never thirst."

Jesus' providing food for the 5,000 is a picture of a greater salvation He would bring. He is not just the multiplier of the fish and the loaves. He Himself is the bread of life.

John 6:40 continues, "For this is the will of my Father, that everyone who looks on the Son and believes in him should have eternal life, and I will raise him up on the last day."

TALK ABOUT IT:

What is the most encouraging verse in this passage? (There is no wrong answer, but John 6:40 is a promise worth remembering. Consider the implications of this verse with your family.)

What does it mean to "look to the Son"? (The question is, who are we looking to for our salvation? If we look to the Son, we look to Jesus and His atoning sacrifice for our salvation. Some look to themselves and think they can get to heaven by the good works they do.)

PRAY:

Ask God to help us "look to the Son" and trust Jesus for our salvation.

THURSDAY

THE STORY: JOHN 6:14,15

Jesus was more than a prophet. After multiplying the fishes and loaves, the people wanted to make Jesus their king. They didn't want to worship Him. They wanted to selfishly make him their king so he could use His power to deliver them from the Rome. God had promised a king - a deliverer. Many of the Jews assumed he would be an earthly king who would reign on David's earthly throne and throw off the foreign domination of Rome. These people were actually prepared to force Jesus to be their king. But Jesus would not be forced to do anything. He was already King of Kings, ruling over heaven and earth. His mission was far more important than overthrowing Rome. Jesus came to overthrow the dominion of sin and death for all who would believe.

TALK ABOUT IT:

Why would the people want Jesus to be their king? (They could use His miraculous power to overthrow the Roman government.)

Why didn't Jesus let them make Him king? (Jesus didn't come to be crowned king over Jerusalem. He came to conquer sin and death, not the Roman Empire.)

PRAY:

Thank Jesus for being our King and Lord, conquering death and sin.

FRIDAY
ON THE ROAD TO EMMAUS

THE STORY: 1 SAMUEL 2:9,10

These verses are the very end of Hannah's prayer of thanksgiving for Samuel, the child God gave her. She prophesied a day when God would raise up His king and exalt the horn of His anointed. Her son Samuel would grow up to be a prophet. He anointed David as God's king. But David would only be a partial fulfillment of this prophetic word. One day God would raise up Jesus the eternal King. Jesus revealed that the Father had anointed Him with the Holy Spirit (see Luke 4:18).

TALK ABOUT IT:

Did Israel have a king when Hannah prayed her prayer? (No. Saul, Israel's first king, was probably not even born yet.)

Why would Hannah talk about God giving strength to His king if there was no king in Israel? (Hannah's prayer was a prophetic prayer that looked forward to the day when God would give strength to His king.)

PRAY:

Thank God for sending His son Jesus to be our King and Savior.

JESUS WALKED ON WATER

Jesus, truly the Son of God, is worthy of our worship.

MONDAY

THE STORY: MATTHEW 14:22,23

Jesus is our example in prayer. Prior to facing Satan, who tempted Jesus, Jesus fasted and prayed. After leaving a crowd who desired to make Him king, Jesus prayed. His retreat to pray is an example of his determination to obey the Father's plan and not yield to the desires of those who would want to make Him King for their own selfish purpose. In Hebrews we learn that Jesus was tempted just like us in every way, but He did not sin (Hebrews 4:15). Jesus' example should guide us in our fight against the sins that tempt us. Jesus prayed. We have no greater weapon than prayer and fellowship with God. God's plan for our lives is always better than some other plan that may arise to tempt us.

TALK ABOUT IT:

What did Jesus do when the people wanted to make him a king? (He left them to pray.)

What can we learn from Jesus' example? (When faced with temptation, we need to pray like Jesus did.)

How can praying to God help us fight temptation? (Temptation offers us fleeting, worldly pleasure. When we pray to God or read His Word, we realize that eternal pleasures are in Christ. With those realities in clear view, and with the help of God's power, we can overcome temptation.)

PRAY:
Ask God to help us grow in our practice of prayer.

TUESDAY

THE STORY: MATTHEW 14:24-32
Jesus walked on water and saved Peter. Peter opened his mouth and said, "Lord, if it is You, command me to come to You on the water." Jesus told him to come. To Peter's credit, he got out of the boat and started to walk toward Jesus. As soon as Peter became afraid and doubted, he began to sink and called out to the Lord to save him. Jesus, without hesitation, reached out and caught him. Jesus stands ready to catch us as well. We simply need to call out to Jesus with the very same words Peter did: "Lord, save me!"

TALK ABOUT IT:
How are we like Peter in this story? (We sometimes start out trusting God, only to doubt when a trial comes. In those trials we should turn to the Lord and ask for help.)

Can you remember a time when you were faced with a trial and were afraid? (Parents, this would be a great opportunity to share a testimony from your own lives. When your children see that you need the Lord and that you are sometimes afraid, they will be encouraged to follow your example.)

PRAY:
Thank the Lord for saving us and protecting us.

WEDNESDAY
WHERE IS THE GOSPEL?

THE STORY: MATTHEW 14:33

Jesus was no ordinary man. He was more than a great teacher. Jesus was, and is, God. When the disciples on the boat saw Jesus walk on the stormy waves, they worshipped Him as God. Little did they know that this same Jesus, who had power over the wind and the waves, who could walk on water and heal all the sicknesses of those who came to Him, would soon die on the cross for their sins.

In this story, Peter cried out, "Lord, save me." His words were more profound than he could realize. In our lives, the storm is one of our own sin. We are separated from God and need to cry out with those same words: "Lord, save me." Just like with Peter, the Lord extends His hand to save and deliver us safely to the shore of heaven.

TALK ABOUT IT:

How are our lives today like Peter walking on the waves? (Like Peter, we need Jesus to save us.)

Why is the disciples' worship of Jesus significant? (Their worship of Jesus signified that they believed Him to be God the Son versus just a good teacher, a kind man, or a magician. The demons on the other side of the lake had called Jesus the Son of God. Now the disciples believed and affirmed that Jesus "truly" was the Son of God.)

PRAY:

Take time to exalt the Lord in praise and words of worship.

THURSDAY

THE STORY: MATTHEW 14:34-36

Once reaching the shore, Jesus continued to heal the sick. Even those who touched him were healed. Mark records that wherever Jesus went, people brought the sick, and all who touched Jesus were healed (Mark 6:56).

TALK ABOUT IT:

What do we learn about Jesus from this passage? (Not only is Jesus all-powerful, but He is full of love and compassion for those who are sick and need His help.)

Should we still pray for those who are sick today? Why? (Yes! Jesus had such compassion on those who are suffering in Scripture, and so we can have faith that he will have compassion on those who are sick today because He never changes. When we pray, we are like the people who are bringing the sick on mats to Jesus.)

PRAY:

Take time to lift up to the Lord anyone who is in need of healing and ask Him to heal them.

FRIDAY
ON THE ROAD TO EMMAUS

THE STORY: ISAIAH 53:4

Matthew connected this passage to Christ in Matthew 8:17. Jesus fulfilled this prophecy in the way He healed those with diseases. Physical healing, like spiritual healing, is possible because of the mercy and grace of God.

TALK ABOUT IT:
Look up Matthew 8:14-17. Did Jesus only heal to fulfill the prophecy? (No. The prophecy describes the care and character of God as one who is compassionate and loving. God is a healing God. That is who He is.)

Why did Isaiah say that he was "stricken by God"? (Those who were crucified were cursed by God. In Jesus, case, Jesus was stricken with God's wrath for our sin.)

PRAY:
Continue to pray for those you know are sick.

TAKE UP YOUR CROSS

Jesus faced the cross, and we must follow Him.

MONDAY

THE STORY: LUKE 9:18-21

Jesus is called the Messiah. Jesus was praying again when He stopped to ask His disciples a question. He first asked them who the crowds thought He was and then He asked the same question to the disciples. Peter, never one to hold back his opinion, answered that Jesus is the Christ of God (the name "Christ" translated means "Messiah"). Jesus warned them not to tell anyone, knowing that the crowds had already tried to force Him to be king. Perhaps wanting to bring more instruction, Jesus went on to tell Peter of His plan to build the church (Matthew 16:17-19).

TALK ABOUT IT:

What did Jesus do that made people think He was a prophet? (God had given prophets the ability to do all kinds of miracles, so it would be natural for the people to think Jesus was a prophet.)

Can you remember any miracles the Old Testament prophets performed? (See if your children can remember some of the miracles that were similar to the things Jesus did. For example, Elijah multiplied the widow's oil and flour, and Jesus multiplied the fishes and loaves. Elisha, similarly, multiplied a widow's oil.)

PRAY:
Thank God for sending Jesus as our Messiah to deliver us from our sins.

TUESDAY

THE STORY: LUKE 9:22
Jesus is called to die. The people were expecting a triumphant king who would lead them to overthrow the Roman rule. After telling his disciples not to spread word that He was the Messiah, Jesus clued them in to the kind of Messiah He was. Jesus' triumph would come later. First, He would endure much suffering at the hands of the Jews themselves. Even worse, He would be killed. On the third day, He would be raised. Jesus would triumph - not over Rome, but over death!

TALK ABOUT IT:
Do you remember when the people wanted to force Jesus to be king? (Yes. See John 6:15, after Jesus fed the five thousand.)

Did Jesus know He would die? How do you know? (Jesus knew He was on earth to die as He described in verse 22. The cross came as no surprise. The writer of Hebrews tells us, "Let us fix our eyes on Jesus, the author and perfecter of our faith, who for the joy set before Him endured the cross, scorning its shame, and sat down at the right hand of the throne of God" [Hebrews 12:2].)

Do you think Jesus was afraid of dying? (No. Although He knew it would be painful, He was willing to obey His Father with joy. The joy Christ anticipated was the joy of restoring people to fellowship with God. What a joy that is!)

PRAY:
Thank the Lord for His willingness to die to save us.

WEDNESDAY
WHERE IS THE GOSPEL?

THE STORY: LUKE 9:22-25

In Luke 9:22 Jesus specifically predicted His death and resurrection, which is the core of the gospel story. He continues in verse 23 to describe how the path to following Him involves our own cross. We must be willing to give up everything, even our very lives. Physical death is not a requirement, but death to self and the pleasures of this world are a definite cost of following Jesus. If we try to secure salvation or save our own lives by any other means, we will fail. Whether by our good works or our own understanding, all paths outside the gospel fail and end in/lead to eternal death. We can only have life if we trust in Jesus and what He has done on the cross on our behalf.

The passing treasures of this life may bring temporary happiness, but even all the treasures of the earth cannot equal our salvation in Christ. Money cannot buy eternal joy. Good works cannot save.

TALK ABOUT IT:

Where do you see the gospel in this passage? (The gospel message is that Jesus died for our sins and rose again from the dead. Both of these components are found in this passage.)

What other parts of the gospel are not found in this passage? (It doesn't talk about the Crucifixion, the Father's wrath poured out upon Jesus, or that He would appear again to the disciples.)

PRAY:

Thank Jesus for His willingness to die. Pray that each member of your family would be willing to give up everything to follow Jesus.

THURSDAY

THE STORY: LUKE 9:26,27

We are called to follow Him. Jesus goes on to tell His disciples (and all of us) that we must be willing to give up everything to follow Him. Most of the disciples would one day be killed for following Jesus. Some of them literally took up their cross. We must be willing to give up anything as we follow Christ. Any sacrifices we make to be His disciples, or any crosses we bear, cannot be compared with having Jesus and His wonderful salvation.

TALK ABOUT IT:

What kinds of things tempt us away from the love and affection we should give the Lord? (Just about anything can take the Lord's place in our hearts. Money and possessions are a big idol for many, but comfort and control can also win our affections over from the Lord. You can always tell if you love something too much when it is threatened to be taken away. We should love nothing more than the Lord, and we must be willing to sacrifice all for Him.)

When are we most likely to be ashamed of the Lord? (The fear of man is a great struggle for many Christians. God calls us to spread the good news of the gospel, but many are afraid of what people might think of them. We need to be sobered by the words of Christ and ask God that His Spirit would fill us and embolden us to share our faith as the Spirit leads us.)

PRAY:

Ask God for courage to be willing to give up anything for the Lord, and for the courage to witness and not give in to the fear of man.

FRIDAY
ON THE ROAD TO EMMAUS

THE STORY: ISAIAH 53:1-3

Isaiah described a suffering servant who would be "despised and rejected by men, a man of sorrows and suffering." Jesus identified with this description when He said, "The Son of Man must suffer many things and be rejected by the elders, chief priests and teachers of the law," in Luke 9:22. Peter also identified Christ as one who was rejected by men (1 Peter 2:4).

TALK ABOUT IT:

What do you think the verse about no beauty or majesty is referring to? (Jesus was a king, but He did not come as a king should come. Rather than arriving dressed in royal robes, Jesus was born in a stable.)

How was Jesus rejected? (Jesus was rejected by the Jewish rulers. He was also rejected by His own disciples, who fled in fear after His arrest in the garden.)

PRAY:

Pray that God would draw every member of your family to Jesus and that no one would reject Him.

THE TRANSFIGURATION

The glory of God is revealed in Jesus.

MONDAY

THE STORY: MARK 9:1-4

Jesus revealed His glory. Jesus took Peter, James, and John up on a high mountain. These three men were brought there to witness the glory of God in Christ. Luke tells us that as the Lord prayed (Luke 9:29), the appearance of His face changed, and His clothes began to radiate in glorious splendor. By revealing His glory, Jesus demonstrated that He could, with the glories of heaven, show His power at any moment. This confirms that Jesus went to the cross freely and willingly, as a lamb led to the slaughter. Elijah and Moses appeared with Jesus, representing the fulfillment of the law and the prophets. The disciples seemed to immediately recognize them even though they had never seen these men before.

TALK ABOUT IT:

What does the transfiguration tell us about Jesus? (Though Jesus became a man and put aside His glory, He never lost His glory.)

Why did Jesus put aside His glory and become a man like you and me? (Paul tells us in Philippians 2 that Jesus humbled Himself by taking on human flesh so that he could die in our place. To put it simply, Jesus became a man to die and take the punishment we deserved.)

Will we ever see Jesus in all His glory? (Yes. When we go to heaven we will be with Him. When He returns, He will come in all his glory and might. There will never be night again, and no lights will be needed because all of heaven will stay lit with the glory of Jesus [see Revelation 21:23].)

PRAY:
Thank the Lord for laying aside His glory that He might die as a man in human flesh in our place.

TUESDAY

THE STORY: MARK 9:5-8
The father affirmed His son. The disciples were very frightened. Peter suggested that three shelters, or memorials, be built. While he was still speaking, Matthew records that a cloud came down and covered them (Matthew 17:5). Out from the cloud, interrupting Peter, came the voice of the Father to settle the matter. Three shelters would not be necessary, because they were to listen to the Son. When the cloud left, Moses and Elijah were gone, and only Jesus remained.

TALK ABOUT IT:
Why were the disciples afraid? (They heard the voice of God. Any exposure to God, whether it be to His voice or a portion of His glory, is a fearful thing for any man.)

Should we be afraid of God? (Yes. All Christians should have a respectful fear of God, much like a person has a respectful fear of a police officer. Those who are not believers should also fear God's judgment.)

PRAY:
Ask God to give us a respectful fear that will help us to obey His law.

WEDNESDAY
WHERE IS THE GOSPEL?

THE STORY: MARK 9:9,10

Here, in a moment of time, three of the disciples had the opportunity to get a glimpse of the holiness, glory, and power of Jesus as God. They knew Jesus, the ordinary man. But they didn't know Jesus, the Son, in glory. If Jesus was not both fully God and fully man, He could not have taken our punishment on the cross and then risen from the dead. Jesus was resolute. He would take that penalty. He would die. And, praise the Lord, He would also rise from the dead.

After the Transfiguration, Jesus gave His disciples strict orders not to tell anyone about what they had seen until Jesus had risen from the dead. They could not understand all that had been revealed to them at that time. They didn't understand what Jesus meant by being raised from the dead or even what His transfiguration revealed. Later they would come to more fully understand that God the Son, Jesus, had come down to earth to take on human flesh that He might die for the sins of man.

TALK ABOUT IT:

What instructions did Jesus give the three disciples on the way down the mountain? (Jesus gave them orders not to tell anyone what they had seen until after the Resurrection.)

Why didn't Jesus want them to tell anyone? (The text does not tell us, but given their confusion and resulting speculation, it is likely everyone would be confused. Also, if the people heard of the Lord's glory, they would likely have wanted to make Him king all the more.)

PRAY:

Thank Jesus again for His sacrifice. We must never tire of thanking Him for His death on the cross.

THURSDAY

THE STORY: MARK 9:9-13

Jesus answered His disciples. Imagine being the disciples. What would you say? They tried to make sense of everything they had seen and heard, but they didn't understand. Jesus explained that the Elijah who was to come had already come. Jesus had already mentioned that to them before (Mathew 11:9-13). Though they didn't understand at the time, they would one day know exactly who Elijah was, why Jesus would need to suffer, and what Jesus meant when He said He would rise from the dead.

TALK ABOUT IT:

Did the disciples understand what had just happened? (No. The disciples didn't understand much of what was taking place.)

Why didn't they understand? (We can sometimes forget just what a crazy experience the whole thing was for them. They had never seen or heard of a transfiguration. They didn't know about people rising from the dead. And they had certainly never seen two men of God from ages past appear at the top of a mountain.)

PRAY:

Thank God for His plan of salvation through His Son Jesus.

FRIDAY
ON THE ROAD TO EMMAUS

THE STORY: PSALM 72:11-13

Jesus is the one to which all kings will bow. Paul tells us that at the name of Jesus every knee will bow (Philippians 2:10). This includes all the kings of the earth from all time. Revelation 17:14 tells us that the Lamb of God, Jesus, is the King of Kings.

TALK ABOUT IT:

When will all the kings of the earth from all time bow to the throne of Jesus? (In the last judgment, all men will know that Jesus is Lord. Those who rejected Him will be sent to eternal punishment, but they will all know that Jesus is King of Kings and Lord of Lords. They will all bow before His authority at that time.)

Why are we blessed to know the kingship of Jesus while we are yet alive? (No one needs to force us to worship at the throne of Jesus. We can pledge our lives to Him right now and call out to Him to save us from our sin.)

PRAY:

Give praise to the Lord Jesus Christ, King of Kings and Lord of Lords, through prayer.

JESUS CLEANSED TEN LEPERS

The forgiveness of our sin is the greatest healing we can receive.

MONDAY

THE STORY: LUKE 17:11-13

Ten lepers met Jesus on His way to Jerusalem. They called out to the Lord to have pity on them. The whole countryside was stirring with excitement regarding the ministry of Jesus. He had multiplied the fishes and the loaves. He had turned the water into wine. He had healed many people of all kinds of diseases. As Jesus approached their village, these lepers called Jesus by name. They called Him "Master," the title given to a teacher or rabbi. Little did they know what was about to happen.

TALK ABOUT IT:

Why did these men stand at a distance? (Lepers were required to keep away from people for fear that others would catch their disease.)

Did they know who Jesus was? (They used Jesus' name and knew He was a teacher. But they didn't know is that He was the Son of God.)

PRAY:

Thank God that we can freely call out to the Lord without fear in our times of trouble.

TUESDAY

THE STORY: LUKE 17:11-14

Ten lepers called out to Jesus for mercy but, Jesus did not immediately heal the lepers. He directed them to show themselves to the priest. Since the priest was the one to verify the healing of a leper, there was hope in Jesus' order. All the men left to see the priest and were healed on the way. The power of God miraculously healed them. These ten men had lived as outcasts, even from their own families who could not go near them. By the power and grace of God, they could return to their families again.

TALK ABOUT IT:

Why did Jesus send the lepers to the priest? (Often Jesus called those He healed to act in faith. In this case, the priest would be the one to pronounce them healed.)

What do we learn about Jesus from His conversation with the lepers? (Jesus sent them to the priest immediately, without hesitation. They called for mercy from the very one who could grant them mercy, and Jesus did just that. Jesus showed compassion and care for the outcasts of the community.)

How should Jesus' response affect the way we pray? (Jesus is the same today. The Bible tells us that we can "approach the throne of grace with confidence, that we may receive mercy and find grace to help us in our time of need [read Hebrews 4:16].)

PRAY:

Take time to lift up the prayer needs of your family to the Lord with confidence.

WEDNESDAY
WHERE IS THE GOSPEL?

THE STORY: LUKE 17:17-19

Only one leper out of ten returned to give thanks for his healing! Jesus commented about his status as a foreigner, suggesting that the other nine were native-born Jews. This episode forshadowed that the message of the kingdom would be missed by the Jews, even those who had seen the power of the kingdom.

Though many Jews believed, the Jewish nation as a whole would reject Jesus as the Messiah. But the Gentiles would gladly receive the gospel. Here we see the Samaritan throw himself down at the feet of Jesus. Clearly this man was affected, not just in an outward healing, but within his heart. The others found healing; this man found Jesus. By healing the man's illness, Jesus saved his life. Our lives are also sick with sin and condemned to death. By dying on the cross, Jesus saved our lives and gave us a greater healing, the forgiveness of our sins.

TALK ABOUT IT:

What did Jesus say healed the leper? (Jesus told the leper that it was his faith that made him well.)

Even though we were not healed of leprosy, we should have the same thankful heart as the one leper in this story. Why is that? (Jesus' death on the cross made a greater healing available to us, the healing [forgiveness] of our sin.)

PRAY:

Pray that we would have the same measure of gratitude for our salvation as the returning leper did for his healing.

THURSDAY

THE STORY: LUKE 17:20,21

Ten lepers were healed. Nine Jews and one Samaritan. Only the Samaritan returned to give thanks to the Lord. Here the Jewish rulers, the Pharisees, asked Jesus (the King of the kingdom) when the kingdom of God would come. They were looking for an earthly kingdom and for their country to be set free from Rome and the surrounding Gentile nations. Jesus told them that the kingdom does not come with their careful observation. It would not be one they could see with their natural eyes. Rather, God's kingdom is one that is built in the hearts and lives of His people. The presence of God had dwelt with Israel in the temple made of stone. Now God's presence, His Holy Spirit, would dwell in the hearts of man. Many of the Jews who were more interested in an earthly kingdom in Jerusalem never came to know the King of the kingdom.

TALK ABOUT IT:

What were the Pharisees in verse 20 missing when they asked when the kingdom of God would come? (They missed the fact that the kingdom of God had already come with the ministry of Jesus and that He was right before their eyes!)

The Pharisees along with the Jews were looking for a deliverer who would overthrow Rome and bring back the kingdom of King David. Jesus was coming to bring victory of a different kind. What was Jesus going to win victory over? (Sin and death.)

How can we be like the Pharisees? (We can expect God to fulfill our desires and wants [our idea of peace and joy] instead of us following the Lord's desires.)

PRAY:

Thank God that we have been given the good news of the kingdom of God.

Thank Him that we know the gospel and that we know Jesus, the great King.

FRIDAY
ON THE ROAD TO EMMAUS

THE STORY: ZECHARIAH 13:1

Zechariah tells of a day when a fountain will come from the house of David to cleanse sin and impurity. Hebrews 9:28 tells us that Jesus was sacrificed once to take away the sins of many. Jesus is the only sacrifice that cleanses us from sin.

TALK IT ABOUT:

Read Psalm 51. What does it mean to cleanse someone from sin? (Psalm 51 gives us the answer: "Wash away all my iniquity and cleanse me from my sin". To cleanse means to clean away, or remove. Our sin will be washed away by the fountain of Jesus.)

What did Jesus do to clean away our sin? (Jesus died on the cross to take the punishment for sin. He lived a sinless life, which He then gives to us. We receive Jesus' righteousness, and, in exchange, He received our sin and God's wrath for our sin.)

What area of sin in your life do you most need to be cleansed of? (Parents, help your children confess their struggles and lead by your own example of confession.)

PRAY:

Thank Jesus for washing away our sin through the pouring out of His blood on the cross.

JESUS CLAIMED TO BE GOD

Jesus, the good shepherd, is God, and is one with the Father in heaven.

MONDAY

THE STORY: JOHN 10:1-6

Jesus is the shepherd. In this passage Jesus introduces the sheep/shepherd figure of speech. The Jews listening did not understand what He was saying. We need to be careful not to judge them too severely, as Jesus at first didn't even tell them who He was talking about.

TALK ABOUT IT:

Why do you think Jesus spoke in a way that the people who were listening did not understand? (The disciples didn't understand much of what Jesus said. We now know that these words recorded in the Bible were not just for those listening, but for us too.)

How does the picture of sheep and the shepherd help us to understand Jesus? (Since we now understand what Jesus was talking about, we can better understand how much Jesus loves and cares for us by knowing just how much a shepherd cares for his sheep.)

How do these verses encourage us when we understand that we are the sheep and Jesus is the Shepherd? (It is a joy to know that when we belong to Him, we will understand His voice or Word and that we will be able to tell the difference between Jesus and someone who might lead us astray.)

PRAY:
Thank Jesus for giving us the Bible that we also might know His voice.

TUESDAY

THE STORY: JOHN 10:7-10
Not only is Jesus the Shepherd, He is the gate. The gate is the only way in. And, everyone who comes in through the gate will be saved. Jesus is the only way to eternal life! We can't work our way in, buy our way in, or sneak in.

TALK ABOUT IT:
What does the sheep pen represent? (The sheep pen represents salvation through Jesus.)

Do you think that Jesus is going to protect the sheep? (Yes. Jesus is the perfect Shepherd. He will protect the sheep.)

Can we get to God another way? (We need to know that Jesus is the only way we can be saved. There is no other way into the sheepfold but through the gate.)

PRAY:
Thank Jesus for dying on the cross to provide a way (gate or door) so we can enter into heaven and enjoy life forever with Jesus.

WEDNESDAY
WHERE IS THE GOSPEL?

THE STORY: JOHN 10:11-21

John 10 is one of the clearest pre-cross explanations of the ministry of Jesus. The Gospel is explained throughout the entire shepherd/sheep analogy. Jesus says that He is the good Shepherd who lays down His life for the sheep. There is no mistaking the gospel here. Perhaps the most beautiful verse in the entire chapter is verse 18, where Jesus demonstrates His incredible love for us all. Jesus said that His death is His willing choice for His sheep. The Transfiguration showed that Jesus had not lost His awesome power. If He wanted to escape the cross, He certainly had the power to do so. But He chose, instead, to lay aside His power and willingly give up His life for us.

TALK ABOUT IT:

Where else do you see the gospel in this chapter of John? (Give your children time to review the chapter and pick up on the analogy of the shepherd and the sheep. If you have younger children, draw them out with simple questions like, "Who do you think the sheep are?")

Did the Jews understand what Jesus was saying? (No. Some thought He was demonized. Others did not. But they did not understand what He was saying. It was only after Jesus died that the disciples even understood what e meant when He talked about dying and being raised up again.)

PRAY:

Thank Jesus for being our Good Shepherd and laying down His life for us.

THURSDAY

THE STORY: JOHN 10:22-42

Jesus claimed to be God. Jesus goes on to say that He is not just the Shepherd, but the Good Shepherd. The Jews became impatient and demanded He tell them plainly if He was the Christ (no more shepherd talk!). That is when Jesus calls God His Father and tells them that He is one with the Father! The Jews picked up stones to kill Jesus because by declaring that He was one with the Father, He made Himself to be God. This was very serious claim, much like if somebody today told you he was God. It would have been blasphemous if it were not the truth – a truth they could not understand. To make things clearer, Jesus told them that He is the Son of God, God is His Father, the Father is in Him, and He is in the Father! They then tried to arrest Jesus, but He escaped! Jesus' description of His relationship with the Father in this passage is one of the passages that helps us to understand the idea of the Trinity.

TALK ABOUT IT:

Why did the Jews want to stone Jesus? (The Jews wanted to stone Jesus because He said He was one with the Father, thus claiming to be God.)

What amazing things did Jesus tell the Jews about what He would do for His sheep? (Jesus said that He would give His sheep eternal life, that they would never perish, and that no one could ever snatch them away from Him.)

What does it mean to hear His voice? (Many people read the Bible, but not everyone believes. Those who hear His voice are those who hear the voice of God, or the call of God, in His Word and obey Him. God's Word touches the heart of every believer. Those who do not believe are not affected by God's Word in the same way.)

PRAY:
Ask God to touch your heart with the gospel message so that you might believe and know the call of Jesus upon your life.

FRIDAY
ON THE ROAD TO EMMAUS

THE STORY: ISAIAH 45:17
Isaiah prophesied the salvation of Israel when he said they would receive an everlasting salvation. Jesus said He came as the Good Shepherd to give eternal life to His sheep and that they would never perish (Read John 10:28).

TALK ABOUT IT:
Is there any everlasting salvation that could come any other way than through Jesus? (No. Jesus said that He alone was the door into the sheep pen.)

This passage tells us that Israel will be saved. But it seems like the Jews rejected Jesus. How could this passage point to our salvation? (Paul tells us that Israel does not just refer to Abraham's natural descendants, but to all who would believe by faith [Romans 9:6-8].)

PRAY:
Thank God for His salvation - which never ends.

THE PHARISEE AND THE TAX COLLECTOR

Our confidence is in the Lord alone.

MONDAY

THE STORY: LUKE 18:9-12

Some are confident in themselves. The Pharisee in Jesus' parable thought he was righteous. He gave God thanks for himself. He exalted himself by comparing himself with robbers, evildoers, and criminals. For further evidence of his righteousness, he lifted up his good works to God. Little did he realize that even our good works, tainted with sin as they are, appear to God as filthy rags.

TALK ABOUT IT:

What did the Pharisee think about himself? (He thought he was good when compared to others he thought were worse than himself.)

When do you find yourself tempted to think more highly of yourself than others? (Parents, help your children reflect on their lives. They might think of themselves smarter because they get a better grade, or more athletic than others who are slower. They might also think of themselves as more righteous than other children who are in their class. If you ask them who are the most misbehaving children in the class, they are not likely to give you their own names!)

The Pharisee was comparing himself to robbers and evildoers. Who does God compare us to when evaluating our righteousness? (God compares every person to His own perfection.)

Can anyone measure up to God's perfection? (No. By ourselves we are all imperfect sinners. It is only by trusting in Jesus and His perfect life that we can measure up to God's standard.)

PRAY:
Ask God to help you see your sin and your need for salvation.

TUESDAY

THE STORY: LUKE 18:13
Some know thier sin. The tax collector knew he was a sinner. The tax collector knew his only hope was in God's mercy. Unlike the Pharisee, the tax collector did not place any confidence in his own good works. He only cried out to God for mercy.

TALK ABOUT IT:
How was the tax collector's prayer different from the prayer of the Pharisee? (Draw the children out on the obvious differences.)

What can we learn about the way the tax collector was standing? (The tax collector was ashamed to look up to heaven. This is an indication that he realized he was unworthy before a holy God. It was a posture of humility.)

Who are we more like: the tax collector or the Pharisee? (We are more likely to behave like the Pharisee. At first your children may not see this. Ask them how they responded the last time you corrected them for sinning. Did they argue for their own righteousness or did they drop their head and seek mercy?)

PRAY :

Take turns confessing your sin and asking God for mercy. (Parents, you need to take the lead in confession. Then help each of your children to be specific.)

WEDNESDAY
WHERE IS THE GOSPEL?

THE STORY: LUKE 18:14

Our confidence can be in the Lord alone for our salvation. We will never be justified by the good works we do. If our body is dirty, no amount of clean clothes can make us clean. We might look clean on the outside and fool our friends, but we would still be dirty. The Pharisee was a sinner just like the tax collector. He was trusting that his good works would get him into heaven. The Bible tells us that our good works can never get us into heaven (Ephesians 2:8,9). If one trusts in one's good works, he will be humbled in the judgment. If we humble ourselves, confess our sin, and trust in Jesus, then, through the gospel of grace, God will raise us up.

TALK ABOUT IT:

Why can't we trust our good works to get us to heaven? (Our good works do put something positive on the record of our lives, but they don't take away our sin. In this life we are not able to do any good work from a totally sinless heart. For instance, if we are proud of our good works, they are tainted by pride. If we serve someone and expect them to be grateful, we are subtly sinning again. Even our best works are so tainted with sin that they are like filthy rags to God.)

If our best efforts are like filthy rags, then why do good works at all? (When we trust Christ, and He gives us His righteousness, He also changes our hearts and motives. Then, changed by God, we become more and more like Jesus. As we become like Him, we glorify Him in all we do. Though sin remains, our good works become less and less stained by our sin. Instead of doing good works to get into heaven, we do them to be like Jesus.)

PRAY:

Pray that each member of the family will trust Jesus and not their good works for their justification.

THURSDAY

THE STORY: LUKE 18:15-17

We must come like children. Very small children were being brought to Jesus. Even though they did not know Jesus, they trusted him. Children trust without questioning. Jesus used this as an illustration to help us understand how we should come to God. We need to trust our lives completely to Jesus. Even children are not too young to come to Jesus.

TALK ABOUT IT:

Who came to God more like a child: the tax collector or the Pharisee? (The tax collector did because he was trusting in God for mercy. In contrast, the Pharisee was not trusting God. He was trusting in himself and his own good works; therefore, he had no need for God, as expressed in his behavior.)

What does it mean to receive the kingdom of God like a little child? (It means we trust God, take him at His Word, and come to Jesus, not trusting a list of good works. It means to receive His gospel in the same way a child receives a gift.)

PRAY:

Ask God to help each person in your family believe and trust in Jesus, not their good works.

FRIDAY
ON THE ROAD TO EMMAUS

THE STORY: ISAIAH 53:11

In this verse Isaiah clearly outlines the gospel of grace through Jesus. Jesus suffered, died, and then rose again to life. He was a righteous servant who justified many by taking their sin upon Himself. When Jesus suffered on the cross, He took our sin upon Himself. Then He bore the punishment for that sin. The penalty we deserved was paid by Jesus. That is why we stand justified.

TALK IT ABOUT:

What are iniquities? ("Iniquity" is just another word for sin, or the things we do against God's law.)

How did Isaiah know so much about Jesus before He was even born? (Isaiah was a prophet who spoke God's words to men many hundreds of years before Jesus was born. When we read this most remarkable account of the gospel in Isaiah's book, we can see how God planned from the beginning to send Jesus to save man. In this prophecy, God was simply giving His people clues ahead of time through Isaiah the prophet. Now, when we look back, these words give us an appreciation of God's control over all things. God has a plan that He is able to make happen.)

PRAY:

Thank God for His wonderful plan through Jesus.

NEW TESTAMENT · LESSON 28

LAZARUS

Jesus is the resurrection and the life.

MONDAY

THE STORY: JOHN 11:1-16

Jesus knew in advance that Lazarus would rise. Jesus received word that His friend Lazarus was very ill, but He delayed His departure for Bethany for two days, announcing that the sickness would "not lead to death." Jesus tells His disciples that Lazarus' illness is for the glory of God and so that the Son may be glorified. Jesus then waited two days and announced that He would go to Lazarus. The disciples objected because the Jews wanted to stone Him. But Jesus remained steadfast. No one could take Jesus' life. Only He could lay it down. Then Jesus told the disciples that Lazarus had died. This time there was no courier with the news. Jesus, the Son of God, simply knew. Jesus knew that Lazarus was dead, but He also knew that Lazarus would not be dead for long.

TALK ABOUT IT:

Why did Jesus say He was glad that He was not in Bethany? (Jesus was glad for the sake of the disciples so that they might believe in Him. Jesus knew He was about to raise Lazarus from the dead and that it would help His disciples and those who love Him to believe.)

How does reading about the miracles of Jesus help us to believe? (Parents, simply draw out your children here. Jesus' miracles are a historical account of His power and tell us about God, just as a history of Abraham Lincoln tells us who Lincoln was. Reading about His miracles builds our faith in an all-powerful God who never changes.)

PRAY:
Thank God for giving us the Gospel accounts of Jesus' life, which help us to know and believe in Him.

TUESDAY

THE STORY: JOHN 11:17-24

Jesus tells Martha that Lazarus will rise again to comfort her. Martha's faith is strong. She believed that Jesus could have healed her brother had He come sooner. She rightly concludes that if Jesus had been there, Lazarus would not have died. Martha, like many of the Jews, believed in a future resurrection. So when Jesus announced that Lazarus would rise again, she agreed, thinking Lazarus would rise on the final resurrection day. But Jesus meant he would rise today!

TALK ABOUT IT:

How long had Lazarus been dead? (Lazarus had been dead four days.)

Why do you think Jesus waited so long? (Jesus said he waited so that His followers might believe. After four days, no one would doubt that Lazarus was dead. When Jesus called Lazarus out from the tomb, they would all see it as a clear and definitive rising from the dead, and Jesus would be greatly glorified.)

PRAY:

Thank God for His kind plan to consider us and shape history that we might believe.

WEDNESDAY
WHERE IS THE GOSPEL?

THE STORY: JOHN 11:25-27

"I am the resurrection and the life." With these words, Jesus revealed that He is the author of life, God over all creation, and the object of our faith. He had already explained to the disciples that He was glad He was not in Bethany to heal Lazarus so that Lazarus might rise again. Now, Jesus declared that He is the one who rules over life itself. Martha, who had earlier complained that her sister Mary was wasting time at the feet of Jesus, declared her faith with two simple words: "I believe." These two simple words are all that God requires. This is not works; it is faith. Her statement points to Jesus, the object of our faith. "I believe" humbles the speaker and looks to the object of its faith. The raising of Lazarus is a picture of the gospel. Death looks to claim people, but the plan of God through Jesus conquers death and saves people from eternal death. Jesus told His disciples that He would lay down His own life that He might "take it up again" (John 10:17). Jesus would soon die, but, like Lazarus, be raised again to new life.

TALK ABOUT IT:

Who is Jesus talking to in verse 25? (Jesus is talking to Martha, but His words are recorded here for us.)

How should this passage challenge us? (Just like Martha, this passage calls us to believe. We have a choice to make. Jesus is saying that those who believe in Him will never die. The question for us is: "Will you believe in Jesus?")

PRAY:

Ask God to help every member of your family believe and place his or her hope and trust in Jesus.

THURSDAY

THE STORY: JOHN 11:28-53

Jesus called Lazarus out. Up until now, Jesus had not demonstrated grief for the death of His friend. But when He saw Mary and all the Jews crying, it touched His heart. Of all our actions in life as sinners, perhaps the purest of all our motives is grief. Death is such a wicked enemy of life that those who grieve are pitted resolutely against it. Life is so precious that when it is gone, those who are close can't help but suffer its loss. When our hatred for death and our love for life come together in grief, it is beautiful in the sight of the Lord.

The family and friends of Lazarus would not grieve for long. Jesus called them to take away the stone. He called to Lazarus to come out. Immediately, Lazarus came out! Many people believed He was the Messiah, and news of this miracle spread. A short time later, Jesus was greeted with praise by a large crowd upon His entrance to Jerusalem. But while some were praising him, others were plotting His death.

TALK ABOUT IT:

How did the raising of Lazarus affect the people watching? (Many Jews believed, just as Jesus predicted.)

How did the raising of Lazarus affect the Pharisees? (They became upset. They were afraid that so many believers following Jesus might result in trouble with Rome. They made plans to put Him to death.)

How does the rising of Lazarus affect you? (Parents, draw out your children here.)

PRAY:

Praise God for how the recorded miracles of Jesus help us all to believe.

FRIDAY
ON THE ROAD TO EMMAUS

THE STORY: HOSEA 13:14

Jesus is the one who ransoms us from the power of the grave. Jesus raised Jairus' daughter. Jesus raised Lazarus. And Jesus Himself was raised from the dead. Jesus said, "I am the resurrection and the life," (John 11:25).

TALK ABOUT IT:

How does Hosea's prophecy point to Jesus? (Jesus is the one who ransomed us by dying for our sins and then rising again from the grave. It is by Jesus, sacrifice that death was conquered [see 1 Corinthians 15:55-58].)

Could this passage be describing anyone else? (No. Jesus is the only one who has the power over death.)

PRAY:

Thank Jesus for defeating death that we might be given eternal life!

JESUS AND ZACCHAEUS

Jesus came to seek and to save what was lost.

MONDAY

THE STORY: LUKE 18:35-43

The blind beggar was healed. On his way to Jericho, Jesus passed near a blind man. Some of those present told the man that Jesus was passing by. The blind man called out to Jesus and would not be quieted by those who were leading him. In fact, he shouted all the louder, "Son of David, have mercy on me." This blind man knew who Jesus was, at least in part. Jesus was the promised descendant of David who would reign on the throne. There would be no other reason to call out His name like this. Why not say "Son of Joseph" or "Jesus of Nazareth"? This man had faith that Jesus was no ordinary man and had the power to heal. After asking Jesus for his sight, Jesus commended his faith and immediately restored the blind man.

TALK ABOUT IT:

What did the man do after Jesus healed him? (He followed Jesus, praising God.)

What was the response of the people there? (When they saw the man healed, they, too, gave praise to God.)

What should our response be when we read this passage? (Our response should be the same as the blind man and the crowd. We should praise God!)

PRAY:
Pray prayers of praise. (Parents, help even your smallest children who can speak praise the Lord. If they are too young to come up with the words themselves, have them repeat after you.)

TUESDAY

THE STORY: LUKE 19:1-8
Zacchaeus pursued Jesus. After the raising of Lazarus, word spread quickly about Jesus. Not only did this amazing man heal the sick, cast out demons, and perform wonders like the multiplication of the fishes and loaves, He also raised the dead. Israel had been without a prophet for a long time. And Israel was under Roman rule, which they would have understood to be God's judgment upon them. They longed for God to restore them. Now, a descendant of David was performing miracles that could be attributed only to God.

Zacchaeus, a short man from Jericho, wanted to see Jesus, so he climbed a tree. Jesus looked up. He called the tax collector by name and invited Himself to dinner at Zacchaeus' home. Zacchaeus gladly came down from the tree and accepted Christ's invitation. Similarly, Jesus seeks after us. He invites himself into our lives. In a sense, the gospel message is an invitation for us to receive Jesus into our lives. We do this by trusting and believing in what He has said and done.

TALK ABOUT IT:
How do we know that Zacchaeus believed Jesus? (Zacchaeus gladly accepted Jesus' invitation and immediately gave away half his possessions to the poor. He also agreed to repay four times over, any-one he had cheated.)

Why would it be significant for a tax collector to be giving away money? (The tax collector's job was to take away money, not give it away. They often took more than the law required so they could keep some for themselves. However, when Jesus came into his life, Zacchaeus agreed to return all the stolen money along with generous interest.)

PRAY
Pray that each member of your family would be so taken with Jesus that they would love Him more than earthly treasure.

WEDNESDAY
WHERE IS THE GOSPEL?

THE STORY: LUKE 19:9,10
Jesus makes the connection to the gospel in this story. Jesus tells us, "Today salvation has come to this house." We also learn that it was the "Son of Man," Jesus, who came to "seek and save the lost."

Though it seems that Zacchaeus was trying to draw near to Jesus, it was in fact Jesus who was coming to save Zacchaeus. This salvation is possible because of what Jesus was about to do on the cross. The evidence of a changed heart in this story is obvious: Zacchaeus gave away half his money.

TALK ABOUT IT:
What did Jesus say had come to Zacchaeus' house? (Jesus said that salvation had come to his house.)

What did Jesus say was the reason? (Jesus didn't say in these verses. Salvation had not come to his house because he gave away half his possessions. Jesus instead said that salvation came to Zacchaeus because Jesus came to seek and to save him.)

PRAY:
Ask God to help you remember that we can not earn heaven by the good things we do. Ask God to help you understand and believe in Jesus. Then you will do good things as a result of a changed heart.

THURSDAY

THE STORY: LUKE 19:11
The people thought the kingdom was about to come. After Zacchaeus came down from the tree and repented, the people were amazed. Not only did Jesus do physical miracles, but he was also able to change the hearts of men. Even tax collectors were giving back to those they had defrauded. Tax collectors collaborated with the Romans and were often considered traitors. Here the people saw a tax collector turn away from his Roman collaboration and turn back to the people of Israel. The people thought, for sure, the kingdom of God was going to appear at once.

TALK ABOUT IT:
Why do you think the people thought the kingdom was about to come? (So many miracles and wonders had taken place that had not taken place for hundreds of years. The people would have thought, "What else could this be, but the restoration of the kingdom?" They knew it would take a miracle worker to bring the deliverance they needed, and now one was among them.)

How was Jesus' kingdom different than the one the people expected? (Jesus came to die, and to defeat sin and death. They thought He was coming to defeat Rome and restore the fortunes, fame, and power of Israel.)

How can we sometimes be like the people of Israel, wanting Jesus to be king over some kind of earthly kingdom? (Rather than seek the Lord for heavenly treasure, we can place our desires on earthly treasure. Rather than praying for earthly riches, we should pray for heavenly riches. Rather than pray for earthly accomplishment, we should ask for grace for eternal accomplishment.)

PRAY:
Ask God to help each person in your family seek heavenly gain over earthly gain.

FRIDAY
ON THE ROAD TO EMMAUS

THE STORY: ISAIAH 11:1-10
Jesus is the banner that will bring all the nations to Himself. He is the one who will bring an end to the hostility of the curse. Jesus, a descendant of Jesse, will bring rest to the people. Paul attributes this passage to Christ in Romans 15:12.

TALK ABOUT IT:
What does it mean that an infant will play near the nest of a poisonous snake? (In creation, prior to the fall, there was no hostility between man and the animals. In heaven, there will be no hostility, no sickness, no dying. God will recreate the earth, removing the curse.)

Will there be animals in heaven? (The Scripture passage refers to animals in heaven. Some think this is merely figurative language, but it is safe to assume that the same amazing creation that we now have will be restored when Jesus makes the new earth and comes to live with men.)

PRAY:
It is good to pray for the return of Christ and the second coming. Pray with your family for Jesus to return, remove the curse, and restore the original beauty of His creation that was tainted by sin.

TRIUMPHAL ENTRY

The people celebrate their King while others plot His death.

MONDAY

THE STORY: JOHN 12:12-16

The crowd celebrated Jesus as king. The crowds assembled for the Passover. Those who saw Jesus raise Lazarus from the dead went out to meet Jesus when they heard that He was on His way into Jerusalem. The people shouted a phrase from Psalm 118:26, saying, "Hosanna! Blessed is He who comes in the name of the Lord!" This was in keeping with the prophecy of Zechariah, who said, "Rejoice greatly, O Daughter of Zion! Shout, Daughter of Jerusalem! See, your king comes to you, righteous and having salvation, gentle and riding on a donkey, on a colt, the foal of a donkey."

The disciples still had no clue of all that was unfolding before their eyes. They, like the people around them, thought Jesus would be a political Messiah. They would be surprised as much as anyone by His arrest.

TALK ABOUT IT:

Did the people know that Jesus was coming to take away sins? (No. They thought he was coming to be anointed king of Israel and bring God's judgment to the Romans.)

Why did God have Zechariah prophesy (about a donkey) if the disciples didn't even recognize the fulfillment of the word at the time? (One of the benefits is that all those who come later get a clear view of God's sovereignty. God demonstrates here, and in many other places, His absolute control over all things to the very last detail. Jesus didn't come by chance, but by the perfect, predetermined plan of God.)

How does knowing God is in control of everything help build your faith? (Parents, draw out your children. Help them to see that if God knows all the details, He knows who they are. If God is in control of all things, He can save them!)

PRAY:
Thank God for His amazing plan of salvation. Pray that it come to each member of your family.

TUESDAY

THE STORY: JOHN 12:17-19
The pharisees jealously watched and waited for a time to kill Jesus. John records several references to the religious rulers wanting to kill Jesus (John 5:18, 7:19, 7:25, 8:40). They even plotted to kill Lazarus because they viewed him as the reason why so many people were flocking to Jesus (John 12:10). Matthew records their scheme: "They plotted to arrest Jesus in some sly way and kill him, 'But not during the Feast,' they said, 'or there may be a riot among the people.'" The crowds believed Jesus would usher in the kingdom. His entrance into Jerusalem at the time of Passover (one of the busiest times of the year) only made for more commotion.

TALK ABOUT IT:
Why did the Pharisees dislike Jesus so much? (The Romans entrusted power to rule over Jerusalem to the Pharisees and other religious rulers. They loved that power. Jesus represented trouble for them and their relationship with Rome. In

addition, they enjoyed exalting themselves and having the people look up to them. Now, the people were looking to Jesus, and they were jealous.)

Do we ever struggle with sin like the Pharises did? (Yes. Any time we want people's attention on us too much, we fall into the same sin pattern as the Pharisees. We want to be admired for our importance or our good works. Because we long to be exalted, instead of exalting God, we are guilty of the same kind of pride we see in the Pharisees. If we reject the words of Jesus and choose not to follow Him, we are also guilty of the same sins as the religious rulers.)

PRAY:
Pray that God would help each member of your family grow in their desire and ability to trust and obey the Lord.

WEDNESDAY
WHERE IS THE GOSPEL?

THE STORY: JOHN 12:20-33
Even as Jesus was riding into Jerusalem, He was aware that the very people who were celebrating His arrival would, in a few days, put Him to death.

Jesus would soon die for the sins of men by suffering on the cross. It is true that Jesus came to earth to be king. But He came as a heavenly king for a spiritual kingdom. That is why He said that if the people did not cry out, the very stones would cry out.

Jesus then predicted His death and announced that the time had come. Some of the very same people, who moments prior hailed Jesus as King in his triumphal entry, would cry out with the religious rulers, "Crucify him!"

TALK ABOUT IT:

Knowing all that was going to take place, what was Jesus saying about His death in verses 23-32? (Jesus was telling them that the time of His crucifixion was near, that His death would result in life, and that He was sad. He also was telling them in advance that Satan would be defeated by His death, and that His death would draw men back to God.)

What is the struggle of Jesus' heart that we see through His comments in verses 27 and 28? (Jesus was aware of the great suffering ahead. Although He could put a stop to the sacrifice and avoid the suffering, He chose instead to continue in order to bring glory to His Father.)

Jesus struggled when facing the upcoming suffering of the cross. How does that struggle affect you when you realize that He died for you? (Draw out your children's thoughts here. Don't rush. Ask follow-up questions.)

PRAY:

Thank Jesus for His willingness to suffer that we might have salvation.

THURSDAY

THE STORY: JOHN 12:37-50

Jesus Is rejected by His own people. In spite of all that Jesus did, Luke records that the Jews still did not believe. Though some did believe, it is safe to assume that more doubted than believed. Once Jesus was arrested, and the crowds saw their hopeful ruler tortured and mocked, they turned against Him.

Some of the rulers who did believe Jesus words, were afraid to say, they did believe. In a similar way we can be afraid to share our faith.

TALK ABOUT IT:
What do we call it when we "love praise from men more than praise from God"? (We call that sin the fear of man. When we are afraid of witnessing because of what people will say or think, we are yielding to the fear of man.)

When are you most tempted to fear man more than God? (Parents, start by confessing your own fears and then helping your children share as well.)

PRAY:
Pray that God would help you overcome the fear of man in the areas you confessed.

FRIDAY
ON THE ROAD TO EMMAUS

THE STORY: ISAIAH 6:9,10
John quotes these words of Isaiah and attributes them to Jesus in John 12:41, saying, "Isaiah said this because he saw Jesus' glory and spoke about Him". What an amazing testimony! Isaiah, who lived hundreds of years prior, saw the glory of Jesus! The real connection is not that Isaiah saw Jesus, but that he saw the glory of God. John talks about the glory of Jesus (John 1:14, 2:11). For John, if you see the glory of God, you are seeing the glory of Jesus - for Jesus is God.

TALK ABOUT IT:
Who does this verse speak about? (This verse speaks about those who do not believe in Jesus.)

Who might these verses apply to? (The Pharisees and many of the Jews refused to believe in Jesus and rejected Him [see John 12:37].)

PRAY:

Pray that you would not be like those who reject Jesus, but that instead, you would turn your heart toward Him and ask Him to heal you of your sin.

THE WIDOW'S OFFERING

The Lord looks into the heart of our offering.

MONDAY

THE STORY: LUKE 20:45-47

Beware of outward obedience. While Jesus was teaching in the temple, He warned the people there about the teachers of the law. Jesus exposed their hypocrisy by showing how they took money from widows and then prayed long prayers for show. This would have been a most serious charge. No wonder the Jewish rulers wanted to kill Him. Jesus was exposing their hidden sinful lives.

TALK ABOUT IT:

How did Jesus know about the sins of the Pharisees? (God knows all our sins. Nothing is hidden from God. Jesus didn't have to spy on the religious leaders; He knew.)

Are we, like the Pharisees, tempted to hide sin and then act as though we are good? (Yes. The nature of sin is for us to hide it. Then, just like the Pharisees, we want the praise of men.)

Can you think of a time when you sinned and tried to hide it? Can you remember a time when you tried to look spiritual so others would see? (Parents, lead in confession so then your children will be more apt to share.)

PRAY:

Pray that the Lord will forgive our hypocrisy and change our hearts that we might serve Him from the heart and not just with outward deeds.

TUESDAY

THE STORY: LUKE 21:1-4

Outward appearances are deceiving. Jesus was sitting next to the place where the offering was being deposited. He then drew attention to a widow's offering. To look at the two small copper coins, one would think it was meaningless amount. But, when we discover it was all she had to live on, we see her great faith in giving it to God.

TALK ABOUT IT:

How was the widow different from the others who were giving? (The widow was giving all she had to live on, while the others were giving from their wealth, with money to spare.)

Does this mean we should give away all the money we have to live on? (No. Money is not evil. This passage is teaching that outward appearances can be deceiving. As God told Samuel, man looks to the outward appearance, but He looks at the heart [see 1 Samuel 16:7].)

PRAY:

Ask the Lord to help you be more like the widow, who was willing to sacrifice all she had in order to worship to God.

WEDNESDAY
WHERE IS THE GOSPEL?

THE STORY: MARK 12:41-44

Mark's description of the widow's offering contains an additional detail. Jesus purposefully sat down opposite the place where the offerings were being placed. He watched the crowd putting money in before He spoke. He had just spoken against the hypocrisy of the teachers of the law who devour widows. Now Jesus used a widow as an example of sincere faith.

Each of us has a choice to make. Will we be like the widow who entrusted her life to God or will we be like the rich men who trusted in their riches? Are we willing to entrust everything we have to God, or is our faith limited to that which does not cost us?

Jesus is present and aware of what is in our hearts. He can see by our actions who or what we really worship. Jesus died on the cross to set us free from the love of money and put love for Himself in our hearts instead. When our hearts are changed by His grace, it is easy to give back to Him because we trust Him with our lives.

TALK ABOUT IT:

Is God most interested in our hearts or how much we give? (God is interested in our hearts.)

How does the gospel change our hearts and our worship? (Before God touches us, we are captivated with the treasures of the world and blind to heavenly treasure. It is when the Lord touches our hearts that our blinded eyes are opened to see heavenly treasure. This affects our devotion, our giving, and every other area of our lives.)

PRAY:
Pray that every family member would be touched by the Spirit of God, being willing to serve God and give sacrificially from the heart.

THURSDAY

THE STORY: LUKE 21:5,6
While Jesus looked at the heart of the widow, the disciples were caughter up with the outer beauty of the Temple building. They failed to understand that the temple was to point to Christ.

Even though some of the stones of the temple were over 30 feet long, Jesus said it would be destoryed. When they wanted to know when these things would happen, Jesus told them a generation would not pass away until these things happened (Luke 21:32). About 40 years later, in the length of a generation, the temple was destroyed by the Romans.

TALK ABOUT IT :
Why is the temple building no longer important in Christianity? (All believers have the Holy Spirit living inside of them, and we are God's living temple [see Ephesians 2:21,22].)

Why do you think God allowed the temple to be destroyed? (Just like the disciples, men are attracted to beautiful things of this world. The temple was to point to Jesus as the place where God dwells and as the place where man and God are reconciled and meet together. Now that Jesus has come, there is no need for the temple building.)

PRAY:
Thank the Lord for making us His temple and for giving us His Holy Spirit to live within us.

FRIDAY
ON THE ROAD TO EMMAUS

THE STORY: ISAIAH 29:13,14

Jesus quotes these verses in Matthew 15:8,9 to speak of the hypocrisy of the Pharisees. Jesus regularly exposed the hearts of the Pharisees. Jesus also frustrated the Pharisees' brilliantly shrewd schemes to trap the Lord.

TALK ABOUT IT:

What does it mean to honor the Lord with your lips, but have hearts that are far from Him? (It is easy to say that you love and worship the Lord, but much harder to love and live for Him inwardly. Only by the grace of God can we live for God from the heart.)

How does this passage fit the lives of the Pharisees as described in Luke 20:45-47? (The outward honoring would be their long public prayers. Their corrupt hearts would be represented by the way they were cheating the widows.)

PRAY:

Ask God to help you honor Him with your words and actions as well as with sincere devotion of heart.

THE LAST SUPPER

The Last Supper was the Last Passover.

MONDAY

THE STORY: LUKE 22:1-6

The trap was laid. The passage tells us that Satan entered Judas, who went to the chief priests to make arrangements to betray Jesus. The chief priests were looking to kill Jesus. But they would likely have known His whereabouts only when He was speaking to the crowds during the day. Judas served their purpose to find Jesus at night, when the crowds were not around.

TALK ABOUT IT:

What does it mean to betray someone? (Literally it means "to give someone over." But the broader meaning can be found in betraying a person's friendship or trust. Friends are loyal; they trust one another. That trust assumes each will honor and protect the other. Judas despised that trust, and with deception, pretending to be a loyal follower, turned Jesus over to those who hated Him.)

How might we betray the trust of people we love? (We could betray them by lying to them or deceiving them. Gossip is also a kind of betrayal.)

PRAY:

Ask God for the grace to love others and not betray them.

TUESDAY

THE STORY: LUKE 22:7-16

The true Passover lamb was soon to be sacrificed. Jesus directed the disciples to prepare for the Passover and accurately predicted just how the preparations would unfold. We are left to wonder if Jesus had really made arrangements administratively or if God supernaturally set up the Passover meal details. In any case, things unfolded just as Jesus said they would. Jesus was eager to eat the Passover before He suffered. There is no question that Jesus was aware of what was about to occur.

TALK ABOUT IT:

What did Jesus mean by "before I suffer"? (Jesus knew He was soon to be arrested, beaten, and crucified.)

What did Jesus mean when in Luke 22:15 He said He would not eat the Passover again until it finds fulfillment in the kingdom of God? (The Passover lamb was a picture of God's salvation through Jesus, the Lamb of God. Jesus was about to die as the sacrifice for the sins of His people. On the cross, the true Passover occurred; God poured out His wrath upon Jesus for the sins of the world. Death and judgment "pass over" us and fall upon Jesus, the Lamb of God, instead.)

PRAY:

Thank Jesus for being our Passover lamb.

WEDNESDAY
WHERE IS THE GOSPEL?

THE STORY: LUKE 22:17-22

The Passover meal was the clearest picture of God's redemption in the Old Testament. The first Passover took place in Egypt, when the angel of death passed over the Israelites' homes where the lamb's blood was painted on the doorposts and lintels.

This night, before Jesus' crucifixion, the disciples learned that Jesus, the Lamb of God, was going to shed His blood for all mankind. For those who believe, Jesus' blood covers their sin so that when the judgment of God comes in their direction, it will pass over and bring them no harm.

The Passover story points to the new covenant, which Jesus introduced at the Last Supper. A covenant is a promise or commitment. Jesus introduced His commitment and promise to the disciples. His blood was shed and His body broken so that we might be forgiven and brought into fellowship with God. Jesus sums up the last Passover this way: "I will not eat of it again until it finds fulfillment in the kingdom of God." Today, we celebrate the Passover in the new covenant celebration of the Lord's Supper, also known as "Communion."

TALK ABOUT IT:

What meal was Jesus celebrating? (The Passover.)

What do we call it when we celebrate it at church on Sundays? (We celebrate a part of the Passover meal, which reminds us of the sacrifice of Jesus. We call this the Lord's Supper or Communion.)

Where is the gospel in the words of Jesus? (When Jesus mentions a new covenant in His blood He is referring to His sacrifice on the cross.)

PRAY:
Thank God for giving up His life on the cross and taking our sins as our Passover lamb.

THURSDAY

THE STORY: LUKE 22:24-34

The disciples didn't have a clue. Right in the midst of Jesus' last moments, they began to argue between themselves about who was the greatest disciple. In spite of all Jesus said about His need to suffer and die, they were more concerned about their own status. Jesus warned Peter specifically when he boastfully replied that he was willing to die or go to prison for Jesus' sake. The disciples still were looking toward an earthly kingdom and had no idea what was about to take place. Jesus, who knew the road of suffering ahead, informed Peter that even he would soon deny Christ. Matthew 26:35 records Peter's response: "Even if I have to die with You, I will never disown You". All the disciples said the same.

TALK ABOUT IT:

Why was Peter so confident he would never deny Jesus? (Peter thought Jesus would fight any opposition and bring victory. In all the Old Testament stories, those who trusted the Lord won the victory even when greatly outnumbered. Peter was probably thinking there would be a battle and that Jesus would use His power and win. He was not prepared for the Savior's unwillingness to resist the men who arrested him. Peter denied the Lord and shrunk back in fear.)

How can we be like Peter? (We can be afraid to tell people we are Christians for fear of what they will say about us.)

What did Jesus say at the Last Supper to teach the disciples about true greatness? (Jesus said in Luke 22:26,27 that we should be like Him and serve others.)

PRAY:

Ask God to help you long for true greatness and not live for worldly greatness.

FRIDAY
ON THE ROAD TO EMMAUS

THE STORY: ZECHARIAH 11:12,13

Zechariah, who lived many hundreds of years before Christ, prophesied the amount of the blood money paid to Judas. Juda betrayed Jesus for 30 pieces of silver. He also prophesied the name of the field in which he was buried. In the amazing providence of God, the prophets spoke truths that we only understand by looking back.

TALK ABOUT IT:

Why did God give the prophets little details like this concerning what He was about to do? (God demonstrated that His plan of salvation was firmly established and that He is able to make all things work together for His glory and our good.)

Can you think of other Scriptures that speak of God's control over all things? (Look up verses such as 2 Corinthians 9:8, Romans 8:28, and Matthew 10:29-31. Have members of your family read them alound.)

PRAY:

Thank God that He is in control of all things and works them all together for our good.

WASHING THE DISCIPLES' FEET

Only those who are washed by Jesus have His salvation.

MONDAY

THE STORY: JOHN 12:44-50

Jesus served the Father. Jesus never exalted Himself. All of Jesus' life was spent demonstrating servanthood and being obedient to His Father. Furthermore, Jesus served us. Jesus sacrificed Himself in service to us that we might be freed from sin. Jesus came to save. The world is already condemned because of sin. Jesus came not to judge but to save. Those who reject Jesus as a harsh judge fail to see His wonderful love demonstrated at the cross.

TALK ABOUT IT:

How was Jesus a servant to His Father? (Jesus only said what the Father told Him to say.)

How is Jesus a servant to us? (Jesus came to die on the cross that we might be saved from wrath of God for our sins.)

PRAY:

Thank Jesus for being a servant that we might come to know the Father and be saved.

TUESDAY

THE STORY: JOHN 13:1-5

Jesus washes the disciples' feet. After supper the disciples got into an argument about who was the greatest (see Luke 22:24). Jesus got up from the meal, and in an outward demonstration of servanthood began to wash the disciples' feet. Luke records the sequence of events. The foot-washing should have been done prior to the meal by one of the servants. If a servant was not present, one of the disciples should have done it. Jesus told them earlier that the greatest should be the servant of all (see Mark 9:35). By washing their feet on the very eve of His arrest Jesus demonstrated true servanthood. Jesus showed that He was indeed the suffering servant prophesied in Isaiah 52:13.

TALK ABOUT IT:

Why was washing feet a dramatic expression of Jesus' love for the disciples? (Jesus was about to die for these men. Rather than seek their pity, Jesus demonstrated His humility by doing something only a servant would do; He washed their feet.)

What can we learn from this story? (We see the amazing character of Jesus in serving the disciples through a wonderful demonstration of true servanthood. As we follow Jesus, we are called to servanthood and true greatness.)

Jesus showed humility in His serving. What stands in the way of our serving those around us? (Our pride stands in the way. We want to be served by others.)

PRAY:

Ask God to help you follow Jesus' example and seek after true greatness by positioning yourself as a servant of all.

WEDNESDAY
WHERE IS THE GOSPEL?

THE STORY: JOHN 13:6-11

Jesus' greatest act of service was not washing feet. Paul tells us in Philippians 2:7,8 that our attitude should be the same as that of Jesus who "made Himself nothing, taking the form of a servant, being born in the likeness of men. And being found in human form, He humbled himself by becoming obedient to the point of death, even death on a cross."

Jesus, God Himself, performed His greatest act of service for us by giving up His life for us. The events in the upper room were pointing ahead to what would soon happen in the Crucifixion. It was demeaning for Jesus to wash the disciples' feet. He was washing away the outward dirt with water and a towel. How much more demeaning was it for him to wash filthy hearts, taking upon Himself all our vile sin and shedding His own blood as an atoning sacrifice?

TALK ABOUT IT:

How should Jesus' death on the cross help motivate us to follow His example in serving one another? (Jesus' sacrifice on the cross goes far beyond foot-washing as an example of servanthood. The least we can do is serve our brothers and sisters here on earth. The more we realize just how sinful we are and that we are forgiven because of Jesus' sacrifice on the cross, the more willing we will be to serve, love, and forgive others.)

What are the things you least like to do in serving others, and why? (Parents - draw your children out on this question.)

How might studying this passage change your perspective? (Knowing what Jesus did for us can motivate us to think more of others and care for them through our service.)

PRAY:
Ask God to give you a willingness to do things for others – and not only the easy things.

THURSDAY

THE STORY: JOHN 13:12-17
Jesus commissioned the disciples to follow His example. After the Master washed their feet, the disciples would have been ashamed of their arguments about who was the greatest. Just to be sure they understood what He meant by this act, Jesus charged them to do as he had done. He did not intend to institute Christian foot-washing ceremonies but to remind them that the greatest among them would be the servant of all.

TALK ABOUT IT:
Why is the servant the greatest? (The servant is building treasure for himself in heaven for all eternity by following Jesus' example and serving others.)

What are some ways we could demonstrate true greatness in serving one another? (Parents, draw out the children and remind them of the charge to pursue true greatness. Like the disciples, they will soon forget.)

PRAY:
Ask God to help you not think of yourself first but to follow Jesus' example in putting others first.

FRIDAY
ON THE ROAD TO EMMAUS

THE STORY: ISAIAH 52:13

Jesus took on the nature of a servant and became a man. Jesus humbled himself and freely offered His life on the cross. Paul tells us in Philippians 2:9-11, "Therefore God exalted Him to the highest place and gave Him the name that is above every name, that at the name of Jesus every knee should bow, in heaven and on earth and under the earth, and every tongue confess that Jesus Christ is Lord, to the glory of God the Father." There is only one to whom every knee will bow: Jesus. Isaiah saw that future exaltation of Christ.

TALK ABOUT IT:

What did Jesus do to posture Himself as a servant? (Jesus' sacrifice and death on the cross was the greatest demonstration of servanthood ever.)

How can we follow Jesus' example as Paul directs in Philippians 2:5? (Every time we serve others, denying our pleasure or comfort, we are following the example of Christ.)

PRAY:

Thank Jesus for humbling Himself and becoming a servant and dying for us when we were His enemies.

JESUS PROMISES TO SEND THE HOLY SPIRIT

Jesus is the Way, the Truth, and the Life.

MONDAY

THE STORY: JOHN 14:1-14

Jesus is the way. By his death on the cross, Jesus would make a way for men to know God and fellowship with Him forever. Jesus, announced that He was God by saying to His disciples that to know Him is to know the Father. Paul said it like this: "He is the image of the invisible God, the firstborn over all creation" (Colossians 1:15). The Father is a spirit. He does not have a human body. We come to know the Father in Jesus Christ, who is both God and man. Jesus is the way to salvation, He is the way to the Father and is the way to heaven. He will return and take us to heaven when He comes again.

TALK ABOUT IT:

Can we understand what Jesus is saying in this passage? (Yes and no. We can understand and believe that Jesus is in the Father and that the Father is in Him, but we cannot fully comprehend how that is.)

Are Jesus and the Father one or two? (They are two distinct persons, but one essence.)

Jesus said He was the "way" to the faterh. What are some of the other false "ways" people embrace? (The greatest false way is to think that "we" are the way. That is, that we can work our own way to God by the good things we do. This lie is behind most false religions. The truth is that none of us could ever be good enough. The second greatest "false way" is to believe there is "no way" and that all we have are the pleasures of life. This is the lie behind those who embrace no religion.)

PRAY:
Ask God to help you believe and place your trust in Jesus as the only way.

TUESDAY

THE STORY: JOHN 14:15-27
Now that Jesus is gone, how can we possibly know the truth? Well, God has given us two wonderful gifts. First, we have His Word, the Bible, which records the life and ministry of Christ. It does not record everything He said but it does record everything we need. The second gift is the Holy Spirit.

Jesus said, "the Counselor, the Holy Spirit, whom the Father will send in My name will teach you all things and will remind you of everything I have said to you". This is the primary mission of the Spirit of God, to point people to Jesus and His words.

In this passage of Scripture we see the Trinity wonderfully displayed. Jesus said that the Holy Spirit will be sent by the Father (see John 14:26). But then He said He was the one coming back (see John 14:28). So it seems that Jesus and the Spirit are one. Jesus also said, "I am in the Father and the Father is in me" (John 14:11). So it seems that Jesus and the Father are one. If Jesus and the Father are one, and Jesus and the Spirit are one, they are all three in one!

TALK ABOUT IT:

Does everyone receive the blessing of the Holy Spirit? (No, not everyone receives the Holy Spirit. Jesus makes a contrast between His followers and the world. The Holy Spirit is given to those who believe in Jesus, not to unbelievers in the world.)

What does the Holy Spirit do for us? (The Holy Spirit does many things, but His main mission is to point us to Christ. The Holy Spirit helps us to understand the Bible. He also equips and empowers us for God's work in the world.)

PRAY:

Ask God to touch each person in your family with His Spirit that you might believe and come to know Jesus better and better.

WEDNESDAY
WHERE IS THE GOSPEL?

THE STORY: JOHN 14:6

Jesus is the way, Jesus is the truth, and Jesus is the life. He is the beginning and the middle and the end. The spiritual food that sustains us is His Word, and His regenerating Spirit gives us everlasting life.

In these final instructions, Jesus told His disciples that He was going to go to the Father in heaven and asked the Father to send the Holy Spirit. The disciples didn't realize that in a few hours Jesus would be arrested, tried, and sentenced to death.

On the cross, Jesus took the penalty for the sins of mankind. The Holy Spirit does not dwell within men apart from Jesus' sacrifice. Jesus paid the penalty for our sin, making us holy and acceptable in God's sight. It is only when we trust the blood of Christ for forgiveness for our sins that we are declared righteous. Then the Holy Spirit makes His home in our hearts. The gospel makes Jesus' promises possible.

TALK ABOUT IT:
How many ways to God are there? (There is only one way to God; Jesus is the way.)

What did Jesus do to make the path to God possible? (Jesus died on the cross for our sins. Parents, draw out the full gospel from your children. You want to make sure they know the gospel. We can't make them believe, but we can make sure they know what to believe.)

PRAY:
Pray that each member of your family would be touched by God so as to believe and place their trust in Jesus, who is the only way to the Father.

THURSDAY

THE STORY: JOHN 15:1-8
Jesus is the life. Jesus is the way and the truth, and now He describes Himself as the life. He uses the picture of a grapevine. Jesus tells us that He is the vine, and we are branches that will bear much fruit. If you cut off a branch, it cannot survive. A branch's only hope of bearing fruit is by remaining in the vine. Our lives must be spent pursuing Jesus and remaining in Him. We do this by following His Word, offering our lives in service to the Lord, and worshipping Him in our hearts every day.

TALK ABOUT IT:
What does Jesus say our relationship with him is like? (Jesus said He is like a vine and we are like branches that need to stay in the vine to be fruitful.)

What kinds of things can tempt us to leave the vine? (There are many idols which can tempt us. Money, possessions, power, fame, the praise of men, control and many other things try to lie to us and claim they can give us a better life.)

What things are most likely to tempt you away from Christ? (Parents take the lead in confession and allow your children to follow your example.)

PRAY:
Ask the Lord to forgive you for the ways you have left Him and ask Jesus to help each member of your family be like a branch in Him that remains in Him.

FRIDAY
ON THE ROAD TO EMMAUS

THE STORY: ISAIAH 29:18-20
There are several key phrases that help us see Jesus in this passage. Jesus is the one who makes the deaf hear and the blind see. This word of Isaiah has its fulfillment in part at the first coming of Christ and will be fulfilled at His second coming. That is when the ruthless will vanish, the mockers will disappear, and when all who have an eye for evil will be cut down (see Isaiah 29:20).

TALK ABOUT IT:
When the Old Testament talks about a future day when the blind see or the deaf hear, does it always point to Jesus? (Yes, it is pointing forward to Christ.)

How does it encourage us to know that God's salvation was planned ahead of time? (The only way God could plan the details of salvation for us through Jesus is if He has always been in control of all things. If God is in control of all things, we can place our trust in Him.)

PRAY:
Thank God for His sovereign control over all things.

JESUS ARRESTED

Jesus offered no resistance to arrest, that we might be saved.

MONDAY

THE STORY: MARK 14:32-42

In one of the clearest demonstrations of the suffering of Christ on our behalf, Jesus took time to pray just prior to His arrest. Jesus was so filled with anguish Mark tells us He was filled with sorrow to the point of death and cried out to the Father to take the suffering away. All the while His disciples were sleeping, and one was about to betray Him.

The sinfulness of man in contrast to the grace of God is clearly portrayed in the failure of the disciples to stay awake to pray with Jesus. The Scripture tells us, "While we were still sinners, Christ died for us, (Romans 5:8).

TALK ABOUT IT:

What did Jesus pray to His Father? (Jesus prayed that the cup be taken away from Him but not according to His will - only by the Father's will.)

What did the cup represent? (The cup represented the suffering on the cross and the rejection by the Father, who would pour out upon his Son the wrath we deserved.

What was important about Jesus' prayer? (Jesus didn't just request relief for His own sake. He said, "Yet not what I will, but what you will." When we pray and ask God for things, we can follow the example of Christ. Sometimes we pray for things that are not in keeping with God's will for us. If we pray like Jesus and use the words "not my will, but your will be done", our prayers will honor the Father.)

PRAY:

Have a person in your family offer a request to God following the pattern of Jesus, who said, "Yet not what I will, but what you will" (Mark 14:36).

TUESDAY

THE STORY: MARK 14:43-50

Jesus was betrayed, arrested, and deserted. Just as Jesus predicted, Judas betrayed Jesus. The kiss was unnecessary, for Jesus identified himself (see John 18:5), yet Judas followed through with his treachery. We learn from John 18:10 that Peter is the one who cut off the ear of the servant of the high priest. Luke 22:51 says that Jesus then touched the man and healed him.

Peter was determined to fight, but did not realize there would be no fighting with swords. Jesus would fight alone. The fight was for our salvation, and the weapon was not a sword, but the cross. Once the disciples saw Jesus arrested without offering resistance, their hope for a restored kingdom was crushed (see Luke 24:21), and they fled. Zechariah predicted this when he said, "Strike the shepherd and the sheep will be scattered" (Zechariah 13:7).

TALK ABOUT IT:

Why did Peter cut off the man's ear? (Peter, in an effort to demonstrate his willingness to defend Jesus, started a fight. He had no idea that Jesus was going to allow Himself to be taken.)

Why did Jesus allow Himself to be taken? (Jesus came to die on the cross at the hands of sinful men. Though there was great suffering involved, Hebrews 12:2

tells us that there was also a joy to which Jesus was looking forward. That is the day when those He came to save will be fully redeemed.)

PRAY:
Thank Jesus for enduring the suffering of the cross that we might be saved.

WEDNESDAY
WHERE IS THE GOSPEL?

THE STORY: JOHN 18:1-11
Jesus did not call down legions of angels or defend Himself. This fulfilled the Scriptures (see Matthew 26:56). Isaiah 53:11 prophesied, "He shall bear their iniquities." The arrest of Jesus was linked to His death, where He bore our sin. When we read of His arrest, we see His willingness to die in our place. This is the greatest demonstration of love in history.

Though Jesus did not defend Himself, John records a fascinating glimpse at His authority and power. When Jesus answered the officials, saying, "I am he," the officials drew back and fell to the ground. Something caused them to fall back. Whether it was a momentary shockwave or simply the command of His voice, we can't help to notice that Jesus' words, match those God used to describe Himself to Moses, saying "I am who I am" (see Exodus 3:14). These men did not fall forward in worship; they should have fallen back since they were mere men arresting God.

TALK ABOUT IT:
Why didn't Jesus defend Himself at His arrest? (If Jesus had defended Himself, he would have won easily, but there would be no salvation.)

What signs did those who arrested Jesus have that He was God? (Not only did they fall back when Jesus said "I am," but they also witnessed Jesus healing the ear of the man Peter had injured.)

PRAY:
Pray that God helps us to recognize Jesus. Many people know His name, but not everyone believes and gives Him their lives.

THURSDAY

THE STORY: MARK 14:53-65

Jesus went on trial. Jesus had done nothing wrong; He was without sin. All the rulers came together and brought false witness against Jesus but their testimonies, all lies, did not agree.

The chief priest asked Jesus directly, "Are you the Christ, the Son of the Blessed?" Jesus answered, " I am." Then He went on to say He, the Son of Man, would come with the clouds of heaven. The high priest, knowing that Jesus was claiming to be God, equal with the Father, tore his clothes and accused Jesus of blasphemy. Jesus was then condemned to die, cruelly beaten, and mocked. The rulers did not realize that everything Jesus said was absolutely true.

Jesus calling Himself the Son of Man brings together Daniel 7:13,14 and Psalm 110:1. The Son of Man in Daniel is given authority and glory, and all the nations worship Him. He is God. Combined with the words "I am," there is no mistaking Jesus' claim to be God.

TALK ABOUT IT:

What is significant about the words "I am"? ("I am" is the name God gave Himself when He spoke to Moses. The Jewish leaders would have known this. Jesus used those words with this in mind.)

What do you think you would have done if you lived in the time of Jesus' arrest? (We can think that we would have acted nobly. The truth is we would have either sided with the religious rulers and accused Jesus, or sided with the disciples and deserted Jesus. We should not look back at these men with judgment. They were all sinners, like us, in need of a Savior.)

PRAY:
Ask God to help each member of your family always remember the cost of the cross.

FRIDAY
ON THE ROAD TO EMMAUS

THE STORY: PSALM 41:9
This is a reference to Jesus' betrayal by Judas and includes a reference to the Last Supper, where Judas shared bread with Jesus. Jesus quoted this passage in John 13:18 and directly attributed it to Himself. Judas betrayed Jesus with a kiss, the greeting of a close friend.

TALK ABOUT IT:
How did Jesus trust Judas even though Jesus knew Judas was going to betray Him? (Jesus allowed Judas to remain with Him and even gave Him the job of carrying the disciples' money.)

Would anyone have understood this passage as referring to Jesus prior to Him making this connection? (No, there were many clues hidden in the Scripture, and in many ways all of the Old Testament points to Jesus.)

PRAY:
Thank God for sending His son Jesus in spite of the tremendous betrayal and suffering He needed to endure.

PETER DENIES JESUS

Even the most confident man will not stand apart from Jesus.

MONDAY

THE STORY: JOHN 18:15-18

Peter and another disciple followed Jesus to the high priest's courtyard, where Jesus was questioned. Peter waited just outside the door. While he was there, a woman recognized him and suggested he was a disciple of Jesus. Peter answered, "I am not." This is hardly the same man who hours earlier at the Last Supper boasted, "Even if all fall away on account of you, I will not" (see Mark 14:29).

TALK ABOUT IT:

Why did Peter deny knowing Jesus? (Peter was afraid.)

What was Peter afraid of? (Peter was probably afraid of being arrested like Jesus.)

How might we deny Jesus today? (We might hide the fact that we are Christians to avoid what people might think. In some countries a believer can still be arrested and even killed for faith in Jesus.)

PRAY:

Pray for Christians in nations where they face arrest and worse for being Christians.

TUESDAY

THE STORY: JOHN 18:19-24

The high priest Annas questioned Jesus about His disciples and His teaching. In His answer Jesus suggested the high priest ask those who heard Him. Jesus was struck for this answer. The irony of Jesus' remark is that one of His disciples, who heard His teaching, was standing just outside the door, denying Him.

TALK ABOUT IT:

Why did the official hit Jesus? (Jesus answered the high priest in a way wrongly perceived to be disrespectful.)

Was Jesus answer disrespectful? (No. Jesus only spoke the truth.)

Why should the high priest have known who Jesus really was? (The high priest would have known the Scriptures better than most and would have been familiar with the prophecies concerning the coming Messiah.)

Is there a difference between knowing about Jesus from your Bible and believing and trusting in Jesus? (Yes. Many people own Bibles, some even study them, and yet in their hearts they do not believe in Jesus. We need to call out to God for grace to believe and to yield our lives to Christ.)

PRAY:

Pray God would give each member of your family grace to believe and place their trust in Him.

WEDNESDAY
WHERE IS THE GOSPEL?

THE STORY: MATTHEW 26:69-75

So often we think we can follow Jesus in our own strength. Peter thought this way. The truth is, even though we think we would do better, we are just like Peter. It is only by the grace of God that we believe. Faith is a gift from God.

Peter needed a Savior. Jesus, the one Peter denied, was moments away from the cross, where He would become that Savior and die for Peter's sin and our sin. What an amazing display of love, that Jesus would go to the cross willingly even while those closest to Him disowned Him. What an amazing Savior who died for us!

TALK ABOUT IT:

What do we learn from this Gospel about Peter's last denial that is different from the account in John? (in Matthew 26:74 Peter's last denial was so strong that he actually began to call down curses upon himself.)

What can Peter's sin teach us? (We, like Peter, are sinners in need of a Savior. Our only hope is in Jesus. We can't follow Jesus in our own strength.)

PRAY:

Ask God to help each member of your family trust in Jesus alone.

THURSDAY

THE STORY: JOHN 18:25-27

Peter denied Christ three times just as Jesus predicted. Peter began the evening a confident man. His pride was evident in the comment, "even if all fall away on account fo you, I will never fall." (Matt. 26:33) Jesus saw Peter's pride and warned Peter. Now in the courtyard of the High Priest, one of the High Priest's servants, who was there when Peter cut off the man's ear, recongnized and challenged Peter. Peter, afraid, denied knowing Jesus. Peter was guilty of assult for cutting off a man's ear. He was afraid. He did not trust in Jesus, he lied.

TALK ABOUT IT:

Why do you think Peter kept on denying Christ? (One lie often leads to another. Like Peter, we all either must put our faith in Christ, or deny Him. There is no middle ground.

How does the proverb "pride goes before destruction" (Proverbs 16:18), fit this story? (Peter demonstrated his pride in boasting that he would not abandon Jesus even unto death. He said this in spite of the Lord's warning that all the disciples would fall away. Peter's pride caused him to think he was different than the other disciples.)

Do you think Peter was sorry for what He did? (Yes, there is evidence Peter was repentant in Luke 22:62.)

PRAY:

Ask God to help you walk humbly and trust in Jesus. Our boasts should only be in the Lord.

FRIDAY
ON THE ROAD TO EMMAUS

THE STORY: ISAIAH 53:7

The prophet Isaiah foretold the arrest of Jesus. Isaiah 53:7 says, "He was oppressed, and He was afflicted, yet He opened not his mouth; like a lamb that is led to the slaughter; like a sheep that before its shearers is silent, so He opened not his mouth."

TALK ABOUT IT:
How does this prophetic passage match the actions of Jesus at His arrest? (Jesus did not resist arrest and did not even say one unkind word.)

How was Jesus oppressed and afflicted? (Jesus was mocked, beaten, falsely accused, given a crown of thorns and crucified.)

PRAY
Thank Jesus for being willing to suffer and die in our place.

THE THIEF ON THE CROSS

God's forgiveness is available even to the worst sinners.

MONDAY

THE STORY: LUKE 23:32-34

Jesus spoke forgiveness, in the midst of His suffering. Jesus was crucified with a criminal on his left and another on his right. Isaiah prophesied about this when he wrote that the suffering servant would be "numbered with the transgressors" (Isaiah 53:12). In Matthew 18:21-22 Jesus told Peter that forgiveness should extend to those who have sinned against us seventy times seven times! Jesus demonstrated here that His forgiveness extends to criminals and even to the men who put Him on the cross.

TALK ABOUT IT:

How is Jesus' prayer an example to us? (If Jesus was willing to forgive those who crucified Him, how much more should we be willing to forgive those who have sinned against us?)

Why is it hard to forgive? (It is hard to forgive because we want payment for our loss. Jesus says we should release others from that debt and forgive them.)

PRAY:

Ask God to help each member of your family remember Jesus' example so that it is easier to forgive those who sin against us.

TUESDAY

THE STORY: LUKE 23:35-38

Even while the people stood and watched Jesus ask the Father to forgive them, they mocked Him. The people, the soldiers and even the rulers mocked Him. Jesus looked powerless as he hung on the cross. The people wanted to see if Jesus would save himself. When He didn't they saw Him as a defeated man. They saw the man who had made great claims about being God now suffering and bleeding like any man. What they didn't know is that Jesus was fully God while also being fully man. Even the sign above Jesus, meant to mock His claims, testified of His true position: Jesus was the King of the Jews.

TALK ABOUT IT:

Why did the people mock Jesus? (It seemed to them that Jesus' claims were hollow, now that he was humiliated and dying. This was made clear by their comment in Luke 23:35: "He saved others let him save himself.")

Did the people know Jesus was saving others by His sacrifice? (No, they did not understand.)

If we were there, what do you think we would have done? (We would likely have either mocked Jesus or fled in fear.)

PRAY:

Thank Jesus for dying on the cross for our sins and for being willing to take insults in addition to the physical pain.

WEDNESDAY
WHERE IS THE GOSPEL?

THE STORY: MARK 15:25-32

Along with the unrepentant theif, the cheif priests, and teachers of the law, Mark tells us that even those people passing by joined in the mocking of Jesus. They challenged Jesus to save himself and came down from the cross. The repeated Jesus' claim to rebuild the temple in three days and jeered.

Jesus would rebuild the temple in three days, the temple of His body. Three days after His death, Jesus would rise again. The mockers called out for Jesus to save Himself, but by dying intheir place Jesus would save the mockers. If we were there, we, like the passers by, would have joined in the mocking. Jesus didn't save Himself so that we could be saved. Jesus gave His life for us.

TALK ABOUT IT:

How is the cross connected to the gospel? (The cross is the main component of the gospel. The cross is where the lamb, Jesus, was sacrificed and received the wrath of God for our sin. The other part of the gospel is His resurrection.)

why should we be thankful taht Jesus died? (Jesus didn't deserve to be killed, but we should be thankful becuase Jesus died for us, taking our punishemetn upon Himself. If we trust in Jesus we can be saved from the punishement of our sin.)

Why did God choose the cross? (The cross was the one method of execution cursed by God [see Deuteronomy 21:23]). Paul makes this connection in Galatians 3:13.)

PRAY:

Thank Jesus for dying for us, that we might be forgiven.

THURSDAY

THE STORY: LUKE 23:39-43

One criminal joined the mocking of the crowd but the other criminal rebuked him. This criminal realized Jesus had done nothing wrong. Then in a remarkable demonstration of grace, the criminal defending Jesus placed His faith in Christ. Then he said, "Jesus, remember me when you come into your kingdom" (Luke 23:42). Jesus replied, "Today you will be with me in paradise." The arm of the Lord is not too short to save even a man who repents at the very last moment. In the midst of so much unbelief, we see here one man's newfound faith. And he was rewarded for that faith with assurance from Christ of life in paradise.

TALK ABOUT IT:

What to happened to the criminal who had faith in Jesus when he died? (Jesus said that he would be with Jesus in paradise, or heaven.)

Where will we immediately go when we die if we believe? (We will go to heaven as well.)

Where do you think the other criminal went? (There is no evidence the other criminal ever repented of his sin and trusted Jesus. If he died without trusting Christ, he went to hell.)

PRAY:

Pray the prayer of the criminal. Confess your sins and ask Jesus to remember you by pouring out His salvation upon you.

FRIDAY
ON THE ROAD TO EMMAUS

THE STORY: PSALM 22:17,18

The whole of Psalm 22, like Isaiah 53, is a prophetic picture of the Crucifixion. Psalm 22:18 accurately predicts the dividing up of Jesus' clothing by casting lots. This is found in Matthew 27:35, Mark 15:24, and Luke 23:34. In verse 17 David also prophesies about Jesus' sufferimg and the mocking of the crowd at the crucifixion.

TALK ABOUT IT:

What do we learn about David (who wrote Psalm 22) by comparing it to the Gospel accounts of the Crucifixion? (We learn that David was a prophet as well as a king.)

How does David's being both prophet and king point to Jesus? (Jesus was both a prophet and a king.)

PRAY:

Thank God for the amazing way the story of Jesus is found in all the Bible.

THE CRUCIFIXION OF JESUS

The death of Jesus brings us life.

MONDAY

THE STORY: MATTHEW 27:27-31

Jesus was crowned with thorns. Jesus, who is King of Kings and Lord of Lords, endured the mocking of sinful men so that we might be saved. The soldiers gave Jesus a crown of thorns, a scarlet robe and a staff. They struck Jesus again and again on the head. This was no surprise to Jesus; He knew the fate that awaited Him. Consider these verses, from the book of Isaiah, He would have known from childhood:

"He was despised and rejected by men, a man of sorrows, and familiar with suffering. Like one from whom men hide their faces He was despised, and we esteemed Him not. Surely He took up our infirmities and carried our sorrows, yet we considered Him stricken by God, smitten by Him, and afflicted" (Isaiah 53:3,4).

TALK ABOUT IT:

Why did the soldiers mock Jesus' claims to kingship? (Jesus admitted to Pilate that he was the King of the Jews. When people think of a king, they think of worldly power. Jesus was a different kind of king, a heavenly king. He looked nothing like a king, so not knowing who He was, the soldiers mocked His claims.)

Why didn't Jesus fight back, or at least correct the soldiers? (Read 1 Peter 2:23-24. It is here that we learn that Jesus offered no resistance because He entrusted Himself to God, the judge, and willingly endured this suffering for us.)

PRAY:
Thank Jesus for enduring suffering for us that we might be forgiven.

TUESDAY

THE STORY: MATTHEW 27:32-44
Jesus was crucified. Jesus was nailed to the cross and crucified. A sign was placed over His head that announced His title as "King of the Jews." The soldiers cast lots for His clothing, and a crowd gathered to mock Him.

Jesus endured crucifixion on our behalf. Crucifixion was a terrible way to be executed. It was so horrible that it was reserved for slaves and the most degraded criminals. If the legs of a person who was crucified were not broken, it might take days to die an agonizing death. Once the legs of a person were broken they could no longer support their weight to breathe so they would suffocate.

TALK ABOUT IT:
Why did people mock Jesus? (They did not believe Him, and now seeing Jesus appear defeated, they felt justified in their unbelief. They thought that if Jesus truly was the Son of God, He would save Himself. When Jesus did nothing against the Romans, they mocked Him as a fake.)

How does reading about the Crucifixion affect you? (Parents, draw out your children here. Be prepared to challenge your children to trust in Christ.)

PRAY:

Ask God to bring salvation to every member of your family that you might all believe and trust in Jesus' sacrifice.

WEDNESDAY
WHERE IS THE GOSPEL?

THE STORY: LUKE 23:44-49

The death of Christ is the heart of the gospel. Without the shedding of blood, there is no forgiveness of sins (see Hebrews 9:22). Jesus was the Lamb of God who was slain for the forgiveness of our sins.

Romans 5:8,9 says "…but God shows his love for us in that while we were still sinners, Christ died for us. Since we have now been justified by his blood, how much more shall we be saved from God's wrath through Him!"

As Jesus was dying, a darkness came over the whole land. At the moment of His death, the temple curtain was torn in two. This is the curtain that divided the Holy Place from the Most Holy Place and blocked men from the presence of God. With Jesus' death, the curtain was torn, and the way between man and God was opened. John records that just before Jesus died He said, "It is finished" (see John 19:30). The wrath of God poured out upon Jesus for the sins of man was exhausted, and the way to God was opened.

Luke 23:46 records that Jesus said, "Father, into Your hands I commit My spirit." He was not entrusting Himself alone but all those who through His sacrifice are "in Christ." Jesus died for all of us.

TALK ABOUT IT:

Why was there a curtain dividing the inner courts of the temple? (The curtain protected the priests from the presence of God. They could only go in once a year and only with blood, which was offered to cover their sins as well as the sins of the people.)

What happened to the curtain when Jesus died? (The curtain was torn in two from top to bottom.)

What did the tearing of the curtain mean? (The way between man and God never need be blocked again. Jesus, the great High Priest, offered His own blood to God, and His sacrifice was able to purchase our redemption forever, according to Hebrews 9:12.)

PRAY:
Thank Jesus for tearing down the curtain that blocked us from the presence of God. Take time to praise God for all He has done for your family.

THURSDAY

THE STORY: MATTHEW 27:45-61
While Jesus was on the cross, Matthew (27:46) tells us He called out, "My God, My God, why have you forsaken me?" For all eternity past, Jesus had been in sweet fellowship with His Father. Now the Father poured out His full wrath upon Christ for our sin, forsaking Him upon the cross. John (19:30) adds that just before He died, Jesus said, "It is finished," signifying that the wrath of the Father had been fully poured out. It did not take long for Jesus to die. He had been so tortured prior to being crucified that his weakened body did not last long.

Imagine being present, mocking Jesus and watching Him die. This was then followed by earthquakes, the tearing of the temple curtain and the resurrections of many. Those watching were terrified, instinctively knowing that Jesus was the Son of God. John (19:32) records that though the soldiers broke the legs of the criminals to hasten their death, they did not need to break the legs of Jesus, for he was already dead. Instead they pierced Jesus' side with a spear.
Joseph of Arimathea requested Jesus' body and buried Him in his own new tomb

(see Mathew 27:57-60).

TALK ABOUT IT:
What did Jesus mean when He said He was foraken? (God the Father did not hlep His son. Instead the Father poured out His holy warther for our sin up on Jesus. The Father had never before turned away from His son.)

Why are the words of John's Gospel account "It is finished" so wonderful? (These words indicate the sacrifice was complete, with the anger of God fully satisfied. The penalty for our sin was paid.)

If Jesus died for our sins why should we think about sin any more? (It is good to remember our sins. It is in remembering our sins that we see our need for the remedy of the cross. Gratefulness for the cross wells up in our hearts.)

PRAY:
Thank Jesus for receiving the punishment for our sins in His body.

FRIDAY
ON THE ROAD TO EMMAUS

THE STORY: ISAIAH 53:5
When we read the account of the soldiers mocking Jesus and striking Him in the head, the connection to Isaiah's words becomes clear. Jesus suffered beatings and was mocked and spat upon by the soldiers on His way to be crucified.

TALK ABOUT IT:
How does reading this account from Isaiah affect you? (Parents, draw out your children and steer them toward gratefulness to Jesus.)

How does Jesus' suffering speak of His love for us? (There is no way to comprehend how much agony He suffered because of the amazing love He has for us. If we thought every hour of every day about the depth of His love, we would still not be able to comprehend its fullness.)

PRAY:
Thank the Lord for enduring so much suffering for us.

THE RESURRECTION

Even though Jesus truly rose from the dead, not everyone believes.

MONDAY

THE STORY: MATTHEW 27:27-31

Soldiers were positioned to guard Jesus' tomb. Even though the disciples did not understand what Jesus meant when He said that He would rise again on the third day, some of the Pharisees seemed to understand. Though they knew, they did not believe. They asked Pilate to order the tomb guarded and sealed until the third day. Consider that around the time of Jesus' death, the sky grew dark, and the moment of His death the earth shook and rocks were split (see Matthew 27:51). In addition, many holy people who had died were raised to life and appeared to many people in the city of Jerusalem. It would be hard to keep quiet when a family member whom you buried months ago, suddenly appeared and shared the account and time of their resurrection. Given that there were many people raised, these reports likely reached the ears of the religious rulers as well. It is interesting to note they did all this "work" on the Sabbath.

TALK ABOUT IT:

What did the chief priests do to Jesus' tomb? (They sealed it and posted a guard.)

Why is it interesting that the priests sealed the tomb on the Sabbath? (The religious rulers criticized Jesus for healing on the Sabbath, yet here they worked to seal the tomb.)

PRAY:
Ask the Lord to help every member of your family to not doubt but believe.

TUESDAY

THE STORY: MATTHEW 28:1-10

Jesus rose with great power. A wax seal and a Roman guard could not stop the resurrection of Jesus from the dead. In fact, if the whole Roman army had been present, Jesus would have risen just the same. Imagine the soldiers' shock as the earth began to shake, then an angel bright as lightning rolled the stone away and sat upon it. What a glorious moment - death was defeated!

The guards were so afraid that they shook and fell to the ground (see Matthew 28:4). The angel spoke to the women, telling them that Jesus had risen from the dead just as He said! The angel sent them to report back to the disciples.

John 20:15 tells us that Mary saw Jesus but mistook Him for the gardener. But when Jesus called her by name, she instantly believed. Matthew 28:9 records that Jesus met the two women on their way to tell the disciples. The women fell down, grasped His feet and worshipped Him. The response of these two women demonstrates their faith. Jesus commissioned them in the same way He commissions all believers: "Go and tell" (see Matthew 28:10).

TALK ABOUT IT:

What is your favorite part of this story? (Draw the children out, as there is much to enjoy in the Resurrection story.)

What can we tell from the women's response to Jesus? (First, their worship indicates their faith. Second, Jesus did not rebuke them. God alone was to be worshipped. If Jesus were not God, He would have corrected them. This might seem obvious, but many today deny that Jesus was God, saying He was simply a good teacher or prophet.)

PRAY:

Take time to worship Jesus through prayers that exalt the name and ministry of Christ. (Parents, help each of your children to pray.)

WEDNESDAY
WHERE IS THE GOSPEL?

THE STORY: LUKE 24:1-12

Jesus is no longer in the tomb! This is the most critical part of the gospel. Paul said it like this:

"If there is no resurrection of the dead, then not even Christ has been raised. And if Christ has not been raised, then our preaching is in vain and your faith is in vain. . . If Christ has not been raised your faith is futile and you are still in your sins" (I Corinthians 15:13,14,17).

Paul goes on to say in 1 Corinthians 15:20-23 that Christ is the firstfruits (the first to be raised) and that we will also be raised! If Jesus had died but not risen again, we would all be lost! The Resurrection is not a tagalong to the cross. It is an integral part of the gospel message without which the gospel would have no power!

TALK ABOUT IT:

Did the disciples believe the women's report? (No, they did not believe at first.)

Did Peter believe when he reached the tomb? (No, but he was puzzled and wondered what could have taken place.)

Why was the resurrection important? (Jesus said He would rise again. If Jesus could not or did not rise from the dead, then He would be a liar. In rising from the dead, Jesus demonstrated that He defeated death. If He was unable to rise again, death would have defeated Him.)

PRAY:
Praise the Lord in your prayers and ask that every member of your family be touched by God's grace to believe.

THURSDAY

THE STORY: MATTHEW 28:11-15
Not all who know the truth will be set free. Some of the guards returned to the chief priests and reported to them everything that happened. Consider that they told the chief priests about the earthquake, the angel, the bright light, the rising of Christ and the visit of the two women who met and conversed with the Lord. They heard all of this, and yet the chief priests did not believe. Instead they hatched a scheme to keep the guards quiet, actually spreading a rumor that the disciples stole the body. The soldiers accepted the money and agreed to lie.

TALK ABOUT IT:
After witnessing the Resurrection, did the soldiers place their faith in Jesus? (No, even after witnessing the Resurrection, the soldiers did not believe and were willing to spread lies in exchange for money.)

Did the chief priests place their trust in Christ after hearing the story? (No, they did not. Instead they paid off the guards to lie about what happened.)

What do we learn about faith from this passage? (Only those who were called were saved. The guards saw the power of God, and yet knowing what they saw to be real, they did not place their trust in Christ. Similarly the chief priests believed the story enough to pay off the guards, but not enough to place their trust in Christ. True faith is more than believing the events of history to be true. True faith is believing the events of the death and resurrection of Christ, and then placing your faith in Jesus for your salvation. Though they saw or heard about what took place, neither the guards nor the chief priests placed their faith in Christ.)

What is the difference between knowing what took place and putting your faith in Jesus? (Draw your children out and help them to see that, as sinners, we must recognize our need for salvation, which can only come through the sacrifice of Jesus. Believing in Jesus requires the "why" to be answered and embraced in our hearts. The "why" is answered when we understand our condition as sinners and understand that God's Son came down to earth to die in our place. Then our trust and belief is placed in Jesus as Savior, not simply in a historic person.)

Is it possible to know about Jesus and yet not truly believe? (Yes, it is possible to know about Him and not believe. The guards and the chief priests are perfect examples of this.)

PRAY:
Pray that every member of your family would not simply know about Jesus but fully place their trust in Him. Ask God to call each of your family members by name, just as Jesus called Mary.

FRIDAY
ON THE ROAD TO EMMAUS

THE STORY: PSALM 34:19,20
While Jesus was still on the cross, the soldiers came to break his legs. But they saw He was already dead, and therefore did not need to break his legs. John tells us those events fulfilled Psalm 34:20 (see John 19:36). In a demonstration of God's sovereign control over every detail, none of Jesus' bones were broken.

TALK ABOUT IT:
Is God able to do what He says? (Yes, God is able to do what He says.)

Was God able to keep Jesus' bones from being broken? (Yes, God did work it out that Jesus' legs would not be broken.)

Why didn't God prevent Jesus from the agony of the cross? (God could have stopped the Crucifixion. Jesus Himself said He could call down legions of angels (see Matthew 26:53). God sent His Son to die for us, which required that Jesus endure great suffering in fulfillment of the Scriptures.)

PRAY:
Thank the Lord for the great suffering He endured that we might be saved.

DOUBTING THOMAS

Jesus calls to faith all those who are His.

MONDAY

THE STORY: JOHN 20:19-23

The disciples believed. After appearing to Mary outside the tomb, Jesus appeared to two disciples on the road to Emmaus. Next He appeared again to Peter, who then informed the others (see Luke 24:34). Even so, the disciples were huddled in a room, afraid of what the Jews might do to them. It is likely the soldiers had already begun to spread the rumor that the disciples had stolen Jesus' body. While they were gathered, Jesus, in His ressurrected body, came into the room even though the door was locked. Luke tells us they thought He was a ghost, so they doubted. Jesus showed them His hands and side. Luke tells us that Jesus opened their minds so they could understand. Once they understood, they were overjoyed. Jesus breathed on the disciples, and they received the Holy Spirit. This was not a symbol of what was to come later. The disciples were converted, and the Spirit of God dwelled in them. They were then commissioned to spread the gospel, but as Luke 24:48 records, Jesus told them to remain until they were clothed with the Spirit's power.

TALK ABOUT IT:

How did Jesus get through the locked door? (We are not told just how Jesus entered through the locked door, but we can be sure He did not have a key! This was a miraculous appearing.)

Why did Jesus show them His hands and side? (Jesus showed them His hands and side where His wounds were. The disciples thought He was a ghost and doubted He was real. By allowing them to touch Him, they would know He was not a ghost. Luke 24:41-43 records that Jesus also ate breakfast with them to help them believe He was alive.).

PRAY:
Ask God to help each one in your family quickly believe and not doubt.

TUESDAY

THE STORY: JOHN 20:24-29
Thomas had been absent during Jesus' first visit and told his fellow disciples he would not believe unless he could touch the wounds of Christ himself. One week later Jesus appeared again and granted Thomas' request. Instantly Thomas' doubts faded and he immediately believed. The words of Thomas, "My Lord and my God!" from John 20:28, declare his faith in Jesus not merely as a great man but as God. Jesus commended Thomas and left us with a great encouragement to faith, saying, "Blessed are those who have not seen and yet have believed."

We are among those who have not seen but do believe. Jesus was not harsh with Thomas. Rather than rebuke Thomas, Jesus called him to faith. Jesus calls us to faith as well.

TALK ABOUT IT:
Is it easier to believe if you have seen Jesus? (Yes and no. Seeing the risen Lord can be used of God to help someone believe, but not everyone who saw the risen Lord responded with faith. It is quite possible that the guards who watched over His tomb never believed. Luke 24:16,31 tells us the disciples on the road to Emmaus were blinded from the truth, and then the truth was opened up to them. It is God who enables us to believe. Whether we have seen the risen Lord

in person, or only through His Word, we need God to open our eyes. There is nothing we can do in and of ourselves to guarantee faith. God is the author of our faith. Faith is His free gift to us.)

If faith is a gift from God which helps us to believe, can we believe without His gift of faith? (No, we cannot believe unless He touches our hearts and opens our eyes and gives us His gift of faith.)

PRAY:
Ask God to open the eyes and heart of every member of your family that you all might believe.

WEDNESDAY
WHERE IS THE GOSPEL?

THE STORY: LUKE 24:36-49
After His resurrection, Jesus opened the minds of His disciples to understand the Scriptures (Luke 24:45). Jesus explained that He Himself was the central theme of Scripture. Jesus very kindly introduced the disciples to the truth. He did not rebuke them for their former doubts; He called them to faith.

Thomas did not believe. He was in need of gospel truth. Jesus knew what Thomas needed and showed him His nail-scarred hands. Jesus called Thomas to faith and opened His mind. Thomas immediately responded by addressing Jesus as God.

The disciples doubted, but when confronted with the risen Lord who was slain for our sins, they believed. Like the disciples, we need to be reminded of Jesus' death to that we, too, might believe. Though we have not seen, we have heard the Word and we can believe.

TALK ABOUT IT:
What three parts of the Bible did Jesus say must be fulfilled? (Luke 24:44 tells us

everything must be fulfilled that is written about Jesus from the Law of Moses, the Prophets, and the Psalms.)

What should we do when we have doubts about Jesus? (We should call out to the Lord in prayer and ask Him for help to overcome unbelief. It is also good to re-read the Bible. Just as Thomas' meeting with the Lord built his faith, so does our reading the Word of God build ours. See Romans 10:17.)

PRAY:
Ask the Lord to help every member of your family to believe and not doubt.

THURSDAY

THE STORY: JOHN 20:30,31
Who will believe? John 20:30,31 adds a bit of commentary. John tells us he did not record every miracle of Jesus but that what was recorded was written so that we might believe. Thomas would not believe until he could see for himself. In His kindness, God reaches out to us in the same way through His Word. The Bible is more than a recollection of history. Hebrews 4:12 tells us that the Word of God is living. When we read the Word, the Spirit of God uses it to transform our lives. In Romans 1:16 Paul said the gospel is the power of God for the salvation of everyone who believes.

TALK ABOUT IT:
Why did God give us the Bible? (That we might believe Jesus is the Son of God and have life in Him.)

Why should we read the Bible? (Some think we should read the Bible because it is the right thing to do. Learning the Word of God increases our faith. Romans 10:17 tells us "Consequently, faith comes by hearing the message, and the message is heard through the word of Christ.")

PRAY:
Ask God to place a hunger for His Word into your heart that you might desire to read the Bible.

FRIDAY
ON THE ROAD TO EMMAUS

THE STORY: PSALM 38:11,12
David's prayer points forward to another king in the line of David who would suffer similarly. Jesus was deserted by His companions. Even those who followed Jesus watched from a distance (see Matthew 27:55). The religious rulers plotted to ruin Jesus and paid Judas to betray Him.

TALK ABOUT IT:
Did David suffer like Jesus? (Yes, David was rejected and had to run for his life from King Saul, and even his own son Absalom wanted to kill him [see 2 Samuel 15:10-14].)

How was Jesus' suffering different from that of David? (Jesus allowed himself to be taken, beaten, mocked, and crucified, knowing that through His sacrifice He was bringing us life and forgiveness.)

PRAY:
Thank God for Jesus' willing suffering and sacrifice on our behalf.

NEW TESTAMENT · LESSON 41

JESUS AND ANOTHER MIRACULOUS CATCH OF FISH

Those who belong to the Lord are sustained by Him.

MONDAY

THE STORY: JOHN 21:1-5

The disciples went back to fishing. Apart from the early appearances by Jesus, the disciples had not seen the Lord for a while. They seem to be without purpose when Peter suggests they go fishing. He gives no good reason. A fisherman by trade, Peter would have likely enjoyed fishing. They fished all night but caught nothing. In the providence of God, this would set the stage for the miracle about to take place. Early in the morning, as they approached the shore, Jesus called to them. Jesus called them friends. Lest we overlook this greeting, we should take a moment to marvel. The Lord of glory is calling sinful men His friends. The disciples, however did not recognize Jesus. How often do we forget, in the midst of our difficulty, that the Lord is but a conversation away?

TALK ABOUT IT:

Why didn't the disciples recognize Jesus? (We could blame the distance, or that they didn't recognize His voice. It is clear from the story, however, that they were not looking for Jesus. Had they been looking for Him, they would have recognized Him.)

Sometimes we forget Jesus as we go about our lives. How might this happen? (The cares and work of this world can capture our attention. In a short while we realize it might have been weeks since we devoted ourselves to the Word and prayer.)

Is this true of you? (Parents, draw out your children and share your own weaknesses.)

PRAY:
Pray for God's grace to keep you ever seeking Jesus.

TUESDAY

THE STORY: JOHN 21:5-14
Jesus appeared tot he disciples again. Knowing the disciples had no clue He was the one speaking to them, Jesus revealed Himself in a humorous way. Surely they would know it was Jesus once they caught the fish. As soon as they drew in the net, they knew it was the Lord. Jesus demonstrated His authority over the fish and the net. A huge number of fish were caught, and yet the net did not break. Jesus was ready with bread and a fire to cook the fish. He ate with the disciples.

TALK ABOUT IT:
Why do you think the Lord provided another miraculous catch of fish? (Jesus was building their growing faith.)

Why do you think it served the disciples for Jesus to eat breakfast with them like any other man? (Jesus had been dead. Earlier they thought He might be a ghost. By eating with them they would quickly relax in His presence. Jesus was not a spirit; he had a real body. Some falsely teach that Jesus rose again in spirit only, but clearly the Scriptures show a man with a body who was able to eat food with his friends.)

PRAY:

Ask God to build and grow your faith as you read and study about Him from the Bible.

WEDNESDAY
WHERE IS THE GOSPEL?

THE STORY: JOHN 21:24,25

When Jesus called Peter, James and John to follow Him, He demonstrated His power by a miraculous catch of fish (see Luke 5:1-11). Jesus demonstrated His power again to the disciples through a second miraculous catch of fish. John concluded his Gospel at the end of this story with a declaration that all he wrote was true regarding the ministry of Christ, the death of Christ, the resurrection of Christ, and even the appearing of Jesus on the shores of Galilee, where He cooked the disciples a breakfast of fish.

John 21:25 goes on to say that Jesus did many other things as well, so many that all the books in the world could not contain them! We can look forward to an eternity of days in heaven where we, who are saved by the death and resurrection of Jesus, can sit at His feet and hear them all!

TALK ABOUT IT:

Why is John's Gospel so believable? (John was an eyewitness and was writing what he saw with his very own eyes.)

What do we call it when we tell others our personal experience with Jesus? (We call our personal experience our testimony. People may doubt what we say about how others experience Jesus, but when we tell them our personal testimony and what Jesus has done for us, they can't easily refute what we say.)

What has Jesus done for you? (Don't pressure your kids for a salvation testimony; rather help them to see all that God has provided for them in general, and remind them of the gift of the gospel. We want to walk the fine line between encouraging our children in their faith and producing false assurance based on our coached interactions.)

PRAY:
Pray that God would give you the courage to tell others about what Jesus has done in your life.

THURSDAY

THE STORY: JOHN 21:15-23
Jesus restores Peter. Three times Peter denied Jesus (see Matthew 26:69-75), and here Jesus asks him three times, "Do you love me?" Jesus appeared once before to Peter in Jerusalem (see Luke 24:34). We are not told what they talked about at that first meeting. Most commentators believe that this passage is Jesus' restoration of Peter. In any case, Jesus is commissioning Peter to feed and take care of His sheep. Some believe the reference to Peter's hands being stretched out is a prophetic word regarding Peter's death. Tradition has it that he was crucified upside down.

TALK ABOUT IT:
How did Peter demonstrate faith in Jesus with his third answer? (Peter appealed to Christ's omniscience and said, "You know all things; you know that I love You." Jesus didn't disagree, for Peter did love the Lord.)

How can the way Jesus dealt with Peter give us hope in the midst of our struggles with indwelling sin? (Peter so completely denied the Lord that he even called down curses on himself in Mark 14:71. In spite of this, Jesus entrusted Peter with the care of His sheep. There is nothing more precious on earth than the Good Shepherd's sheep. If Jesus can forgive Peter and entrust to him a measure of care for His most precious sheep, He can forgive us and use us as well.)

PRAY:
Thank Jesus for the forgiveness of sin and His willingness to use us to reach the lost.

FRIDAY
ON THE ROAD TO EMMAUS

THE STORY: ISAIAH 32:1-4
Jesus is the King who will reign in righteousness. Jesus calmed the storm that blew in suddenly on the lake, and He is our refuge in time of trouble. Jesus opened the eyes of the blind and the ears of the deaf, and He also opened the minds of men so they could understand who He is.

TALK ABOUT IT:
How does this Scripture apply to our relationship with Jesus today? (Jesus is still the one we call upon for physical healing and in times of trouble. Jesus is still opening the minds of men to understand and believe in Him.)

Has there ever been a king apart from Jesus who has reigned in righteousness? (Though many of Israel's kings did honorable things, they were all sinners. Even their good deeds were corrupted by their sinful motivations. Jesus is the only truly righteous king.)

PRAY:
Thank Jesus for becoming our Savior.

THE GREAT COMMISSION

The nations must be taught the instruction of the Lord.

MONDAY

THE STORY: MATTHEW 28:16,17

Some of the disciples struggled to believe. The eleven disciples were asked to meet Jesus on a particular mountain. When they saw Jesus, some worshipped Him, while others doubted. Rather than rebuke those who doubted, Jesus commissioned them all! What an encouragement to us when we struggle at times with our faith.

TALK ABOUT IT:

How are we like the disciples in this passage? (Even when we know the truth about Jesus, we can still doubt Him.)

What are some areas where we can struggle to believe and trust God? (Parents, lead by confessing your own unbelief. Many times this manifests when we lose faith that God is able to take us through difficult times for our good.)

How can we be encouraged by the doubt of the disciples? (They saw the risen Lord! If they doubted, then we, who have not seen the Lord, will also doubt. When we doubt, we can be encouraged that Jesus uses doubters. Jesus reveals himself to doubters and helps us in our unbelief.)

PRAY:
Ask God to strengthen your faith.

TUESDAY

THE STORY: MATTHEW 28:19
Jesus commissioned the doubters. In spite of the fact that some doubted, Jesus commissioned all eleven to go forth and teach all nations to obey everything commanded, baptizing them in the name of the Father and the Son and the Holy Spirit. Here, contained in a very small portion of Scripture, are some astounding truths. First, the apostles were not to limit their teaching to other Jews. They were to spread the teaching of Jesus to the Gentiles as well! In this Great Commission, Jesus applied this to us as well. Jesus also revealed the doctrine of the Trinity here when He says we are to baptize in the name of the Father, the Son, and the Holy Spirit. By including Himself, Jesus again declared His deity.

TALK ABOUT IT:
Who did Jesus say they should teach? (Jesus told the disciples to go to all nations.)

How does the Great Commission remind us of the promise given to Abraham about his offspring in Genesis 18:18, 22:18, and 26:4? (God promised to bless all nations through Abraham and his offspring. Jesus, a descendant of Abraham, is the means by which all nations will be blessed.)

PRAY:
Thank Jesus that His salvation has been extended to all nations.

WEDNESDAY
WHERE IS THE GOSPEL?

THE STORY: LUKE 24:46-49

The Great Commission of Matthew 28:16-20 is not found in the other Gospels, but has a companion passage in Luke. Jesus had earlier commissioned the disciples to spread the message of His death and resurrection (Luke 24:46). Both passages tell us that the gospel is to be preached to all nations. The salvation of Jesus Christ is not limited to the Jews, but is to go to all nations and all peoples. Mathew records that those who receive the message are to be baptized. That baptism, Paul later explains, is an identification with the death and resurrection of Jesus in the life of the individual believer (Romans 6:3,4).

TALK ABOUT IT:

Where do you see the gospel in Luke 24:46-49? (Verses 46 and 47 basically outline the gospel. Even though this might be obvious for your children, we should never tire of pointing out the gospel. We want to ensure that our children immediately recognize the gospel.)

What does it mean to be a witness of something? (Being a witness means that you saw it happen.)

Are we witnesses even though we didn't see Jesus? (We are witnesses of what we read in the Bible. We can't tell people that we were alive and saw Jesus die on the cross, but we can tell them that we believe what the Bible says happened. We can also tell others about our relationship with God. In that way we are also witnesses.)

PRAY:

Thank Jesus for each part of the gospel outlined in this passage: His suffering on the cross, rising from the dead, and granting of repentance and forgiveness of sins in His name.

THURSDAY

THE STORY: MATTHEW 28:20

Jesus is with us as we go. Matthew concluded his Gospel with amazing encouragement from Christ. Jesus told us that He will be with us always, to the very end of the age. Whenever we run into difficulty, we need to remember that Jesus is with us. Whenever we doubt, we should remember that Jesus is near. This is a verse we should remember!

TALK ABOUT IT:

Why is this verse so encouraging? (We are all going to face trials. What a joy to know that Jesus is always with us and that we can call on Him.)

Is it easy to forget this? (Yes. In our struggles we often rely on our own strength, ideas, opinions, and feelings. We forget that Jesus is ready to help us.)

PRAY:

Thank the Lord for being with us forever.

FRIDAY
ON THE ROAD TO EMMAUS

THE STORY: MICAH 5:4,5

Jesus is the shepherd whose greatness will extend to the ends of the earth. The promise to Abraham was that all the nations of the earth would be blessed through his offspring. Through Jesus, this promise is fulfilled. Those of us who believe are called the sheep of His flock who know His voice. Jesus is our peace. He said in John 14:27, "Peace I leave with you; My peace I give you. I do not give to you as the world gives. Do not let your hearts be troubled and do not be afraid."

TALK ABOUT IT:

What part of this passage sounds like the Great Commission? (This passage tells us that Jesus' greatness will reach to the ends of the earth. In the Great Commission, the message of Christ, which conquers death, is to go into all the earth.)

What kind of peace does the Lord give? (Jesus does not promise us freedom from earthly trials. He does promise us freedom from the wrath of God, along with forgiveness, rather than judgment, for our sin. The result is an unshakeable peace, even in the midst of earthly trials.)

PRAY:

Thank the Lord for being your Good Shepherd, your Savior, and your Prince of Peace.

THE ASCENSION

Jesus left, but He will return.

MONDAY

THE STORY: ACTS 1:1-5

Luke is the author of the Book of Acts, which is really just a continuation of the Gospel he wrote. We have four Gospels, but we only have one Book of Acts, thanks to Luke. In his opening, Luke gives a recap of Jesus' life, death, and resurrection. He mentions that Jesus gave many convincing proofs that He was alive again. Many have tried to discredit the resurrection, but it is one of the most documented ancient events, with multiple witnesses. Luke reminds us of Jesus' charge to the disciples to wait in Jerusalem for the outpouring of the Holy Spirit. Although Jesus had breathed on them to receive the Holy Spirit, they were expecting and waiting for a greater outpouring of the Spirit's power.

TALK ABOUT IT:

Does Luke believe Jesus rose again? How do you know? (Yes. Luke tells us that He appeared and gave many convincing proofs that He was alive.)

What are some of the convincing proofs Jesus gave? (Jesus ate with His disciples and allowed the disciples to touch the nail scars on His hands.)

PRAY:
Thank Jesus for all the testimony He left, which makes it easy for us to believe that He, indeed rose again from the dead.

TUESDAY

THE STORY: ACTS 1:6-11

Jesus ascends into heaven. Just before Jesus was lifted up to heaven, the disciples asked the Lord if He was going to restore the kingdom to Israel. They seemed to still be a bit confused about what the restored kingdom was all about. It is a good thing for us that Jesus did not restore the kingdom because we wouldn't have been a part of it. Now we get to enjoy everlasting life with God in heaven!

After He answered the disciples, Jesus was taken up while they were watching. A cloud hid Him. Like we might search for a balloon floating up in the sky, the disciples looked intently, hoping to catch another glimpse of the ascending Lord. Suddenly two men dressed in white appeared and made a wonderful announcement. Jesus would return one day just as He left! Today, we still look forward to His return. Though it is not for us to "know the times or dates," we should pray for His soon return.

TALK ABOUT IT:

Although the ascension would have been a sad parting for the disciples, Jesus gave them hope for the future. What hope did Jesus leave them with? (Jesus told them He was going to send the Holy Spirit and would return again one day.)

Do we have the same hope? (Yes. Every believer has the Holy Spirit living within. Imagine, God living in our hearts! And we, too, should long for the return of Christ.)

PRAY:

Thank Jesus for the Holy Spirit and pray for Christ's quick return.

WEDNESDAY
WHERE IS THE GOSPEL?

THE STORY: LUKE 24:50-53

If there were any lingering doubts that Jesus was God, they were silenced at His ascension. During the forty days before the Ascension, Jesus had appeared on a number of occasions to the disciples. Each time He was met with doubters. This time, doubters and fear are not mentioned. What a tender moment it was as the Lord said goodbye. For three years these men had lived with the Lord. They had learned much and were arguably the most privileged men on earth. They not only saw the Lord, but they also walked with Him, laughed with Him, were afraid with Him and for Him, watched Him die, and then saw Him risen.

Jesus blessed them and was taken up into heaven. Their last act was to worship the man they had come to believe was God. From there, they went to the temple, where they praised God continually. Likely the curtain, torn in two at the death of Christ, was sewn together again. These men, however, now understood the gospel. Never again would another sacrifice for sin be needed. Jesus, the Lamb of God, had been slain - for them, for you, and for me.

TALK ABOUT IT:

What did the disciples do after Christ's ascension? (The disciples worshipped Jesus and then, filled with great praise for God, returned to the temple.)

What does this tell us about the kind of men they were? (They clearly believed and obviously loved the Lord with all their hearts.)

Will we ever get to share the privilege of seeing Jesus face to face? (Yes! When we go to heaven, not only will we see Him face to face, but we will also have all eternity to hear these same stories from His mouth!)

PRAY:
Thank the Lord for His ministry on earth and His ongoing ministry in our hearts.

THURSDAY

THE STORY: ACTS 1:12-14
The disciples return to Jerusalem to wait. The disciples returned from the Mount of Olives and met together in the upper room. They were joined by Mary, the mother of Jesus, along with His brothers. What a joy it must have been for them to relay the story of Jesus' ascension to Mary. She had an incredible life. She experienced the visit of the first angel, witnessed His miracles, agonized through the suffering of her son, rejoiced at the joyful news of His resurrection, and, now, learned of His ascension into heaven. This is the last we hear of Jesus' mother Mary.

TALK ABOUT IT:
Why were the disciples meeting? (They were waiting for the Holy Spirit, as Jesus had commanded them.)

Was Mary special? (Mary is not given any special attention in Scripture except when Christ, on the cross, charged John with her care. Mary was a blessed woman, but she was a sinner like me and you. It is good to see her, and the brothers of Jesus, present as believers in the upper room. We will see the whole family in heaven!)

PRAY:
Thank Jesus for the way He preserves the faith of those who believe in Him.

FRIDAY
ON THE ROAD TO EMMAUS

THE STORY: ZECHARIAH 12:10,11

This passage is filled with words that have prophetic meaning regarding Jesus. The House of David is the lineage of kings out of which Jesus would come. Jerusalem is the city in which Jesus would be crucified. Grace for those who believe is poured out as a result of Jesus death on the cross. We can connect these words to Jesus because John connects this passage to Jesus in his Gospel (John 19:37) in talking about how the soldiers pierced the side of Jesus.

Long before Jesus' day, God was revealing a plan in small clues through His prophets. Now we, in looking back can see through the fulfillment of these clues that Jesus didn't just die by accident, but according to God's plan.

TALK ABOUT IT:

Have one of your children look up and read John 19:34-37 and compare it to today's scripture in Zechariah. What similarities do you see? (They are identical.)

What is the grace that is poured out as a result of Jesus death on all the people of God? (Grace means something that is a gift. We receive God's gift of salvation. That is forgiveness and freedom from the penalty we deserved for our sins. This is the grace that is poured out to everyone who believes and places their trust in Jesus' death on the cross.)

What does the house of David have to do with Jesus? (Jesus was born in the line of the house of David and became a king in the line of king David.)

PRAY:

Thank the Lord for suffering for us for us so we could be forgiven.

PENTECOST

The promised Holy Spirit is poured out.

MONDAY

THE STORY: ACTS 1:15-26

The disciples replaced Judas the betrayer. Peter addressed about 120 believers and explained that a witness had to be chosen to replace Judas since he had betrayed Jesus and killed himself. Peter laid down the requirements: He had to be a man who was with them from the time of John's baptism through the Ascension. Two men were chosen who filled these requirements. Rather than make the final choice through debate, they prayed for God's will, cast lots, and allowed the sovereignty of God to guide the choice.

TALK ABOUT IT:

Why did Peter think it necessary to replace Judas? (The apostles became known as the "Twelve" [see Luke 9:1]. It would be strange for them to only have eleven. God revealed to Peter a passage in Psalms which prophesied Judas' replacement.)

Is the number twelve significant? (Yes. There were twelve tribes of Israel, and in Revelation we read that the city of God will have twelve foundations and on them will be written the names of the twelve apostles of the Lamb [see Revelation

21:14]). We can assume the name Matthias will be listed there instead of Judas.)

What part of Jesus' ministry was most important for them to have witnessed? (Peter places particular emphasis on the Resurrection, which validated all of Jesus' claims.)

PRAY:
Thank the Lord again for His ministry from the time of John the Baptist through to the Resurrection. Invite your children to thank Jesus for a specific part of His ministry such as being born, healing the sick, dying on the cross, etc. Make sure that if the cross is not mentioned by your children, you mention it.

TUESDAY

THE STORY: ACTS 2:1-4
The Holy Spirit is poured out. On the day of Pentecost, fifty days after the Passover was celebrated and about ten days after Jesus ascended into heaven, the waiting for the Holy Spirit ended. As the Holy Spirit was poured out, a wind from heaven came and filled the whole house. They saw what looked like tongues of fire settle upon each one of them. All of them, not just the twelve, began to speak in other tongues as the Spirit enabled them.

TALK ABOUT IT:
Did Jesus keep His promise? (Yes. Jesus kept His promise to send the Holy Spirit.)

Did they have to wait long? (No. Jesus walked among them for forty days [see Acts 1:3]). The feast of Pentecost was fifty days after the Passover, so we can approximate that their wait was about ten days.)

What promise are we now waiting to see fulfilled? (Jesus said He would return.

We are now eagerly waiting for Him to return.)

PRAY:
Thank the Lord for His faithfulness in keeping His promises and ask Him to return soon so we can be with Him and so that sin and death can be finally destroyed.

WEDNESDAY
WHERE IS THE GOSPEL?

THE STORY: NUMBERS 28:26-31
In the Old Testament, the feast of Pentecost was called the Feast of the Harvest or First Fruits (see Exodus 23:16). In Numbers 28:26-30 the offerings for this day are described. Bulls, lambs, and a goat were offered, in addition to the regular offering, to make atonement.

Now that Jesus has been sacrificed, no goat for atonement needs to be killed. The promised blessing to Abraham was about to be fulfilled. The gospel can be spread from the very first believers to people of every tribe, language, and nation!

TALK ABOUT IT:
Why are the sacrifices normally offered on the Feast of First Fruits? (The sacrifices were offered in worship to God, who provided the harvest.)

Do we need to continue this practice today? (No. Both the killing of lambs without defect and the killing of goats for atonement were completely fulfilled on the cross. Jesus, the Lamb of God, was sacrificed. The debt of all men who would believe has been paid for all time. God's wrath against man for his sin has been fully and completely satisfied.)

PRAY:

Thank God for Jesus - our perfect sacrifice.

THURSDAY

THE STORY: ACTS 2:5-13

The assembly was amazed. The people from various nations heard the disciples speaking in their own language. They could not understand how the disciples, Galileans, could do this.

Those who mocked heard only a loud babble of foreign languages they could not understand. They wrongly assumed drunkenness. And this crowd may have included those who had already turned against Jesus and had called for His crucifixion.

This event marked a major development in God's salvation plan for man. It signaled that the gospel was for all peoples and all tongues. God was now going to take initiative by His Spirit, through the followers of Jesus, to reveal Himself to people outside of Israel. From this point on, people did not have to identify with the nation of Israel and learn the Jewish tongue to know God. He was now speaking by His Spirit, through his disciples, to the whole world in order to reach every tribe and tongue.

TALK ABOUT IT:

What does the outpouring of the Spirit tell us about God's mission? (The gospel of the kingdom is to reach all men, not just the Jews. Here at Pentecost men from all over the world could hear the message of the disciples in their own language.)

What did Jesus say the disciples would receive from the Holy Spirit? (They were to receive power. [see Luke 24:49.)

Can we be filled with the Holy Spirit today? (Yes. The Spirit of God dwells in the heart of every believer. But we are also called to be continuously filled with the Holy Spirit [see Ephesians 5:18] and we are to pursue the gifts of the Spirit [see 1 Corinthians 14:1]. Paul said he wished everyone would speak in tongues and even more, would prophesy. [see 1 Corinthians 14:5].)

PRAY:
Thank the Lord for sending His Holy Spirit to us all.

FRIDAY
ON THE ROAD TO EMMAUS

THE STORY: ZECHARIAH 9:10,11

Jesus is the promised king. He will proclaim peace to the nations. Jesus said, "Peace I leave with you; My peace I give you. I do not give to you as the world gives. Do not let your hearts be troubled and do not be afraid" (John 14:27). At the outpouring of the Spirit we see further evidence that the kingdom will go to all nations, as men from all over the world heard the disciples speaking in their own language!

TALK ABOUT IT:

How do we know that passages like these point to Jesus? (Often they are quoted in the New Testament. This passage is quoted in Matthew 21:5. Other times we can tell by the description. For instance, there is only one righteous king who brings salvation.)

What is the greatest peace offered by Jesus? (The greatest peace offered is the freedom from judgment, which comes when we trust Christ. When we believe, our sins are taken away and we have peace with God.)

PRAY:

Thank the Lord that His salvation and peace extends to all nations, especially your own.

NEW TESTAMENT · LESSON 45

PETER AND THE PROPHET JOEL

The Spirit - empowered gospel call goes forth.

MONDAY

THE STORY: ACTS 2:14-21

Peter explains the outpouring of the Spirit. Some of the people who witnessed the outpouring of the Spirit thought those who received the Spirit and were speaking in other tongues were drunk. So Peter stood up with the eleven other disciples and explained what was happening. God was pouring out His Spirit just as the prophet Joel had foreseen and Jesus had promised. Peter did not want to simply correct their poor judgment. He wanted them to be saved. That's why he went on to share the gospel.

In the days of old, God only spoke through a few choice men, and God's Spirit would not be poured on all God's people. This new outpouring, however, would be for all kinds of people, and God would speak through men and women, young and old.

From this very first sermon we can see the Spirit at work in the life of Peter. No sermon would be given without pointing back to Jesus.

TALK ABOUT IT:

What does Joel's prophecy say about the outpouring of the Spirit? (It says that all God's people can be filled and that God will speak through young and old alike.)

How is Peter different here than in the courtyard during Jesus' trial? (The Holy Spirit has filled Peter with boldness, courage, and power to preach to the people. Peter is no longer thinking of himself and is not afraid to proclaim the gospel to the crowd.)

PRAY:
Thank Jesus for the outpouring of His Spirit. Ask God to change the heart of every member of your family and pour out the Spirit upon each of you so that you will have boldness to share the gospel just like Peter did.

TUESDAY

THE STORY: ACTS 2:22-28
Peter shares the gospel. After Peter explained the outpouring of the Spirit, he connected it to the gospel. His courage is evident as he accused his hearers of nailing Jesus to the cross. That could have stirred up trouble. Peter also connected these events to the sovereign plan of God. Jesus was handed over as a part of God's predetermined plan. Peter shows them how King David foresaw the resurrection of Jesus.

TALK ABOUT IT:
According to Peter, what proves that Jesus was from God? (Miracles, wonders, and signs.)

What does it mean when it says Jesus was handed over by "God's set purpose and foreknowledge"? (God was not surprised by Jesus' crucifixion. Even Jesus chastised Peter when he cut off the ear of the servant of the high priest's. He could have called down legions of angels, but that was not the plan. God planned that His Son would be handed over to die for our sins.)

PRAY:
Thank God for His wonderful plan of salvation through Jesus.

WEDNESDAY
WHERE IS THE GOSPEL?

THE STORY: 1 PETER 1:10-12

Immediately following the outpouring of the Spirit on Pentecost, Peter addressed the crowd. Emboldened by the Holy Spirit's power, Peter interpreted the prophets and connected their prophecies to the outpouring of the Spirit and the gospel message. Jesus, he said, "was handed over to the Jews by God's set purpose and foreknowledge." He further explained that the Jews put Him to death, but that God raised Him from the dead. The gospel, delivered at Pentecost, became the core of Peter's life message.

In his subsequent letter, Peter gives us a wonderful glimpse back into the mind of the prophets (see 1 Peter 1:10). What exactly did they know? He tells us they searched with the greatest care because they knew the words they spoke were not for them, but for all those who would come after them. Moses knew. David knew. And Joel knew that God had a glorious plan of salvation. They searched intently to know more.

With the coming of Christ, the secrets of the kingdom of God were revealed by Him and through Him. We reveal them to others just as Peter did in his first sermon at Pentecost: through the gospel message. This mystery, revealed to us, is a message even the angels longed to know.

TALK ABOUT IT:

Why are we so privileged to know the gospel? (Many of those who believed in the Old Testament did not understand the whole gospel. They were placing their faith in God to save them, but they only saw a shadow of the full reality. We have been given the clear gospel message.)

Where do you see the gospel in Peter's sermon? (Parents, walk your children through Peter's sermon and help them pick out the gospel.)

PRAY:
Thank the Lord for the gospel, which we have been given without riddle or mystery.

THURSDAY

THE STORY: ACTS 2:29-37

Peter connects the scriptures to Christ. Peter, having shared the gospel once, continued his explanation of the prophets and how David looked forward to Jesus. And then Peter shared the gospel again! When he spoke of the Resurrection, he calls it a fact. There would be no room for doubters. Peter ends with a resounding call to all of Israel to believe. The people were so affected that Luke says they were "cut to the heart" and asked what they should do!

A true sign of repentance in a person is when they realize they are guilty, give no excuses, make no argument, and simply say, "What should I do?"

TALK ABOUT IT:

What does it mean to be "cut to the heart"? (Hebrews 4:12 gives us the answer: "For the word of God is living and active. Sharper than any double-edged sword, it penetrates even to dividing soul and spirit, joints and marrow; it judges the thoughts and attitudes of the heart." The people's thoughts and attitudes were judged by Peter's words, and they wanted to repent for killing Jesus and not believing.)

Should our response to the gospel be the same? (Yes. We need to repent of our sins against Jesus and believe.)

PRAY:

Ask God to help every member of your family see the need for the gospel, repent from sin, and believe in Jesus.

FRIDAY
ON THE ROAD TO EMMAUS

THE STORY: ISAIAH 49:7,8

Jesus is the Redeemer and Holy One of Israel. He was despised and abhorred by the rulers and people of Israel who mocked, beat, and crucified Him. Jesus rose from the dead. One day all kings will bow their knees to Him.

TALK ABOUT IT:

Who is the Redeemer referenced in this passage? (Jesus is the ultimate Redeemer. Only Jesus, by His death on the cross, can redeem us.)

How was Jesus faithful? (Jesus did everything the Father asked of Him. The Bible tells us that Jesus is a faithful high priest [see Hebrews 2:17], a faithful Son [see Hebrews 3:6], and His name is called Faithful and True [see Revelation 19:11].)

PRAY:

Thank Jesus for being our faithful Redeemer, who set us free from the bondage of sin and the wrath of God.

NEW BELIEVERS

The message of the gospel is effective to save and change the sinful hearts of men.

MONDAY

THE STORY: ACTS 2:36-39

Peter's audience was undone by the message of the gospel. They asked Peter, "What shall we do?" Peter answered that they should repent of their sins. He told them that the promised Holy Spirit was for them too. Peter continued with a wonderful extension of the promise. The promise was for them, their children, and all who are far off. We fall into the category of all who are far off. What a blessing to read and know that we, too, can be transformed as these early believers were.

TALK ABOUT IT:

Peter told the people there was something they must do. What was it? (The people must repent, or turn away from their sins.)

Peter told the people there is something that God must do. What is it? (The Lord must call them. The promise extends to all people of all ages whom the Lord calls. Apart from the transforming work of God, and call of God, none of us would repent and turn to God.)

PRAY:

Call out to the Lord and ask Him to call you and grant you repentance and cause you to be transformed by the power of His Holy Spirit.

TUESDAY

THE STORY: ACTS 2:40,41

The gospel reaps a harvest. Jesus said that the disciples would do even greater things than He did because He was going to the Father (see John 14:12). When we read these words, our minds may first think about more incredible miracles. What Jesus meant, however, is that after He ascended, the Holy Spirit would work through the disciples to gather in the harvest. Jesus preached to the multitude, but never saw three thousand converts! In fact, after all the miracles of Jesus, there were only about 120 believers who waited in the upper room for the promised Holy Spirit. Peter preached the gospel, and 3,000 believed and were added in just one day!

TALK ABOUT IT:

What does Acts say the people who were added did? (They accepted the message, believed, and were baptized.)

What were the people added to? (The people were added to the other believers. This is the first local church. Jesus told Peter, "I will build my church" [see Matthew 16:18]. These people represent the body of Christ, the first church.)

PRAY:

Thank God for the power of the gospel to transform our lives.

WEDNESDAY
WHERE IS THE GOSPEL?

THE STORY: 1 PETER 1:13-16

The behavior of the very first converts in the Book of Acts is the fruit of the gospel. These people were transformed from being mockers of Christ. In fact, some of them were probably in the crowd who yelled "Crucify Him!" And yet now, we see them selling their possessions to share with other Christians who had need. Peter, affected by this first dramatic gospel transformation, went on to exhort all new believers in his first letter to reject their sinful past and live holy, upright lives (see 1 Peter 1:14-15).

The gospel takes someone's worldly self-focus and turns their gaze heavenward. The first converts went from Jesus-haters to being people who loved Jesus. They served others and worshipped God through Christ. Only the Spirit of God can change hearts this way. The gospel continued to transform lives as more new converts were added each day.

TALK ABOUT IT:

What does Peter mean when he says, "As obedient children, do not conform to the evil desire you had"? (Peter means that once we become Christians we should live for Christ and not for the sinful desires that once captured our affections.)

What are the sinful desires that most threaten to capture your attention? (Parents, you should lead in confessing your weaknesses to set the example for your children. Then make sure to help draw your children out.)

PRAY:

Ask God for help to say "no" to your sinful desires and "yes" to the gospel and living for God.

THURSDAY

THE STORY: ACTS 2:42-47

The gospel brings change. The three thousand converts were added to the initial one hundred twenty believers, and together they were the first local church.

Immediately we see the fruit of the Spirit at work in their lives. They willingly shared what they had, regularly praised God, were devoted to the preached word by the apostles, and continued to add more and more people to their number.

TALK ABOUT IT:

Peter called the people to repent. What evidence do you see that they turned away from sin? (Draw your children out and help them see how remarkably they were changed.)

Do we all need to sell everything we have to follow Jesus? (No. God does not call all of us to sell everything we have. He does, however, call us to be willing to sacrifice what we have for the good of others. Some may be called to sacrifice or share everything they have. Others may not. The issue is not our outward giving, but the posture of our hearts. Having said that, most of us could stand to give away much more than we do. Few people need to be corrected for giving away too much, as our sinful desires keep us from being that selfless.)

Who might you bless by giving away something you have or own? (Consider this question seriously and act on your ideas.)

PRAY:

Pray that God would transform the desires of every person in your family so that you are looking for opportunities to bless those who are in need.

FRIDAY
ON THE ROAD TO EMMAUS

THE STORY: ISAIAH 35:5-8

Jesus certainly did open the eyes of the blind and restored hearing to the deaf. But there is a greater meaning to this passage than physical healing. Jesus opened our eyes and ears to understand the message of the gospel. The early church understood how their eyes and ears were opened. They were even called "the Way" (see Acts 9:2) because they followed the way Jesus spoke of when He said, "I am the way" (John 14:6). The way is the name given to the path of righteousness, which Isaiah says will be laid down for all those who repent. The early church understood this. Their eyes were opened and their ears unstopped to the truth of Christ.

TALK ABOUT IT:
What did Jesus mean when He said He is the way? (Jesus is the only way to salvation, the only way to the Father, and the only way to forgiveness.)

Do we call ourselves the Way today? (No. The followers of Christ were called Christians starting in Acts 11:26. That became a clearer way to describe those who follow Christ. See also 1 Peter 4:16 and Acts 26:28. "The Way" is never used to describe Christians outside of the Book of Acts.)

PRAY:
Thank God for opening up our eyes and ears to understand and believe the gospel.

THE LAME BEGGAR WALKS

There is power in the name of Jesus.

MONDAY

THE STORY: ACTS 3:1-8

The lame begger was healed. In a story reminiscent of Jesus, we see Peter and John on their way to the temple when they were interrupted by the call of a crippled man who asked for money. Peter called for the man's attention and then, in the name of Jesus, ordered the man to walk. Peter helped the man up, and instantly the man's feet were healed! Recognizing this, he leapt to his feet and went into the temple praising God. The power of Jesus continued even after His death, resurrection, and ascension!

The temple had been quiet for some time. The agitation Jesus and His ministry once caused had passed. Though there were rumors of His rising from the dead, they likely did not carry much weight because Jesus was nowhere to be found. He was gone. The Jewish leaders probably did not realize there were now four thousand Christians about to break the message out to the whole world. With the words "in the name of Jesus," there was commotion in the temple again!

TALK ABOUT IT:

What does this story remind you of? (Look up Luke 5:23-26 and read it to your children.)

What does the ongoing healing tell us? (The authority Jesus gave to the disciples to heal did not depend on Him remaining on the earth.)

PRAY:
Take time to lift up those who you know are sick. God is still a healing God!

TUESDAY

THE STORY: ACTS 3:9-16
Peter addressed the amazed crowd. The people came running to see the miracle that had just taken place. They were astonished. Peter wasted no time giving credit for the miracle to Jesus. Peter shared the gospel with the crowd. His message was not mild. In fact, he accused them of killing Jesus. Peter testified that he was a witness to the resurrection.

Peter's actions were in keeping with the charge Jesus gave the disciples just before His ascension. Jesus said in Acts 1:8, "But you will receive power when the Holy Spirit comes on you; and you will be My witnesses in Jerusalem, and in all Judea and Samaria, and to the ends of the earth." The mission to touch all people began in Jerusalem.

TALK ABOUT IT:
Who did Peter credit for the healing? (Peter gave Jesus credit for the healing.)

Did Peter draw any attention to himself? (No. Peter gave all the glory for the healing to God.)

Who might God want you to share the gospel with? (Parents, take time to think of a person you and your family might reach out to. Pray for an opportunity to share the gospel with this individual.)

PRAY:

Thank Jesus, the author of life, for the gospel. Ask him to give you the same courage Peter had so that you might share the gospel with those around you.

WEDNESDAY
WHERE IS THE GOSPEL?

THE STORY: ACTS 3:17-26

After healing the crippled beggar, Peter was not going to miss an opportunity to share the gospel. Peter explained that if they repented and believed in Jesus, their sins could be forgiven. He appealed to them from the words of the prophets and he quoted Moses (see Deuteronomy 18:15). Peter ended his appeal by reminding them of Jesus' call for them to abandon their wicked ways. The gospel was the theme of Peter's appeal.

TALK ABOUT IT:

Why did Peter talk about the prophets so much? (We need to remember that they only had the Old Testament. The New Testament was not yet written. Peter was simply using Scripture as his authority so that faith did not depend on his testimony, but on the testimony of God through the prophets.)

Where do you see the gospel mentioned in Peter's message? (Help your children locate the gospel in the passage. We never want to tire of making sure they know and can clearly recognize the gospel message.)

PRAY:

Thank the Lord for the good news! Have your family thank God for the ministry, death, and resurrection of Jesus, the call to repentance that comes to us as a result, and the willingness with which God forgives those who place their hope in Jesus.

THURSDAY

THE STORY: ACTS 4:1-22

Peter and John stirred up so much commotion that the Sadducees put them in jail. But many who heard the message believed, and continued praising God. This posed quite a problem for the religious rulers. They could see the man who was forty years old and crippled from birth standing there. Because the crippled man begged at the temple, many people became aware of his healing and praised God. This made it difficult for the religous leaders to speak against Peter & John. They were surprised by the courage of Peter and John. They decided to simply ask them to stop talking about Jesus. Peter and John refused. After the rulers threatened them again, Peter and John were released.

TALK ABOUT IT:

Where did Peter get the courage to speak to the rulers and elders? (Peter was filled with the Holy Spirit. The Holy Spirit emboldened him and helped him. See Acts 4:8)

What did Peter share with the religious rulers? (Peter shared the gospel. Review Acts 4:10-12.)

Why does the gospel keep getting repeated? (The gospel is the power of God unto salvation for everyone who believes. See Romans 1:16.)

PRAY:

Ask the Lord to give us courage and humility as we share the gospel with others.

FRIDAY
ON THE ROAD TO EMMAUS

THE STORY: PSALM 49:7-9

No mere man can redeem the life of another or give to God a ransom for him. But Jesus was no mere man. Paul told Timothy, "For there is one God and one mediator between God and men, the man Christ Jesus, who gave himself as a ransom for all men (see 1 Timothy 2:5,6). Not only was Jesus sufficient as a ransom for one man, Jesus, life was sufficient as a ransom for all men!

TALK ABOUT IT:

Why can't a man give up his life to ransom another from God? (All of us are sinful. We don't have the worth of a sinless man; therefore, we can not pay the debt of another man who has fallen into sin. Imagine trying to make amends with a neighbor if your son broke his window by giving him a broken window!)

Why can Jesus pay the ransom for all men? (First, as a man, Jesus lived a sinless life here on earth. Secondly, His worth is far greater than all the people of the earth combined.)

PRAY:

Thank the Lord for giving up His life as a ransom for ours.

ANANIAS AND SAPPHIRA

The Spirit of God is poured out in grace, discipline and power.

MONDAY

THE STORY: ACTS 4:32-37

The Spirit of God is poured out in heart-changing power. It is amazing to read about the early Christians and how the Spirit of God worked grace into their lives. We can forget that the descriptions are of brand-new believers, not people who had been Christians for years and years.

The first believers were so affected by the gospel and the infilling of the Spirit that they were glad to sell their possessions and share with those in need. Joseph sold a field and brought the money to the apostles so that those who were in need could be cared for.

TALK ABOUT IT:

How were the lives of the early believers changed by the gospel and the power of the Spirit? (They began to share their possessions to care for one another. We assume this is new behavior for them. Before believing the gospel and receiving the Spirit, they would likely have been quite the opposite. When the Spirit of God brings new life, the grace of God frees us from the bondage of sin and the love of our possessions.)

Do all Christians automatically live such unselfish lives? (No. This kind of sacrifice is not automatic for all new believers. It is also not automatic for us. In the power of the Spirit, we can do as they did. With His heart-changing power at work within us, we, too, can overcome selfishness, greed, and coveting. We can help those who are in need and share what we have.)

Who do you know that is in need? How can you help them? (Parents, take this question seriously and take the opportunity to bless those who are in need.)

PRAY:
Ask God to pour out His Spirit upon the lives of each member of your family so that you might increasingly desire to glorify God by sharing what you have with those who are in need.

TUESDAY

THE STORY: ACTS 5:1-6
The Spirit of God is poured out in discernment. Acts 5:1-6 starts out, "But a man…" Luke is contrasting the generosity of Joseph with the deception of Ananias and Sapphira. Perhaps Joseph was praised or esteemed for selling his field and giving the money to those in need. Ananias did not have to sell his field. Nor did he need to give all the money from its sale. Bur Ananias sinned. He sold the field and pretended to give all the money while keeping some for himself. This was treated by God as a very serious matter. The Holy Spirit brought severe discipline for the good of all.

Peter confronted Ananias for lying. His words help all of us to remember that when we sin against each other, our greater sin is against God. Immediately, Ananias fell down dead, and a great fear of sin came upon those who saw. The Holy Spirit was working to keep the church pure.

TALK ABOUT IT:

To whom did Ananias lie? (Peter tells us in verse 3 that he lied to the Holy Spirit, and then, in the next verse, he says Ananias lied not to men, but to God.)

Why does it say Ananias lied to God? (All of our sin, even those sins we commit against one another, are sins against God.)

When we sin against our brothers, sisters, or parents, should we also confess to God when we repent? (Yes. You should always confess your sin to God.)

PRAY:

Take time for each person to confess the sin of their past week to the Lord. (Parents, help your children by your example and by helping them to remember this past week.)

WEDNESDAY
WHERE IS THE GOSPEL?

THE STORY: ACTS 5:7-11

The Holy Spirit was poured out on the early church with great power. There was a mighty outpouring of grace in the lives of the new Christians. This move of the Spirit of God helped launch the advance of the gospel.

Ananias and Sapphira threatened to discredit the gospel and the work of God as the church was becoming established. They sold their property, but they wanted praise for giving everything. So they decided to keep some of the money secretly for themselves. God would not tolerate this lying selfish ambition. With the credibility of the gospel on the line, the Spirit of God killed them both. Thus, a holy fear fell upon all the people, and the integrity of the gospel was protected.

TALK ABOUT IT:

How could the lying of Ananias and Sapphira discredit the gospel? (Others may have followed their example. Probably many more would have drifted carelessly into other kinds of selfish ambition and falsehood had God not brought this discipline. The gospel is all about a change that takes place in a person's heart. By faking generosity and keeping back some of the money, Ananias and Sapphira looked good on the outside, but their hearts were full of sin. When God disciplines one, everyone searches their hearts and is more careful to not sin.)

What does the sin of hypocrisy look like in the lives of people today? (We are guilty of hypocrisy any time we pretend to be holy to look good but hide sin. If we live ungodly lives Monday through Saturday, but pretend to be good Christians on Sunday, we would be guilty of the same compromise we read about in Ananias and Sapphira's lives.)

PRAY:

Ask God to genuinely touch the lives of each member of your family so that the good you display flows from heart-transforming grace and not your own proud efforts to look good in front of others.

THURSDAY

THE STORY: ACTS 5:12-16

The Spirit of God is poured out in power. Many people were healed in the early church as the power of God was poured out for healing. Verse 14 tells us that more than ever, believers were added. We need to remember that three thousand were converted after Peter's explanation of the outpouring of the Holy Spirit. That means that thousands were being converted here as well. When people understood the gospel and saw the power of God, many put their faith in Jesus.

The compromise of Ananias and Sapphira had the potential to hinder this move of God. That is why the Lord judged them so severely. This swift judgment served to warn the early believers of the dangers of sin and of the fearful holiness of God.

TALK ABOUT IT:
How did the people demonstrate faith in what God was doing? (They brought out the sick and hoped that even the shadow of Peter would touch them.)

What was the result of their faith? (God had compassion on them, and they were all healed.)

How can reading stories like this encourage our faith today? (God is the same today as He was then. God is able to heal the sick! We need to pray in faith and trust the Lord when we pray for those who are sick. Reading about what God did in the early church can help build our faith for what God can do today.)

PRAY:
Lift up in prayer those around you who are sick, asking God to heal them.

FRIDAY
ON THE ROAD TO EMMAUS

THE STORY: ISAIAH 56:7
In Matthew 21:13 Jesus quotes this verse as He rebukes the money-changers and those who are turning the temple into a marketplace. Jesus was zealous that the house of God not be defiled by sin.

Similarly, in this week's passage in Acts, Ananias and Sapphira are judged swiftly for bringing sinful behavior into the house of God, the church.

TALK ABOUT IT:
Why does God judge sin? (God is holy and has no sin. Sin by definition is disobedience toward God. Just as light must cause darkness to disappear, so must God judge sin for the sake of His holiness.)

Why did Jesus drive out the money-changers from the temple? (The focus of the temple was to be worship of God. These men were not at the temple to worship God. Rather they were there to make money.)

PRAY:
Ask God to help you never forget the important place true worship is meant to play in our lives.

THE DEATH OF STEPHEN

The gospel cannot be stopped by persecution.

MONDAY

THE STORY: ACTS 6:8-15

Stephen is filled with the Spirit and with power. Jesus said, "If they persecuted me, they will persecute you also" (John 15:20) Stephen, like Jesus, was spreading the gospel of the kingdom with power. The religious rulers were angered that the old covenant was being minimized for a new covenant of grace. They didn't think it was right that their customs be replaced (Acts 6:14). However, they could not withstand Stephen's wisdom and could not deny the power of God upon him.

They incited men to testify that Stephen was a blasphemer, just as they had done to Jesus. But Stephen was not afraid. The Spirit of God was upon him. Even those who sat in the council saw that his face "was like the face of an angel."

TALK ABOUT IT:

How was Stephen's ministry like Jesus' ministry? (Stephen was doing great wonders and signs among the people. And he was sharing the gospel with such wisdom that the leaders could not argue against him.)

What kinds of things might Stephen have said that would have angered the religious leaders? (Jesus is the Lamb of God who takes away the sins of the world. This meant there was no longer any need to continue to sacrifice at the temple.

Imagine telling people they can be forgiven by trusting in Jesus and that they would no longer need to sacrifice at the temple, which had been the tradition for years!)

PRAY:

Thank Jesus that His sacrifice on the cross is good once and for all to cover our sin; that no further work is needed to be acceptable to God. We simply need to trust in what Jesus did!

TUESDAY

THE STORY: ACTS 7:1- 53 (THIS IS A LONGER READING, BUT A WONDERFUL SUMMARY OF ISRAEL'S HISTORY)

The rulers of Israel had always rejected the plan of God, each step of the way. Stephen summarized the history of God's dealing with Israel and ended with a stinging rebuke, accusing the present leaders of murdering Jesus, the Righteous One.

These men were not innocently unaware of the gospel or confused. They were actively opposing the work of God, just as leaders of Israel did when they turned away from God and when they killed the prophets. Then Stephen, with great courage, rebukes them for not keeping the law they are claiming to defend.

TALK ABOUT IT:

What did Stephen accuse the Jews of doing? (Stephen accused the Jews of killing Jesus, just as they killed the prophets before Jesus.)

Who do we know that does not believe and needs the grace of God? (Parents, help your children see that we all need the grace of God to repent and believe. don't be afraied to suggest the names of your younger children and also point out that we are all sinners who need God's grace.)

PRAY:
Ask God for grace for each member of your family to repent and believe. Take time to lift up those you know who currently reject the gospel.

WEDNESDAY
WHERE IS THE GOSPEL?

THE STORY: 1 JOHN 2:1,2
Just like Stephen's description of Jesus in Acts 6:52, John also calls Jesus the "Righteous One". The "Righteous One" means the only person who did what was right. The reason that Jesus can be called the "Righteous One" (Acts 7:52) is because he never sinned, not even once! Not only that, but Jesus obeyed all of God's laws completely. No one before Jesus and no one after Jesus can keep God's Law. The Bible tells us that there is no one who is good, not even one (read Psalm 14:3 and Romans 3:10).

Because we have broken God's laws, like the Ten Commandments, we deserve the punishment of hell. Jesus died on the cross to pay the penalty for our sin. He lived a righteous life, obeying all the laws for us. Jesus took our sin and gives us his obedience so we can enter into heaven. He is the only Righteous One!

TALK ABOUT IT:
How does John connect Jesus as the Righteous One to the gospel? (John tells us that Jesus, the Righteous One, is our atoning sacrifice - one sacrifice for the sins of all.)

Based on Psalm 14:3, how many of us sin? (We are all sinners, no one is righteious, except for Jesus, the "Rightous One")

Can you remember what Jesus does now in our defense before His Father in Heaven? (Jesus is interceding, or praying, for us before the Father. The nail marks in his hands and feet forever plead our case before the Father, Hebrews 7:25. Jesus took our penalty. So now when we sin, we need not fear the eternal judgment of God.)

PRAY:
Thank Jesus for His atoning sacrifice on the cross which paid for our sins and brought us life!

THURSDAY

THE STORY: ACTS 7:54 – 8:8

Stephen is stoned for his faith and the gospel is spread. The Jews, along with the Jewish leaders, became very angry at Stephen's vision of heaven. They took him out of the city and stoned him. Their anger spilled out toward other Christians. As a result of the persecution, the Christians in Jerusalem were scattered. At first that might seem like a defeat. But God had a plan. The Christians that were scattered began to preach the gospel in the surrounding countryside. The result was that many, who would not have otherwise heard the gospel, were saved. We are told of the results of this scattering later in Acts Read Acts 11:19-21 and see just how God used the persecution in Jerusalem to spread the Gospel.

TALK ABOUT IT:

Stephen was a man of great faith and great courage, where do you see his faith and courage in this passage? (Stephen trusted God, even at the cost of his own life. Stephen gave praise to God and trusted the Lord, even to his last words.)

How did God work the death of Stephen for His own glory? (Those who fled the persecution, which began with Stephen's stoning, spread the gospel to the surrounding countryside.)

PRAY:

Thank God that nothing stands in the way of His plan, even persecution!

FRIDAY
ON THE ROAD TO EMMAUS

THE STORY: ISAIAH 24:16

Isaiah speaks of the Lord as "the Righteous One" to whom all the ends of the earth will sing "Glory." In Revelation 5:12-13 we read that every creature in heaven and on earth and under the earth and on the sea will sing glory and praise to the Lamb. Isaiah gives us a glimpse of that day.

When Stephen gave his defense, he called Jesus the "Righteous One" (Acts 7:52). This declaration enraged the crowd and led to the stoning of Stephen. Luke records that, at that moment, the heavens opened and Stephen himself saw the righteous Son of Man, the Righteous One.

TALK ABOUT IT:

Why is Jesus called the Righteous One? (Jesus never once committed sin. Jesus also kept the whole law.)

Why was it so important that Jesus never sinned? (Perfect righteousness is what God requires. Jesus met that requirement for us. Only a sinless man could meet the standards of God's holiness for us.)

PRAY:

Thank Jesus for being the Righteous One who is without sin, who is able to redeem us by His sacrifice.

SAUL KNOCKED TO THE GROUND

No man is a match for the grace of God.

MONDAY

THE STORY: ACTS 8:26-40

The persecution spread the gospel to many. As a result of the persecution of Christians by Saul and others, the church in Jerusalem was scattered. During this time of scattering, an angel instructed Philip to travel south. There he met an Ethiopian eunuch who was reading the scroll of Isaiah. Philip explained to him how the Old Testament pointed to Jesus. The Ethiopian man was so affected by the gospel, he commanded his chariot to be stopped so that he might be baptized! After Philip baptized the eunuch, the Spirit of God carried Philip away to preach the gospel elsewhere.

TALK ABOUT IT:

How does the Isaiah passage ready by the Ethiopian remind you of Jesus? (Jesus is the sheep who was led to slaughter on the cross. Jesus is the lamb who did not open His mouth. Jesus willingly died so that we might be saved.)

How did hearing the gospel affect this man? (When the Ethiopian man heard and understood the gospel, he was immediately converted from unbelief to faith, and he ordered his chariot to stop so he could demonstrate his faith in baptism.)

PRAY:
Pray that God would convert each member of your family and give them the gift of faith to believe.

TUESDAY

THE STORY: ACTS 9:1-19

Saul threatened to kill anyone who believed in Jesus. He received letters which gave him authority to arrest anyone who belonged to "the Way" in Damascus. The Way was a name given to early Christians who followed Jesus. Jesus said that He was the "Way" (John 14:6).

While traveling to Damascus, Saul was stopped in his tracks when Jesus appeared before him. Saul was blinded and had to be led into the city. For three days he remained blind until God sent Ananias to him. Ananias prayed for Saul and laid hands upon him. Immediately, his sight was restored. Like the Ethiopian, Paul was immediately baptized in confirmation of his conversion. In God's words to Ananias we are given a glimpse of the difficult life that was to come to Saul. God said that Saul, later called Paul, would suffer much for His name (Acts 9:16).

TALK ABOUT IT:

How is God's calling of Saul like His calling of other men in the Bible? (God took initiative. Saul was not calling out to God. It was God who called out to Saul. This is true of Abraham, Moses, and the disciples. In our lives it may seem that we call out to God first, but God is at work arranging circumstances and drawing us before we even know it!)

What is the other name Saul is known by? (Saul is also called Paul in Acts 13:9.)

Are people still converted like Saul was? (Yes - People are dramatically changed in a moment. Saul's experience in seeing Jesus and being knocked to the ground is unique. But God does dramatic things when He saves some men. Many are delivered from great wickedness in a moment by the power of God.)

How can Saul's conversion increase our faith for unbelievers today? (Seeing such a wicked man converted helps us to remember that no man is too sinful for the saving arm of God to reach him.)

PRAY:
Pray that the power of the gospel touches the lives of every member of your family.

WEDNESDAY
WHERE IS THE GOSPEL?

THE STORY: ACTS 22:4-21
When the voice came out to Saul asking, "Saul, Saul, why are you persecuting me?" Saul did not know who was speaking. He questioned, "Who are you, Lord?" What an amazing answer came to him saying, "I am Jesus."

We, like Saul, are sinners who do not know Jesus. Saul knew that Jesus was a teacher, a man who lived and died on the cross. But Saul did not yet know and believe that Jesus was Lord, the Son of God, raised in power!

We come to know Jesus in a similar way that Saul did - not with a visionary appearance of Christ, but by God's initiative while we were still sinners. Saul was on his way to kill more disciples when Jesus revealed Himself to him. Saul immediately realized that the stories of Jesus' resurrection were true. Jesus was, and is, alive!

TALK ABOUT IT:
What do we call it when a person shares the story of his or her conversion? (We say the individual is sharing his or her testimony.)

Do all Christians have a testimony? (Yes. All Christians have a testimony, even those who were touched by the gospel at a very young age. Once we were enemies of God. Then our hearts were changed by the power of the Spirit of God.) Parents take time to share your testimony with your children.

PRAY:
Ask God to reach each member of your family with the gospel and give you the courage to share your testimony with others.

THURSDAY

THE STORY: ACTS 9:19B - 25
The gospel bears fruit in Saul's life. After his conversion Saul remained with the disciples and immediately proclaimed Jesus in the synagogues. People were amazed because he was a Pharisee who had been persecuting the followers of Jesus. His dramatic conversion served to confound the Jews there. This was further evidence that Jesus was alive and could transform lives.

Jesus once said to His disciples, "You did not choose me, but I chose you and appointed you to go and bear fruit – fruit that will last." See John 15:16. No place is this more true than in the life of Saul. It was by God's initiative that Saul was converted, and the fruit of that conversion was dramatic.

TALK ABOUT IT:
Are all Christians changed when they are converted? (Yes. We are all changed and all bear fruit for God's kingdom. If a person thinks he is a Christian but bears no fruit of conversion, that person should consider himself unconverted and should continue to call out to God for salvation.)

What do you think the Jews did about Saul's conversion? (As with Jesus, they plotted to kill him, but he escaped. See Acts 9:23-25. Just as God told Ananias, Saul would suffer much for the sake of Christ. That suffering began almost immediately. Paul, the persecutor, was now the one being persecuted.)

PRAY:
Thank God for the power of the gospel to change our lives.

FRIDAY
ON THE ROAD TO EMMAUS

THE STORY: PSALM 130:3-8
The psalmist recognizes that we all deserve to be punished for our sins, and that every man is a sinner. If the Lord, in His glory, were to appear to us as He did to Saul on the road to Damascus, we would not be able to stand. Just as Saul fell to the ground, so would we. But we need not fear the Day of Judgment. We can, instead, hope in the Lord because He has redeemed us. The redeemer of Israel is Jesus. The psalmist would die waiting for his redemption. We, however, have no need to wait for our redeemer. Jesus, our redeemer, has come!

TALK ABOUT IT:
Why couldn't this passage be referring to anyone else beside Jesus? (Jesus is the only redeemer who can remove Israel's sins. Plenty of men were redeemers of Israel, saving them from an earthly enemy. But only Jesus brings eternal redemption. Only Jesus brings full redemption.)

If Jesus has already come, what good are these words of hope to us? (Although Jesus has already come, salvation has not automatically come to all men. We are required to place our faith and hope in Jesus. Only those who place their hope in Christ will be saved. This psalm urges us to trust in Jesus and assures us of His forgiveness.)

PRAY:
Thank God for not keeping a record of our sin. Thank God for redeeming us.

THE GENTILES WERE CONVERTED

The promise of the gospel is for all men.

MONDAY

THE STORY: ACTS 10:1-23

Cornelius, a Gentile soldier, received a vision of an angel telling him to send men to Joppa to get Peter. While these men traveled, Peter received a vision from the Lord concerning animals, both clean and unclean. Peter was commanded to kill and eat both the clean and unclean animals. Peter refused because Jews were commanded not to even touch unclean animals, much less to eat them.

God repeated the command and told Peter not to call unclean those things that God has made clean. We learn from Peter's later account in Acts 11:10 that the vision and command came to Peter three times. Still, Peter did not understand. While Peter pondered the vision, the men sent by Cornelius arrived. The Spirit of God told Peter to go with them without hesitation. When the Gentiles invited Peter, a Jew, to go with them, Peter agreed.

TALK ABOUT IT:

Read Deuteronomy 14:4-20. Name some unclean animals.

Why did God tell Peter he could eat unclean animals? (God was going to show Peter that Jesus broke down the barrier between Jews and Gentiles, the clean and unclean. The unclean animals represented the Gentiles. Salvation would be extended to Gentiles. Through the sacrifice of Jesus, they would be made clean.)

PRAY:
Thank the Lord for dying for both Jews and Gentiles.

TUESDAY

THE STORY: ACTS 10:24-34

When Peter arrived, Cornelius tried to worship him as if he was divine. But Peter refused, explaining to Cornelius that he was only a man. Peter went on to explain the meaning of his vision to the people gathered there. Gentiles, formally considered to be unclean by God were to be welcomed into God's family.

After telling his story and encounter with God, Cornelius asked Peter to share all that God had commanded. Peter saw that God spoke and directed Cornelius just as God had directed Peter himself. He concluded and announced that God shows no favoritism or partiality for the way had been opened up to accept men into the family of God from every nation. This marked the beginning of God's promise to Abraham to bless all nations. Partiality, but accepts men from every nation. Peter went on to freely share the gospel with those present.

TALK ABOUT IT:

How are Cornelius and Peter similar in this story? (God visited both men with amazing visions and words even though Cornelius was a Gentile.)

Why is this significant? (God had defined Himself as the God of the Hebrews - the God of Abraham, Isaac, and Jacob. He was the God of Israel. Now, God was saying that He was the God of all nations. Through the sacrifice of Jesus, all men, no matter what nation they are a part of can believe and become a part of God's family.)

PRAY:

Thank God for drawing all men to Himself, both Jew and Gentile.

WEDNESDAY
WHERE IS THE GOSPEL?

THE STORY: ACTS 10:39-44

The gospel is clearly spoken by Peter in Acts 10:39-43. Even while Peter was still speaking, the Holy Spirit fell on the Gentiles, filled them, signaling their conversion. It was the power of the Gospel, not Peter, which affected Cornelius and his household.

Clearly what the apostle Paul wrote is true when he said in Romans 1:16-17, " … it (the gospel) is the power of God for the salvation of everyone who believes: first for the Jew, then for the Gentile."

TALK ABOUT IT:

Where do you see the gospel in Peter's message to Cornelius? (Help your children pick out the components of the gospel from Peter's exhortation.)

How did Peter connect the gospel to the Old Testament? (Peter explained in verse 43 that all of the prophets bore witness to Christ.)

PRAY:

Thank the Lord for the gospel, which was foretold by the prophets and lived out by the death and resurrection of Christ.

THURSDAY

THE STORY: ACTS 10:44-48

The Holy Spirit was poured out on the Gentiles. While Peter preached the gospel, the Holy Spirit fell on all who heard the Word and they spoke in tongues and were praising God. Peter described it this way in the next chapter: "The Holy Spirit fell on them just as on us at the beginning," and "God gave the same gift to them as he gave to us when we believed in the Lord Jesus Christ" (see Acts11:15,17). The gift of tongues became a regular occurrence in the early church among believers.

TALK ABOUT IT:
Why were the people, who came with Peter amazed? (The people who came with Peter were amazed that the Holy Spirit was poured out on the Gentiles. The saw them speaking in tongues and praising God. They saw the Holy Spirit's moving on the Gentiles as proof that salvation was not limited to the Jews.)

What is the gift of tongues? (Tongues is a gift of the Spirit that the apostle Paul described in 1 Corinthians 14 as words that can not be understood without the gift of interpretation, that they are prayers directed to God, (See in 1 Corinthians 14:2, 14. A note to parents: This is a great opportunity to teach your children your understanding of the gift of tongues as it relates to each of us today.)

PRAY:
Thank God for His marvelous gifts. Pray that God would touch the lives of each member of your family, just as He touched Cornelius and his household.

FRIDAY
ON THE ROAD TO EMMAUS

THE STORY: PSALM 53:1-6
After saying that all men are sinners and that everyone has turned away from God, David prays a prophetic prayer for salvation in verse six that points to salvation through Jesus.

Peter said that all the prophets bore witness to Jesus. This is also true of the Psalms. In Psalm 53:6 we read that salvation for Israel would come out of Zion. This was a name given to Jerusalem from the days of David. Salvation, indeed, did come out of Zion. Jesus was crucified there.

TALK ABOUT IT:

When Psalm 53 tells us that Israel will be saved, how does that leave room for the Gentiles? (The true Israel of God includes many who are natural descendents of Abraham. But it is not limited to his natural children. And not all of Abraham's descendents inherit the promise. The blessing of salvation comes to those who have faith in God's promise, like Abraham did. The true Israel of God is made up of Jews and Gentiles who have put their faith in the promise of God's salvation, which came through Abraham's descendents. That salvation came through Jesus Christ, Abraham's promised seed [see Galatians 3:16]).

Think of the New Testament passage for this week. Was Peter surprised that the Gentiles were included in God's plan of salvation? (Yes. It is easy to see how men like Peter were only thinking of the nation of Israel and not the Gentiles.)

What Scriptures did men like Peter, who thought salvation was only for Israel not understand? (Peter didn't understand many Scriptures. But primarily he forgot the very first covenant promises to Abraham where God told Abraham that all of the nations on earth would be blessed through him [see Genesis 12:3]).

PRAY:

Thank the Lord for dying on the cross for people of every nation.

THE FRUIT OF THE SPIRIT

The fruit of the Spirit marks the lives of Christians.

NOTE: THIS PASSAGE CONTAINS SEVERAL REFERENCES TO CIRCUMCI-
SION. GIVEN THE KEY ROLE OF CIRCUMCISION IN THE BIBLE, IT MIGHT
BE GOOD TO TACTFULLY EXPLAIN ITS MEANING TO YOUR GRADE-
SCHOOL CHILDREN. ONCE YOUR CHILDREN LEARN TO READ, THEY
WILL DISCOVER REFERENCES TO CIRCUMCISION THROUGHOUT THE
BIBLE.

MONDAY

THE STORY: GALATIANS 5:1-15

Christ has set us free from the law. Paul wrote the letter to the Galatians to correct problems in that local church. After Paul first brought the gospel, men who were "false brothers" came in distorting the gospel by claiming that a person needed to be circumcised to be saved (see Galatians 2:3-5). In this passage Paul reclaims the purity of the gospel by explaining that those who are believers in Christ are free from the law. In other words, we are accepted by God because of what Jesus did. We cannot earn our way to God by any work we do.

Paul goes on to say that all believers are free from the bondage of trying to earn salvation, but all remain bound to love one another. Because we are saved, we are free to obey without threat of punishment. In addition, we are not to use our freedom (from the slavery of the law) to indulge the flesh (sin). Instead we are to use our freedom to live for God by loving one another.

TALK ABOUT IT:

Does the gospel require us to do any outward work to be saved? (No, there is nothing we can do, no work we could do, that can save us. None of us could ever be good enough to earn salvation. Salvation is a free gift that comes to us while we are sinners. What we must do is believe the gospel and accept the free gift of God's grace.)

What do we do to the gospel when we try to earn salvation by something we do? (Jesus paid the price for our sin. When we tell someone they have to do something extra [some work] to be saved, we are saying Jesus' work was not enough to save us. Jesus' sacrifice and death are sufficient to save us from our sin. Nothing needs to be added to what Jesus did. We obey out of worship and gratitude for what Jesus did, not to earn salvation or mercy from God.)

Do men still try to add works to the gospel today? (Yes, sometimes we feel better about ourselves if we are doing good things. We need to be careful that we do good things for the right reasons. All believers are accepted by God even though they continue to sin. We strive to obey in order to honor God, not to earn salvation. Salvation is completely free!)

PRAY:

Thank God that His salvation is free. Our sin -- past, present, and future -- was fully paid by Jesus on the cross. Because He died for us, ask God to help us to live for Him.

TUESDAY

THE STORY: GALATIANS 5:16-23

In this passage Paul directs our attention to the internal war that goes on in the life of every believer. The desires of the flesh (or the old, sinful nature) are in opposition to the desires of the Holy Spirit (which come to the new nature as a result of our conversion). We must fight the sinful nature because its desires seek to entice us and drag us away (see James 1:14). Each day we have choices to make. The Spirit within us gives us power to overcome remaining sin inside us and live righteously for God. For every sinful temptation, we find within us the opposite holy desire. We are no longer bound to sin but instead can put sin down and follow the way of the Spirit. So we cultivate godly desires from the Spirit and "put to death" sinful desires from the flesh. Paul tells us that it is not complicated. Our sinful desires are obvious, and so is the fruit of the Spirit in our lives.

TALK ABOUT IT:
Where do you see the fruit of the Spirit at work in the lives of your family members? (Parents, help your younger children here. Go through the list and help them remember when they saw these evidences of God's grace in the lives of their brothers, sisters, and parents.)

Where do you see the desires of the flesh or sinful nature at work in your life? (Parents, help your children go through this list and confess their weaknesses. It would be good for you to set an example in leading in confession.)

PRAY:
Ask God to help each member of your family with their weaknesses. Thank God for the grace you see in each person as well.

WEDNESDAY
WHERE IS THE GOSPEL?

THE STORY: GALATIANS 5:24
Apart from Christ, none of us are good, and the only way we can demonstrate the fruit of the Spirit is if we have been given a new nature by God through the gospel of Christ. Notice that Paul doesn't call the fruit of the Spirit the fruit of the good man. Instead Paul says in Galatians 5:24, "Those who belong to Christ Jesus have crucified the flesh with its sinful passions and desires."
The gospel is the doorway to Christ, and He is our only help. Apart from the

sacrificial death of Christ and the work of the Holy Spirit, all our efforts fall short, and we would at best be doing good works with mixed, self-honoring motives. The Spirit of God is the one who changes our desires from sinful to truly righteous.

TALK ABOUT IT:
What does it mean to belong to Christ? (When we surrender our lives to Christ and believe the gospel, we become a part of the body of Christ - the church. Christ comes to live in us by His Spirit and we become forever linked to Christ [see John 15:4-7 and 17:21].)

What does it mean to crucify the flesh (the sinful nature) with its passions and desires? (We need to be killing sinful desires. When we say "no" to sinful desires we are putting our sinful flesh to death.)

PRAY:
Ask the Spirit of God to empower you to recognize your sin and put it to death by refusing to indulge your sinful desires and walking away from sin.

THURSDAY

THE STORY: GALATIANS 5:25-6:1
We need to help each other in our fight against sin. Although the desires of the flesh and the fruit of the Spirit are obvious, we need others in our lives to help us obey. Rather than becoming prideful in our accomplishments, we are called to humbly serve those who have stumbled. We are to restore them gently and be careful so that we do not stumble ourselves.

None of us are perfect. We are all sinners and continue to sin. Therefore, none of us perfectly walks in step with the Spirit. We all have areas where we stumble, and often we are blind to those areas ourselves. We need to help each other see these areas of compromise. What is difficult for us to see is usually easy for others to see. When we restore each other humbly, in a spirit of gentleness, bearing one another's burdens, we fulfill the law of Christ in loving our neighbor as ourselves.

TALK ABOUT IT:

Why is it important to restore someone in a spirit of gentleness? (We always need to keep in mind that we are fellow sinners who are also in need of forgiveness for the sins we commit. Apart from the grace of God we would be hopelessly fallen in sin. Humility demands we be kind and gentle. In addition, God has been kind and gentle with us, not treating us as our sins deserve.)

What does it feel like to be corrected harshly? (Parents, draw out your children here.)

When are you most tempted to be harsh in your corrections? (Parents, take the lead and confess first, d then raw out your children.)

PRAY:

Ask God to help each member of your family bring corrections to one another with gentleness, always remembering the cross and how God has been gentle and forgiving toward us.

FRIDAY
ON THE ROAD TO EMMAUS

THE STORY: JEREMIAH 9:23-26

Our boast can only be in knowing the Lord Jesus Christ. Jeremiah prophesied about a day when it would not be sufficient to simply be circumcised in the flesh. One would also need to be circumcised in his heart. In Romans 2:29 Paul tells us that circumcision of heart is the way true believers are marked. Physical circumcision pointed forward to the day when Jesus would die and circumcise the hearts of believers by the work of the Holy Spirit in regenerating them. This is only possible through the work of Christ, the one who brought righteousness to the earth.

TALK ABOUT IT:
What does this passage say we are to boast in? (We are to boast that we understand and know God.)

Read 1 Corinthians 1:27-31. Where Paul refers back to Jeremiah's prophecy. How does Paul's teaching compare to Jeremiah's prophecy (Paul connects Jeremiah's prophecy to the Gospel and the work of Christ.)

How did God teach Peter (we learned this in lesson 51) the same things? (God gave Peter the vision of the sheet with the clean and unclean animals to show him that God does not show favoritism. In the New Testament the mark of God's people would no longer be physical circumcision but circumcision of the heart.)

PRAY:
Ask God to help you boast only in the Lord and not in your own accomplishments apart from Him.

PAUL'S WORK IN EPHESUS

Apostles care for the local church and preserve sound doctrine.

MONDAY

THE STORY: ACTS 18:24-19:8

Paul corrects the disciples of Apollos. Apollos was an eloquent man who came to Ephesus and taught about Christianity but he did not have the complete Gospel. When Paul reached Ephesus he found some disciples of Apollos who did not understand the complete Gospel. They had been instructed on the ministry of John the Baptist and the need to turn away from their sins but not the ministry of Jesus and trusting in his work on the cross. They didn't have a complete gospel nor did they even know about the Holy Spirit. After Paul spoke to them they believed and were baptized. Paul laid his hands upon them and the Holy Spirit came upon them. Although this was only a small group of men, Paul saw an opportunity to serve this group of men and spent three months in the synagogue laboring to teach them sound doctrine.

TALK ABOUT IT:

What important doctrine (beliefs) were the men Paul met missing? (They didn't understand the complete Gospel story, they didn't know about Jesus command for all believers to believe in Him and be baptized, and they didn't know about the Holy Spirit.)

God used the Apostle Paul to correct their mistakes, what do we have today to help us follow sound doctrine (right beliefs) today? (Today, we rely on the Bible, both the Old Testament and the New Testament to guide our doctrine [beliefs]. The New Testament we are reading today was not yet written. The teachings of Jesus came through the disciples who had been with Jesus and others, like Paul, called by God into ministry.)

PRAY:
Thank God for preserving the Apostles teaching for us in the Bible and pray God would give you a love for His Word.

TUESDAY

THE STORY: ACTS 19:9,10
Paul trained the local leaders. After three months of teaching in the synagogue and meeting with opposition, Paul turned his attention to the local leaders to train them for the work of ministry in the local church at Ephesus. For two years he taught them daily.

It is reasonable to assume that as a result of Paul's work in Ephesus, local churches were formed all over Asia. This occurred both from Paul's teaching directly to people who came to hear him over those two years and from the leaders he trained to take the message elsewhere in Asia Minor. By the time Paul returned to Ephesus (see Acts 20:17) there were elders and a thriving local church. The work of Paul, as an apostle, in correcting false and incomplete doctrine cannot be underestimated.

TALK ABOUT IT:
Why did Paul withdraw with the disciples from the synagogue? (The people at the synagogue persisted in their unbelief and spoke evil of the Christians.)

What did Paul give the next two years to doing? (Paul took the next two years to teach the disciples and Christians the Word of the Lord.)

How do we receive the kind of teaching Paul brought to the people of Ephesus? (We learn the Word of the Lord by reading and studying our Bibles, listening to the preached Word on Sundays, and through fellowship with other believers who can also speak into our lives what they themselves have learned.)

PRAY:
Pray that God would give you a love for His Word and motivation to read the Bible every day.

WEDNESDAY
WHERE IS THE GOSPEL?

THE STORY: ACTS 20:17-24
God used Paul to bring an accurate Gospel message to the Ephesians. As a result, the work which began with a small group of disciples grew into a thriving church. After working with the Ephesians for three years Paul left. After some time Paul returned and paid a visit to Ephesus. He called for the Ephesian elders. After they arrived Paul reflected back on his time of teaching to the Ephesians. He said, "I did not shrink from declaring to you anything that was profitable . . . .testifying both to Jews and Greeks of repentance toward God and of faith in our Lord Jesus Christ.

When Paul first arrived the twelve disciples of Apollos seemed to only have the first half, repentance toward God. Paul corrected them, teaching them to place their trust in Jesus Christ, giving them the complete gospel message. It is always good for men to repent of their sins against God but apart from placing our faith in Jesus and what He did on the cross we will not be saved. It is only through Jesus that we are saved. Acts 4:12 says, "And there is salvation in no one else, for there is no other name under heaven given among men by which we must be saved."

The result of bringing the gospel to the Ephesians was that many were healed, delivered, converted, and people repented of every evil practice.

TALK ABOUT IT:

Why did Paul leave his friends in Ephesus? (Paul knew God was calling him to preach the Gospel in other places.)

What in today's scripture gives us a picture of Paul's dedication to the Gospel? (Even though the Holy Spirit revealed to Paul that he would be sent to jail and suffer, he was still willing to go preaching the Gospel.)

Paul had courage in following Jesus. In what kinds of situations might we need to have courage in following Jesus? (It takes courage to tell others about Jesus because not everyone will welcome our message. It also takes courage to do the right thing when other people are doing the wrong things.)

PRAY:

Ask God to actively lead you by His Holy Spirit and give you a love for the establishment of your local church.

THURSDAY

THE STORY: ACTS 20:1-6

Paul moved on from Ephesus to coarry the Gospel mesage to Macedonia and Greece. Paul was not called as a pastor but as an apostle. A pastor shepherds a local congregation. An apostle's task is to plant and care for local churches. Once the church in Ephesus was strengthened with an accurate understanding of the gospel, with local leaders in place, it was time for Paul to move on to continue his apostolic work. A quick survey of Paul's life reveals an amazing apostolic mission. A great deal of the advance of the gospel in his generation can be attributed to his ministry. Paul's journeys through the Mediterranean area saw churches planted in Ephesus, Philippi, Thessalonica, and Corinth. From these key cities the message spread throughout the nations of that area.

TALK ABOUT IT:
Why didn't Paul stay with the church at Ephesus? (Paul was called of God to be an apostle, not a pastor. God commissioned Paul to go to the Gentiles with the gospel [see Acts 9:15].)

What effect did Paul's ministry have on the people and leaders? (Paul's ministry was an encouragement to them.)

PRAY:
Thank God for the ministry of Paul that spread the gospel to the Gentiles. Thank God that much of our New Testament is comprised of Paul's letters to the Gentile churches.

FRIDAY
ON THE ROAD TO EMMAUS

THE STORY: ISAIAH 45:21,22
Jesus is the only Savior to whom we can turn to be saved. Jesus said, "I am the way and the truth and the life. No one comes to the Father except through me" (John 14:6). Compare Isaiah's words with those recorded in Acts 4:12 by Luke: "Salvation is found in no one else, for there is no other name under heaven given to men by which we must be saved." Surely Isaiah's prophecy points forward to Jesus.

TALK ABOUT IT:
Could the passage in Isaiah be fulfilled by any other person but Jesus? (No, Jesus is the only way to salvation.)

What does this say about all the other religions in the world that follow leaders such as Buddha, Mohammed, Vishnu, or others? (All other paths to salvation, all other gods are false. Jesus is the only way. Even if men who follow other gods do so believing they are correct, those other gods cannot save them.)

PRAY:

Pray that God would help every person in your family trust in Jesus, the true God.

THE BODY OF CHRIST

Christians are called to work & serve together

MONDAY

THE STORY: 1 CORINTHIANS 12:1-11

The Corinthian church was struggling. In the church there could be found immorality (See 1 Corinthians 5:1), lawsuits among believers (see 1 Corinthians 6:1-11), and divisions (see 1 Corinthians 1:11-12, 3:1-4). Instead of being an interdependent, connected family of believers, the Corinthian church was competitive and divided.

In addressing spiritual gifts within this church, Paul first reaffirmed the solid foundation upon which the Spirit of God operates. First, the Spirit of God testifies to Christ. No true Christian testimony can come except by the Spirit of God. Secondly, all gifts come from the same Spirit and are therefore given for the ministry of Christ. Third, God's gifts, though given to individuals, are for the common good - that is, the good of the body of Christ, which is the church.

TALK ABOUT IT:

Why does God give spiritual gifts to the church? (God gives them for the common good.)

Why is it important to remember that spiritual gifts are given by God for the benefit of the church? (It would be very easy for a person to think he is better than others because of his gifts. People often use these gifts to exalt themselves and not Christ. This is what was happening in the Corinthian church. People were boasting that they were more spiritual because of their gifts.)

How have you been tempted to boast in your accomplishments? (Help your children see how they might have boasted in their accomplishments. How much more might they be tempted if God used them powerfully through a spiritual gift?)

PRAY:
Pray that God would help you always remember that all our gifts are meant to serve the body of Christ for the glory of God, not our own glory.

TUESDAY

THE STORY: 1 CORINTHIANS 12:12-26
Every Christian is a dependent part of the body. One of the most helpful pictures of the church is Paul's analogy of the church as a body. Though each member is different, we are all important for the effective functioning of the body. None of us can say we don't need others in the church. Since we have all been given different gifts, we need each other. Our gifts and placement in the body have been sovereignly directed by God (see 1 Corinthians 12:18).

TALK ABOUT IT:
How does the picture of the body help us to know we need each other in the church? (Imagine a leg trying to walk around without an eye, or an eye trying to get somewhere in its sight without legs to take it there. The only way the body works is if all its parts work together, each with its own special gift.)

Paul talks about two separate problems in the body. What are they? (In 1 Corinthians 12:14-17, the first problem is jealousy or self-pity among members who long to be a different part of the body. The second problem is in 1 Corinthians 12:21-25, when one part of the body is proud and thinks it does not need the other parts of the body. We are not to reject the church because others are more gifted than us, or cause division in the church because we think we are more gifted than others.)

Which of the two problems noted above might you be most tempted to struggle with? (Parents, help your children by answering first and then help your children to answer. They are not likely to refer to spiritual gifts but rather to general gifting. Even so the principle and the sinful patterns are the same.)

PRAY:
Ask God to help you trust Him for your gifts and the way they fit into the body.

WEDNESDAY
WHERE IS THE GOSPEL?

THE STORY: 1 CORINTHIANS 12:27
Through Paul's entire discussion regarding the gifts, Christ is at the center. As he begins the chapter, Paul tells us that the Spirit helps us to exalt Christ in our words. The gifts are also meant to exalt Jesus. The gifts are given not for individual benefit but for the benefit of the church. The gifts of God and are not given merely for our individual pleasure.

The Spirit of God poured out the gifts of God to grow and build the church. The church is called the body of Christ because the Spirit of Christ lisves in us. We are to use oru gifts to belss one another and to reach out to others with the Gospel. This is only possible because God has changed our hearts. Apart from the Gospel we are only selfish using our gifts for our own glory. Though God has given various gifts to individual members, all believers are to pursue their spiritual gifts to strengthen the body of Christ.

TALK ABOUT IT:
Who is at the center of all the gifts? (Christ & His spirit are at the center of all the gifts.)

Why is the church called the body of Christ? (God's spirit lives in each believer.)

PRAY:
Ask the Spirit of God to save each family member and help you use your gifts to build the body of Christ.

THURSDAY

THE STORY: 1 CORINTHIANS 12:27-31
Christ is the head of the body. Paul tells us that we are the body of Christ (vs 27). In Ephesians Paul also explains that Christ is "the head of the church, His boyd, and is Himself its Savior." (Eph. 5:23b) The whole church, all the people in it, are called to work together in unity under the direction of Christ. (See Ephesians 3:6)

TALK ABOUT IT:
Who is the head of the body? (Jesus is the head)

How does Ephesians 3:6 relate to today's Bible passage? Look up Ephesians 3:6 (We are all called together by the gospel so we should all work together in the body, the church)

How does God's plan for the gifts keep the church united? (Since everyone is gifted differently, we all need each other.)

PRAY:
Pray that God would pour out His Spirit and His gifts on each member of your family. Take time to pray for each one by name.

FRIDAY
ON THE ROAD TO EMMAUS

THE STORY: HOSEA 2:18-20

Hosea foresaw a day when God would betroth Himself to His people forever. This betrothal would be in righteousness, justice, love, and compassion. One day we, the church - the bride of Christ - will join Him at the wedding supper of the Lamb (see Revelation 19:7).

TALK ABOUT IT:

Who does the bride refer to in the Bible? (The bride is the church.)

Who is the bridegroom? (Jesus is the bridegroom.)

What else do you see in the Hosea passage that points forward to Christ? (Hosea talks about a new covenant, which will result in the end of violence and death - a reference to the end of the curse from the Fall. That covenant is the new covenant in Christ's blood.)

PRAY:

Thank the Lord for sending Jesus to die on the cross for our sins that we might become His bride.

LOVE

Love is the most important gift of all.

MONDAY

THE STORY: 1 CORINTHIANS 13:1-3

Although Paul encouraged the Corinthians to pursue the gifts, he took time to interrupt his discussion of the gifts to teach them about love, the greatest of God's spiritual gifts. In 1 John 4 we are told that we can love because God first loved us. So, even love is a gift from God. The Corinthians were using the spiritual gifts to pridefully show off their spiritual abilities. All the while they were sinning through immorality and taking one another to court (see 1 Corinthians 5 and 6).

Unlike the other spiritual gifts, which a person may or may not have, everyone can love. Love is required and ensures the proper operation of all the other gifts. To use a spiritual gift in an unloving way gains nothing.

TALK ABOUT IT:

Why can we consider love a spiritual gift? (Every good thing we do is only by the free gift and grace of God. Likewise, love, the most excellent way, is also a gift from God.)

Why is love the greatest gift of all? (Love is the required foundation for all the gifts. It glorifies God and serves others. If we exercise the gifts for our own benefit, we exalt ourselves but not Christ.)

What happens in your famiy when you don't love one another? How is that noisy like a gong or cymbal? (Parents, draw our your children and help them to see how boasting or anger disrupts the peace of your home.)

PRAY:
Ask God to help you demonstrate love to each member of your family.

TUESDAY

THE STORY: 1 CORINTHIANS 13:4-7
Love is action. Love is a word cheapened by overuse today. We say we love pizza, candy, the beach, and a million other things. Love is defined as something we feel, not something we do. Here in Paul's description, not a single item refers to feeling. Paul doesn't say love is wonderful, delightful, or intense. Each description of love demonstrates a godly action toward another. Each of these godly actions requires sacrifice. Each of these sacrifices points to the ultimate sacrifice and demonstration of love: "This is love: not that we loved God, but that He loved us and sent His Son as an atoning sacrifice for our sins" (1 John 4:10).

TALK ABOUT IT:
How do you use the word Love in everyday conversation? (Draw your children out regarding both the meaningful and trite ways they use the word love.)

How is the word love connected to the cross? (The cross is the greatest demonstration of love. If we review the list in Paul's description of love, we can find the gospel in each one of them. For instance, God was patient not to judge sin, but in kindness He sent His son, Jesus. Jesus honored the Father by submitting to the cross and giving up His glory in a demonstration of humility, the opposite of envy and boasting.)

Review the list of the characteristics of love. Take time to encourage one another by sharing the evidences of God's grace you see in each other's lives, where one or more of these characteristics of love are observable and at work.

PRAY:
Thank God for His demonstration of love on the cross.

WEDNESDAY
WHERE IS THE GOSPEL?

THE STORY: 1 CORINTHIANS 13:10

Many quote 1 Corinthians 13 on love. Portions of this passage might sound wonderful at a wedding ceremony, but without an understanding of the gospel and its connection to it, Paul's description of love cannot be fully appreciated. The gospel defines and gives meaning to love. The Bible tells us, "God is love." And the apostle John in 1 John 4:8-11 describes God's demonstration of love as the death of His Son on the cross. John goes on to explain that the cross should be our reason for loving one another. Paul also points to this in 1 Corinthians 13:10 when he says, "when the perfect comes..." "The perfect" is Jesus.

Since God is love, love never ends! All other worldly gifts and knowledge will be superseded, but the love of Christ will remain forever.

TALK ABOUT IT:

Can we separate genuine love from the gospel? (No, genuine love grows out of the gospel. We love because God first loved us.)

Why is it difficult for us to love perfectly? (Although believers have been set free from the bondage of sin, we still have sin remaining within us, which wars against love. That is why Paul tells us to pursue love [see 1 Corinthians 14:1]. We must put off selfishness and put on love, as well as put off impatience, pride, anger, lies, and every other sin, and put on love.)

PRAY:

Ask God to help you put on love in honor of the way God loved us by sending Jesus to die on the cross for our sins.

THURSDAY

THE STORY: 1 CORINTHIANS 13:8-13

Love never ends. When Jesus, the perfect, comes, we will no longer have a need for tongues or prophecy, healing or wisdom. All the gifts of the spirit will pass away because we will be in the presence of perfect wisdom, perfect knowledge, and perfect truth. Love, however, will not pass away. The cross - the greatest demonstration of love and the basis of our salvation - will be celebrated forever. Sin will be destroyed, and we will all live in perfect love toward one another and toward God. The theme of heaven is love. When we recognize this and live in the good of it today, we bring a little bit of heaven to earth. Perhaps there is no greater earthly expression of the love of Christ than when someone sacrifices for another. When we do, whether we realize it or not, we are honoring the sacrifice of Jesus, the author of love.

TALK ABOUT IT:

Why does Paul say prophecy and knowledge will pass away when Jesus (the perfect) returns? (We know only a small part, but when Jesus comes, we will see Him as He is. Our former understanding, all we knew about Jesus, will be nothing compared to seeing Him face to face.)

Why won't love pass away? (Love is the basis of our relationship with God. The cross is the way to heaven and our guarantee of remaining in heaven.)

How can we demonstrate love toward one another? (Parents, draw out practical examples.)

PRAY:

Pray that God would help you love one another just as Jesus loved you.

FRIDAY
ON THE ROAD TO EMMAUS

THE STORY: PSALM 31:5

Just before Jesus died, He spoke the words of this verse, "into your hands I commit my spirit" (Luke 23:46). The centurion who saw what happened praised God and said, "Surely this was a righteous man" (Luke 23:47). Jesus had finished the work He set out to do. The wrath of the Father was satisfied. Our sins were paid for on the cross, which was the single greatest demonstration of the love of God.

TALK ABOUT IT:

Read aloud the parelell passage in Luke 23:46,47. How did Jesus' words affect the centurion? (The centurion saw that even in Jesus' very last breath, He spoke not a single ill word to anyone. He could tell that Jesus was no ordinary man and that He was righteous.)

Why is it important that Jesus finished well, without sin? (Not only do we depend on Jesus taking our punishment on the cross, but we also depend upon Christ's perfection for our righteousness. Jesus takes away our sin and gives us His perfect life in exchange. His perfect life, given to us, fulfills the requirements of God's law.)

PRAY:

Thank Jesus for His death on the cross and for His perfect life. He truly is "the perfect"!

A NEW CREATION

Every Christian is a new creation.

MONDAY

THE STORY: 2 CORINTHIANS 5:11-15

False teachers moved into the Corinthian church in Paul's absence and undermined Paul's ministry and the gospel. Paul's second letter to the Corinthians is designed to refute false teaching and affirm gospel truth. Here Paul is absolutely caught up in love for Christ and shows us where right motivation for all we do as Christians must come from.

Christ's love compels us and affects the way we live. Paul was telling the Corinthians what motivated him as well as declaring a standard for all Christians. The cross is the greatest declaration of love there could ever be. When our hearts open to the wonder of the cross, we are given the power to live for Christ. Jesus died on the cross so that we could die to sin and live for Him. Our whole lives are changed by the gospel. When we live by the love of God in Jesus, we are compelled to live for Christ.

TALK ABOUT IT:

What motivated Paul? What lies behind all he does? (Paul is motivated by God's love demonstrated in the sacrifice of Jesus on the cross.)

How does Christ's death help us to obey? (It is hard to obey an evil king who demands hard labor in return for a place in the kingdom. But it is easier to obey a righteous king who treats you with kindness and only gives you good gifts. Jesus, our King, gave us His life. How can we not obey His Word?)

Paul said that we are convinced that when Jesus died, all died (see 2 Corinthians 5:14b). What does Paul mean by "that all died"? (Jesus died that the power of sin might be destroyed. If we are convinced of this, we have confidence to live for Christ and say no to sin. Jesus' victory on the cross ensures our victory over sin! This gives us confidence.)

PRAY:
Thank the Lord for the cross and ask God to help us live for Him by saying no to sin.

TUESDAY

THE STORY: 2 CORINTHIANS 5:16,17

Anyone in Christ is a new creation. Not only can we live for Christ because sin has been defeated, we have also been changed! This change is so significant that Paul describes it as being created again! Our old self, which was a slave to sin, has been changed. Now we are free to live for Christ. The old has gone and the new has come; we have been created again! The word used for "come" does not mean "to arrive" or "to get somewhere." Rather, it signifies change and could be translated "generated". In other words, if anyone is in Christ, he is a brand-new creation. What was old has passed away, and something new has been generated. When a person becomes a Christian, this passage teaches us that he has been regenerated or re-created.

TALK ABOUT IT:

What did God do to make us a new creation? (God sent His Son, Jesus, to die on the cross so that we could be free from the bondage of sin and live for Jesus.)

Can we recognize a Christian by the way he or she lives? (Yes, unbelievers live for this world, but Christians have been freed from sin to live for Christ. When we see a person living for Christ, we can recognize him as a Christian. If a person consistently does not live for Christ, we can recognize him as an unbeliever who needs to be re-created by the Spirit of God.)

Can we re-create ourselves? (No. That is why we believe in Jesus and call out to Him to change us. There is no work that a person could do to change themselves in this way. Becoming a new creation is a work of God's grace that God promises to those who believe and place their faith in Jesus and His sacrifice on the cross.)

PRAY:
Ask God to regenerate every member of your family.

WEDNESDAY
WHERE IS THE GOSPEL?

THE STORY: 2 CORINTHIANS 5:18-20
This passage, and indeed all of 2 Corinthians 5, is filled with the gospel. Through Christ's work on the cross we have been reconciled to God. That, in short, is the Gospel!

2 Corinthians 5:21 says, "For our sake he made Him to be sin who knew no sin, so that in Him we might become the righteousness of God." If we take out the pronouns this passage reads: "For [add your name]'s sake God the Father made Jesus to be sin who knew no sin, so that in Jesus [add your name] might become the righteousness of God".

This is the message of reconciliation that has been entrusted to us. We call this message the gospel. The message applied in our lives so transforms us that we become new creations (see 2 Corinthians 5:17).

TALK ABOUT IT:

Where do you see the gospel in this chapter? (Parents, help your children find the gospel in this passage. If they can read, have them look for verses. If they can't read, help them remember what you read together, or read through the passage again and have them raise their hand whenever they hear a part of the gospel.)

Why is it important to put our names in the Scripture to make it personal? (We need to remember that God is not just speaking to people in general. God is speaking to each one of us specifically. That is why it is good to see your own name in the verses of the Bible. God is speaking to you!)

PRAY:

Ask God to change each member of your family, make them a new creation, and help each one to see that the message of the gospel is especially addressed to them by God.

THURSDAY

THE STORY: 2 CORINTHIANS 5:20-6:2

Christians speak for Christ. When God regenerates us or re-creates us, we become His ambassadors. We take His message to others. We don't just take the message of the cross without emotion, as though we were delivering a package. Instead we are to implore others to be reconciled to God. We are to tell others the gospel - that God made Jesus, who had no sin, to be sin for us so that in Christ we could be righteous! We are to convince others. We are to appeal, to urge, to passionately implore them to turn to God. We are to explain to them that there is no time to wait; today is the day of salvation.

TALK ABOUT IT:

What is the message God has asked us to take to others? (We are to take to others the message of reconciliation. God has made a way for man to be at peace with Him. This is possible through the death of Jesus, His Son, who took our sins upon Himself so that the wrath of God against us would be satisfied and we could be forgiven.)

What do we call God's message of reconciliation? (We call it the gospel.)

Do most people know the gospel? (Although many people have heard about Jesus, a lot of them do not understand the gospel message. They don't understand that God is holy and that our sin separates us from Him. They don't realize they are enemies of God; they don't think they need to be saved or reconciled with God. When, by the Spirit of God, they understand they are enemies of God, bound for judgment in hell, the message of the gospel is good news. We have the privilege of giving them the best news they will ever receive in their lives!)

PRAY:
Ask God to give your family opportunities to share the message of reconciliation with those around you who need to hear.

FRIDAY
ON THE ROAD TO EMMAUS

THE STORY: PSALM 31:9-16
Jesus quoted from Psalm 31:5 just before He died. In looking at the rest of the psalm, although it is written by David to describe his own suffering, we see the suffering of Christ as well. Jesus was consumed by anguish on the road to the cross, and his strength failed Him as He fell carrying the cross. He was deserted by the disciples, his friends. People slandered Him on every side.

Although these verses are not directly attributed to Christ, David's life itself is a shadow of the life of Jesus and points us forward to Christ. When we read this psalm, though we know it speaks of David, we should know that it also speaks of the sacrifice of our Savior and His suffering.

TALK ABOUT IT:
Read through Psalm 31. Where do you see Jesus and His sacrifice in the sufferings and trials of David? (Help your children look for connections.)

How did David's faith in God reflect our Lord's trust in the Father? (David demonstrated great faith and trusted God in the midst of his suffering just as Jesus trusted His Father while on the cross.)

PRAY:
Thank God for giving up His Son, Jesus, to suffer on the cross for our sins.

GOD LOVES A CHEERFUL GIVER

Everything we do, including our giving, should spring from grace.

MONDAY

THE STORY: 2 CORINTHIANS 9:1-9

Cheerful giving is grace-motivated giving. Paul had written earlier to the Corinthians (1 Corinthians 16:1-3) and asked them to give an offering for the poor Christians in Jerusalem. In this letter Paul wrote to remind them to complete the work of giving they and had begun to offer the gift they promised cheerfully. Paul reminded them that everything comes from the Lord by His grace. Even the act of giving is the result of a work of grace. It was Paul's desire that their faith be stirred so that their giving would bring them joy and be offered cheerfully.

TALK ABOUT IT:

God has provided all that we need. How does that help us to be generous in our giving? (If God could supply all that we have, He can also re-supply all that we give away.)

What does Paul mean when he talks about sowing and reaping? (If we only sow a few seeds, we will only harvest a few plants and a small crop. If we sow generously, we will get many plants and a large crop. If we give a little, we will only reap a small blessing. But if we give generously, we will reap a large blessing.)

What do we reap when we give? (Some might see this as a way to get more money. If you give money away, they conclude, you will get a lot of money in return. While God often rewards generosity by providing more to give away, the greatest harvest we receive is a spiritual harvest. People give glory to God through our generosity, and we receive treasure in heaven for our sacrifice.)

Who might you bless as a family? (Parents, work with your children to think of an individual or family you might bless with a gift.)

PRAY:
Thank God for all he has blessed your family with and for the grace of giving.

TUESDAY

THE STORY: 2 CORINTHIANS 9:10-12
Generous giving flows out of God's generosity to us. When we understand that everything we have comes from God, it is much easier to give it away. God supplies both the seed and the harvest. He is the one who makes us rich so that we might be generous on every occasion. Our giving is a demonstration of thanks to God. We thank Him for what He has given us by giving it away! When we give to others, we are actually participating in God's generosity to them, which results in their giving thanks as well. Our giving is an expression of thanks toward God, resulting in others giving thanks toward God!

TALK ABOUT IT:
Who gives us everything we have? (God gives us everything we have.)

Does what we have belong to us or to God? (Everything we have still belongs to God. We are stewards of the things God gives us. We are to use them faithfully. Sometimes that means we give them away to others. Other times we enjoy them ourselves.)

Why is it a sin to refuse to share or be reluctant to give? (God doesn't give us what we have just so we can keep it selfishly for our own use alone. God desires to bless others through what He gives us. When we are selfish, we are actually trying to take for ourselves what does not really belong to us.)

PRAY:
Ask God to help you be a cheerful, generous giver.

WEDNESDAY
WHERE IS THE GOSPEL?

THE STORY: 2 CORINTHIANS 9:13
Paul was excited about the cheerful giving of the Corinthians. He was not excited because it was an empty work, but because it flowed out of their "confession of the gospel of Christ" (2 Corinthians 9:13).

Our giving will not get us to heaven. Rather, our giving should be out of thanksgiving for our salvation and in confidence that our heavenly Father will provide. The giving of the Corinthians resulted in thanksgiving to God from Paul and from the recipients of the gift. Because of the cross, God is able to make "all grace abound" (2 Corinthians 9:8) to us so that the treasures of this world no longer have a grip on us.

TALK ABOUT IT:
Why should we ultimately give to others? (Our joy for giving should flow out of our thankfulness for what God did in sending Jesus to die for our sin on the cross.)

What sins stand in the way of our being generous? How do you see those sins at work in your own life? (Parents: We all struggle with greed, selfishness, unbelief, and coveting. All of these sins rob us of our generosity. Confess how they affect your life, then draw out your children.)

PRAY:
Confess your weakness and love of material things and ask God to help you be a generous, cheerful giver.

THURSDAY

THE STORY: 2 CORINTHIANS 9:14,15
Grace-motivated giving results in praise to God. When we give to others, it results in their hearts going out to us. They will be grateful and thankful for us. When we give to others, it also results in praise and thanks to God. Paul knew that the Christians in Jerusalem would also offer prayers of thanks to God for the Corinthians.

TALK ABOUT IT:
How has God provided for you through the generosity of others? (Parents, help your children see just how little they contribute to their own daily needs and how much is given to them by others.)

How can remembering God's faithfulness to you in the past help you to be generous in the future? (We know that if we give something away, God will be faithful to provide our future need. When we doubt God's faithfulness, we can be reluctant to give something away. We think we may need it later for ourselves. For example, the person with extra money today might not be willing to give it any of it away because he doesn't trust God's faithfulness for tomorrow.)

PRAY:
Give thanks to God for the many ways He has provided for you through others. Ask God to help you be generous.

FRIDAY
ON THE ROAD TO EMMAUS

THE STORY: ISAIAH 53:9

In Matthew 27:57 we are told that Jesus was buried in the tomb of a rich man from Arimathea named Joseph. Jesus was crucified among thieves, died among thieves, and was assigned a grave among sinners. Isaiah 53 paints the picture of the passion and suffering of our Lord. It is interesting to note here that a rich man became a disciple of Jesus. His transformed heart is evident in the generous giving of his own tomb, which had never been used. Joseph also displayed great courage to go before Pilate and ask for the body of Jesus. Where as others deserted Christ, Joseph, a converted rich man, cared for our Savior's body. Our money, placed under the submission of the King, can be used to advance the kingdom.

TALK ABOUT IT:

How does the second half of Isaiah 53:9 also speak of our Savior? (Jesus never lied or was violent.)

Why didn't Jesus fight back when they crucified Him? (Jesus willingly died that He might be crucified and was cursed to take the punishment that we deserved. He did this with joy, in spite of the great suffering, out of love for us.)

PRAY:

Thank Jesus for sacrificing His life on the cross for your sins.

A GIFT OF RIGHTEOUSNESS

All men are sinners in need of the gospel.

MONDAY

THE STORY: ROMANS 3:9-20

All men, Jews and Gentiles alike, are under sin and condemned by the law. Our sin affects every part of our being. Paul pulls together a string of Old Testament texts here to make his point. The collective whole leaves a convincing argument for the total depravity of man. Paul concludes the argument with a clear statement of the lost condition of all men. No one will be declared righteous in the sight of God by his good works (observing the law). The best the law does for us is to show us our sin and inform us where we have failed.

TALK ABOUT IT:

Who is Paul describing when he uses the description of throats like open graves, the poison of vipers on their lips, and mouths that are full of cursing? (Paul is describing you and me. Paul is describing all men and women apart from the saving grace of God.)

Is there any way for a person to become good in God's sight by what he does? (No. There is nothing we can do to make ourselves righteous or good before God.)

Do you see yourself like Paul describes us, or do you think of yourself as being pretty good? (Parents, help your children identify with the sinful description of man that Paul gives.)

What's wrong with thinking you're a pretty good person? (It is not until we see our real need for a Savior that we run to the Savior. Pride and self-righteousness deceive us by making us think we are good enough and, therefore, do not need a Savior. We make our sins seem small with this kind of thinking. In reality, these sins separate us from God - a much more serious condition.)

PRAY:

Ask God to pour out His grace upon your family members who are hopelessly lost in sin apart from Jesus.

TUESDAY

THE STORY: ROMANS 3:21-24

Our righteousness must come by faith in Christ. If Paul had ended his message at the end of verse 20, we would have no hope. But Paul doesn't leave us lost in our sin. He goes on to describe how a man can be made righteous, or good, in God's sight. We can receive righteousness from God when we have faith in Jesus Christ. Paul then, in verses 23 and 24, summarizes our problem and God's solution. All men have sinned, but we can be saved by grace through the work of Jesus on the cross. The whole Old Testament (the Law and Prophets) points forward to this most amazing truth. The sacrifice of Jesus on the cross to make a way for sinners to be saved is what God's story is all about!

TALK ABOUT IT:

What does it mean when it says that the Law and the Prophets testify about God's plan for righteousness? ("The Law and the Prophets" is the way Paul refers to the books of the Old Testament. When Paul says they testify, he means that you can read about God's plan there. The prophets foretold a day when God would save His people from their sin. When they talk about God's plan for salvation, they are talking about Jesus and His death on the cross.)

How much do we have to pay or what do we have to do to be saved? (We don't need to do anything except trust in what Jesus already did. God's gift is freely given. That is what grace means.)

PRAY:
Thank God for His free gift of grace available to us through the sacrifice of Jesus on the cross.

WEDNESDAY
WHERE IS THE GOSPEL?

THE STORY: ROMANS 3:25,26
Paul is basically defending the gospel in Romans 3. In verse 25 and 26 we see some important components of God's plan. First, it was God's willing plan. He presented Jesus as a sacrifice. Secondly, Jesus' sacrifice was an acceptable payment, or atonement, for our sin. Thirdly, this sacrifice was required to ensure the justice of God, who had allowed sins to go unpunished.

Earlier in this passage Paul clearly wanted to help us to see our total depravity and our utter inability to stand righteous apart from God's grace. Paul said, "None is righteous, no, not one," and "No one understands; no one seeks God," and "All have turned aside." He left absolutely no possibility that someone might be good apart from Christ.

After giving this convincing argument, Paul goes on to declare one of the best "buts" of Scripture: "But now the righteousness of God has been manifested apart from the law... the righteousness of God through faith in Jesus Christ for all who believe" (Romans 3:21,22).

Faith is not in Jesus as a good teacher, but in Jesus as the Savior who died on the cross taking the penalty for our sin. We deserve death - yet, in exchange for our sin, Jesus Christ gives us His righteousness. Jesus was able to live the sinless life we could not live. He freely gives us His clean and righteous record when we place our trust in His sacrifice for us on the cross.

TALK ABOUT IT:
How did God demonstrate His patience and forbearance until Jesus died? (God did not immediately judge men for their sin, but allowed the future sacrifice of Jesus to hold back His wrath for sin.)

How did God satisfy judgment for sin? (God poured out His judgment for sin upon Jesus on the cross. Our punishment was given to Jesus.)

PRAY:
Thank God for His amazing mercy. Thank Him for withholding complete judgment and sending His only son to take the penalty for our sin.

THURSDAY

THE STORY: ROMANS 3:27-31
Our only boast is in Christ. If everything we have is based on what God has done, and if we have nothing based on what we have done, then we have nothing to boast about. The only thing we can take credit for is our sin. All our salvation, from start to finish, is by God's grace. Even the faith we have is a gift of God. Apart from the work of the Holy Spirit in our lives, we would remain enemies of God. Paul lived his life this way. He celebrated his weaknesses and admitted his sin (1 Timothy 1:15), and he made his boast in the Lord (Galatians 6:14).

TALK ABOUT IT:

What does it mean to boast? (Boasting is a form of pride where one takes credit for what one does. If a person tells everyone how well he did in a race, he is boasting about the race.)

Why would it be wrong to boast about our salvation? (We did nothing to gain salvation. Jesus did it all. We have nothing to boast about because we added nothing to the salvation Jesus gained for us.)

What does it mean to boast in Jesus? (When we celebrate or tell others about what Jesus did for us, we are boasting in Jesus. When we tell them we are weak without His strength and we are lost without the cross, we are boasting about Jesus.)

PRAY:

Ask God to help each member of your family remember that hope is found in Christ alone, and we have no room to boast, because He did it all.

FRIDAY
ON THE ROAD TO EMMAUS

THE STORY: ISAIAH 52:14,15

These verses are found in the middle of Isaiah's description of the suffering servant. Jesus suffered greatly. Blood poured from wounds upon His face and head. The face of Jesus would have been bruised and swollen from being repeatedly struck by the soldiers' fists. The back of Christ would have been torn from the scourging. Clearly, people would have been appalled to look at Him. The blood shed upon the cross by Jesus would sprinkle many nations. The sprinkling of water was done as a rite of cleansing (Numbers 8:7 and 19:18,19). Blood sprinkled on those who were ceremonially unclean would sanctify them (Hebrews 9:13). The blood of Jesus sprinkled on the nations speaks of the cleansing of the nations by His sacrifice (Hebrews 10:22 and 12:24).

TALK ABOUT IT:

Why is it helpful to think about the suffering of Jesus? (We never want to forget the great humiliation and suffering Jesus went through to take away our sins.)

How can remembering the suffering of Christ motivate us toward godly living? (When we realize that it was our sin that nailed Him to the cross and was the reason for Jesus' suffering, we hate sin all the more and look to live righteous lives by saying no to sin.)

PRAY:

Thank Jesus for His suffering so that we could be spared the penalty for our sin. Ask God to help you live for Christ. Pray that He would give each member of your family grace to avoid sin.

ABRAHAM: FATHER TO ALL BY FAITH

Abraham is the father of all who place their trust in Christ.

MONDAY

THE STORY: ROMANS 4:1-8

Abraham is our example of faith. Paul uses Abraham, the patriarch of the Jewish faith, to demonstrate that our standing of righteousness before God has always been by faith and not by works. Paul quotes Genesis 15:4, where, after God told Abraham that his children would be as numerous as the stars, the text simply reads, "Abraham believed the Lord, and He credited it to him as righteousness." Abraham did no work to earn his righteousness. He simply believed God's promise. Righteousness, was God's free gift.

TALK ABOUT IT:

Is there any work we need to do to become righteous before God? (No. There is no work we could do. We need to simply follow Abraham's example and believe.)

Abraham believed God's promise. Who do we believe? (We are called to believe in Jesus Christ and His saving work on the cross.)

PRAY:

Ask God to help each member of your family come to saving faith in Jesus.

TUESDAY

THE STORY: ROMANS 4:9-17

Abraham is the father of all who would believe. The Jews would have believed Abraham to be their father. They even called themselves the "children of Abraham." They also believed that their right standing before God was marked by circumcision. In this text, Paul explodes their thinking. Abraham was counted as righteous before circumcision. Abraham, Paul informs us, is the father of all those who have faith, whether they are circumcised or not. Abraham is the father of all who believe! Later, in the Book of Romans, Paul goes a step further and tells us that God's children are those who are children of the promise by faith, not those who are the natural children of Abraham (Romans 9:7,8). Abraham is not just the father of the Jews, but the father of "many nations" (Romans 4:17).

TALK ABOUT IT:

How can Abraham be the father of many different nations? (The descendants of Abraham's natural children became several nations in the ancient world, especially Israel. But more importantly, Abraham is the father of those who believe because they have the faith of Abraham.)

What do we need to do to become members of God's family? (We need to believe the gospel message, putting our faith in the work of Jesus Christ on the cross.)

What does God give us when we believe? (God credits the righteousness of Christ to our account.)

PRAY:

Thank God for His free gift of grace available to us through the sacrifice of Jesus on the cross.

WEDNESDAY
WHERE IS THE GOSPEL?

THE STORY: ROMANS 4:23-25

Paul directly ties the faith of Abraham trusting in God's future redemption with our trusting in God's past work on the cross and through the Resurrection. Abraham's faith was "counted to him as righteousness" (Romans 4:22). In the same way, "It will be counted to us who believe in him who raised from the dead Jesus our Lord, who was delivered up for our trespasses and raised for our justification" (Romans 4:24,25).

TALK ABOUT IT:

What does it mean to have something credited to you? ("Credited" means "added". If you return something to the store, the store will give you credit for what you returned and add back the money to your account.)

What does Paul say is special about the words written about Abraham, "It was credited to him"? (Paul tells us that they were also written for all of us who would later believe in Jesus).

PRAY:

Thank God for His mercy in crediting our account with the work of His Son Jesus.

THURSDAY

THE STORY: ROMANS 4:18-25

Abraham believed against all hope. He trusted God's plan. This is a wonderful picture of our need to trust in Christ. Abraham's body was as good as dead just as we are dead, in our sins. There was nothing Abraham could do in his own strength to renew his own body so that he could have children. Likewise, there is nothing we can do to work our way to heaven. If Abraham was going to have children, it would have to be the work of God. If we are to be saved, it can only come by the work of God. Abraham believed that God had the power to do what He promised, and we must believe that God has the power to fulfill His promise of salvation through the work of Jesus on the cross. Like Abraham, we have no other hope. We are hopelessly lost in our sin apart from Jesus.

TALK ABOUT IT:

How did Abraham demonstrate his faith? (Abraham needed to believe God's promise that he would have many children even though he was too old to have children.)

What does our faith look like? (We need to believe that Jesus suffered, died, and rose again for our sins even though we did not witness these events. We need to trust the Scriptures by faith. Jesus said, "Blessed are they who have not seen but yet they believe" [see John 20:29].)

PRAY:

Ask God to help each member of your family to believe in the sacrifice and resurrection of Jesus as payment for sin.

FRIDAY
ON THE ROAD TO EMMAUS

THE STORY: ISAIAH 53:10

Jesus is the Lamb of God, the guilt offering that takes away the sin of the world (John 1:29). God presented Jesus as a sacrifice of atonement through His blood (Romans 3:25). Jesus did not remain crushed. On the third day He rose again, and the will of the Lord in bringing many to salvation was accomplished.

This wonderful verse, in the midst of Isaiah's prophetic look at the Crucifixion, once again opens our eyes to see the willingness of the Father to crush His Son for our redemption.

TALK ABOUT IT:

What does this verse tell us about God's plan to offer up Jesus? (This verse tells us that it was the Lord's will or God's plan. John 3:16 tells us that God gave up Jesus out of love for us.)

What does it mean when it says His life is a guilt offering? (In the Old Testament an animal would be killed as a guilt offering or sacrifice for a person's sins. Those sacrifices never actually took away sin. Jesus was crushed by God as a sacrifice that did take away sins. Jesus' sacrifice paid the price for all the sins of those who believe.)

PRAY:

Thank God for lovingly giving up His only Son as a guilt offering for us that out sins might be forgiven.

NEW TESTAMENT · LESSON 60

BELIEVE AND CONFESS

Salvation in Christ is free for all to believe.

MONDAY

THE STORY: ROMANS 10:1-4

Salvation can not be earned. Paul hammers away at the idea that righteousness can not be earned. Paul repeats that we are saved by faith and not by our own works. He wants to ensure that his hearers know that our righteousness comes from Christ and not from what we do. This is important because some, especially in Paul's day, rejected the message and insisted on continuing to follow the law as a means to justify themselves before God. Paul's desire and prayers were for the salvation of Israel.

TALK ABOUT IT:

Why did Paul have such a love for Israel? (Paul was a Roman Jew who was a Pharisee prior to his conversion. He knew what it is like to hear the gospel and reject it.)

Why was the gospel difficult for the Jews to believe? (Most Jews placed their faith in their nation and the law. They saw salvation as freedom from Rome for their country. They were expecting another kind of messiah, one who would free them from the Romans. Jesus came to free them from sin. Paul tells us Christ is the end of the law. This was very difficult for the Jews to accept.)

PRAY:

Thank God for doing the work of salvation for us so that we are no longer under the curse of the law.

TUESDAY

THE STORY: ROMANS 10:5-13

Paul wanted to be sure that everyone was clear that the required work of righteousness has been done by God. Paul suggests that to try and be righteous by the law is like bringing Christ down from heaven by your own power or causing Christ to rise from the dead by your own power. The point is that God has already done these things! There is no more work to be done but to believe the word that is near us. The word is already in our mouths and in our hearts. We simply need to believe what we know and confess our belief and trust in the Lord. Then we will be saved. Salvation is not far away. Salvation is near.

TALK ABOUT IT:

Why does salvation seem far away for a person who tries to earn it by works? (We are all sinners. Perfection is impossible. Anyone who tries to earn salvation is faced with the reality that our lives are filled with sin.)

Why can salvation seem close when you accept God's righteousness by faith? (God did all the work. There is nothing left to do but accept what He already did.)

Why is accepting God's salvation difficult for some? Why does anyone refuse? (People refuse because of sin. Men are in rebellion against God. It is only by God's grace that anyone can have faith and believe. Apart from God's saving grace, we reject all knowledge of God. That is why so many deny the world was created by God. See Romans 1:20-21.)

PRAY:
Ask God to pour His saving grace upon each member of your family that they might repent of their rebellion against God and trust the Lord.

WEDNESDAY
WHERE IS THE GOSPEL?

THE STORY: ROMANS 10:9,11
This is one of the clearest passages which addresses our responsibility toward God in salvation.

We must believe that the Jesus who was crucified was also raised from the dead. Though this belief is a requirement for salvation, we cannot simply believe unless God first extends His saving grace. This is because we were completely dead in our sins. When we hear the words of the gospel, the Spirit of God uses them to give us a new heart so that we might believe and confess.

TALK ABOUT IT:
Why does salvation seem so easy? (Salvation seems easy because the hard work has already been done by Jesus. We simply need to place our trust in Him.)

Why is salvation so hard for some? (Trusting in Christ means that you no longer trust yourself. Turning to Christ means that you turn away from the world. People reject Christ because they want to trust in their own works and/or don't want to turn away from the world. A person can't have it both ways.)

PRAY:
Pray that God would give each member of your family grace to turn away from the world and trust in the finished work of Christ.

THURSDAY

THE STORY: ROMANS 10:14-18

Salvation is spread by preaching the gospel. The good news is the message that all the requirements of the law have been met in Christ! All the work is done! All across the land people were and are trying to earn their salvation. We need to share the good news that the work is done. All that is left is for us to believe!

It sounds simple, but Paul was aware that not everyone who heard the message accepted the message. Many of the Jews refused to believe, just as the prophets had predicted. Often the Gentiles accepted the message of the gospel which the Jews rejected.

TALK ABOUT IT:

How does the kingdom of God advance and grow? (The kingdom of God advances through the proclamation of the gospel, by telling others about Jesus.)

What is the most important question we should take away from this passage? (Will I believe and trust in Christ?)

PRAY:

Pray for those you know who have rejected the gospel. Ask God to soften their hearts to the truth.

FRIDAY
ON THE ROAD TO EMMAUS

THE STORY: ISAIAH 65:1,2

Paul connects this passage to Christ in Romans 10:20. Paul pulls the rebellion of

Israel in Isaiah's day forward and speaks of Israel's rejection of Jesus. Jesus is the subject of this passage. Jesus is the one who was rejected by the Jews, the very ones who sought after the Messiah. The Gentiles, however, who did not seek after the Messiah, found a Savior in Jesus.

TALK ABOUT IT:

How does verse two also accurately describe Jesus? (Jesus ministered among the Jews. He healed them, delivered them, and taught in their synagogues proclaiming the good news of the kingdom. But they rejected Him.)

What is the message we should take away for our own lives? (We need to be careful not to reject the Lord, but to place our trust in Him. Every sin that led the Jews to reject Christ is active in our own hearts.)

PRAY:

Pray that God gives grace to each member of your family to accept the gospel and live for Christ.

PAUL IN CHAINS

Nothing can stop the advance of the gospel.

MONDAY

THE STORY: ACTS 28:11-20

Paul was in chains because of the gospel. Paul was arrested after sharing his testimony when the Jews began to riot in opposition (Acts 21:27-36). While in custody the Jews swore they would kill Paul (Acts 23:12-13). Rather than be handed over to the Jews, Paul appealed to Caesar. He knew that he was called to Rome by our Lord. After a difficult journey, Paul finally reached Rome.

TALK ABOUT IT:

Why was Paul arrested? (Paul was arrested for proclaiming the gospel which caused a lot of commotion among the Jews.)

Paul said it was because of the hope of Israel that he was bound in chains. What is the hope of Israel? (Jesus is the hope of Israel. The gospel is the hope of Israel.)

Is the gospel our hope as well? Why? (The message of good news is our hope. It is our hope because it is the only way by which people are saved from their sins and brought back into a right relationship with God.)

PRAY:

Thank God for the gospel - our only hope for salvation.

TUESDAY

THE STORY: ACTS 28:17-23

In spite of his chains, Paul continued to preach. In Acts 23:11 Jesus appeared to Paul and told him he would proclaim the gospel in Rome. Once in Rome, Paul wasted no time. Paul explained the gospel, God's story, from the Old Testament from morning to evening. Some were convinced by what Paul shared, but others did not believe.

TALK ABOUT IT:

How is Paul an example of faith for us? (In spite of difficult circumstances, Paul remained steadfastly committed to the proclamation of the gospel message.)

How should Paul's example of preaching the gospel in chains affect us who are able to share the good news freely without threat of arrest? (We should recognize the wonderful opportunity we have in our freedom to share the gospel. Too often we stop to enjoy the pleasures of life and forget that we are on a mission to proclaim God's word.)

PRAY:

Pray that God would help your family to look for and take opportunities to share the good news about our salvation with your family, friends, and neighbors.

WEDNESDAY
WHERE IS THE GOSPEL?

THE STORY: PHILIPPIANS 1:12-18

Paul knew that he was being detained in a house arrest situation so that the gospel could be widely proclaimed. In Philippians 1:12 Paul said that the advancement of the gospel was the reason for his imprisonment in Rome.

For two years Paul stayed under house arrest, sharing with anyone who would come to listen. Acts 28:31 tells us that he proclaimed the kingdom of God and taught about Jesus with all boldness and without hindrance. Even when others were preaching with false motives (to make a name for themselves) and in competition with Paul, Paul rejoiced. To him, the most important thing was that the message was going forth.

TALK ABOUT IT:

What effect did Paul's imprisonment have on other Christians? (Paul's example motivated others to spread the word of God more courageously.)

How could Paul's example motivate them and not cause them to fear their own imprisonment? (Even after being arrested and placed in chains, Paul continued to preach. If Paul was not afraid to talk about Jesus while under arrest, how could those who were free not take the message to others?)

How are you doing in spreading the gospel as a family? Who can you be reaching out to? (Parents, draw out your children and come up with a plan to reach out to one of your neighbors or someone you know that does not know the Lord.)

PRAY:

Pray for the person you are planning to reach out to.

THURSDAY

THE STORY: ACTS 28: 24-31

Paul was not hindered by the unbelief of the Jews. In spite of the fact that many did not believe Paul, Paul remained committed to spreading the message. For two years Paul welcomed all who came to see him and preached the gospel without hindrance. Paul knew that many of the Jews would reject Jesus, but he also remembered that the Lord had called him to proclaim the message to the Gentiles. Even while under house arrest, Paul continued the work God had assigned him.

TALK ABOUT IT:

According to Isaiah, who were the people that would not be able to see or hear the truth of the gospel? (Israel, who should have welcomed Jesus, rejected Him.)

Who did Paul say the gospel was sent to when Israel rejected it? (Paul said that God's salvation was sent to the Gentiles.)

Who are we like - the Jews who rejected the message or the Gentiles who received it? (Each man can either reject or accept the message. There were many among the Jews who accepted the message, and there were many Gentiles who rejected it too.)

PRAY:

Pray that the Spirit of God would touch each member of your family so that each one might receive the message of the gospel and place their trust in the finished work of Christ.

FRIDAY
ON THE ROAD TO EMMAUS

THE STORY: PSALM 22:22-31

The writer of Hebrews quotes Psalm 22:22 attributing this verse to Christ (Hebrews 2:12). This passage speaks of the adoption we have as brothers of Christ because of the work of Christ. This passage also speaks of the advance of the gospel to all nations.

TALK ABOUT IT:

What is the message of righteousness future generations will be told about? (The gospel is the future message of righteousness that we proclaim.)

Who are the future people Psalm 22:31 mentions? (We are a part of the future people who were, at that time, yet unborn. This prophetic psalm prophecies the future spread of the gospel to us, our children, and to those yet unborn until our Savior returns.)

PRAY:

Thank God for reaching your family with the gospel.

THE SUPREMACY OF CHRIST

Christ is supreme over all.

MONDAY

THE STORY: COLOSSIANS 1:15-17

Christ is head over creation. After Paul's opening remarks to the Colossians, he exalts Christ. First, Paul exalts Christ as the image of the invisible God. This is similar to what John tells us in his Gospel: "No man has ever seen God, but God the One and only, who is at the Father's side, has made him known" (John 1:18). Paul then opens our eyes to the work of Christ in creating the world. Not only did the Son create the world, but He also sustains it and holds it together. When Jesus wanted to feed the multitude, he multiplied the bread and fish. When Jesus rebuked the wind and the waves, they listened. And when Jesus commanded Lazarus to come forth, he came forth.

TALK ABOUT IT:

How could Jesus be the Creator when He was born after the creation was already created? (We need to remember that the Son of God is God's eternal Son, who always existed with the Father. Although the person of Jesus did not exist prior to His birth and His taking a human body, the eternal Son of God was with the Father and created the world. Paul finds no need to be careful to make any distinction when he describes the eternal nature of the Son, whom he introduced in Colossians 1:3 as the "Lord Jesus Christ.")

Is there anything that Jesus is not in control of? (No, all things are in subject to Christ.)

Why is sin such a terrible thing when we consider this passage? (Sin is man's rebellion against the rule of Christ. Sin is saying "no" to God's authority and rule in our lives.)

PRAY:

Ask the Lord to pour out His grace upon your family so that you might love Him and obey His commands.

TUESDAY

THE STORY: COLOSSIANS 1:18,19

Christ is head over re-creation. Christ is not only head over the original creation but also the new creation that comes to men via the Holy Spirit. Christ is the head of the church so that He has supremacy over all things. The sacrifice of Jesus on the cross restored peace between God and man. Jesus did this by taking the punishment we deserved.

TALK ABOUT IT:

Where do you see the gospel in today's passage? (Draw out your children so they tell you why they believe their answer is the gospel.)

When will we experience the reconciliation of all things, which Paul tells us will come through Christ? (The full restoration of peace will come when Jesus returns. Read Romans 8:18-25.)

PRAY:

Ask Jesus to come back soon and put an end to all sickness, sin, and death.

WEDNESDAY
WHERE IS THE GOSPEL?

THE STORY: COLOSSIANS 1:21-23

After introducing the peace that resulted from Christ's sacrifice on the cross in verse 20, Paul goes on to more fully describe this wonderful miracle. We were separated - alienated - from God as His enemies. Right from the very beginning with Adam and Eve, sin separated people from God. After sinning, Adam and Eve were afraid of God. Now, through the sacrifice of Jesus, people can be reconciled to God. Not only that, but also our sins can be taken away so that we are presented without blemish (that is, without sin). We who have been saved are then called to continue in faith and hope in the promise of the gospel.

TALK ABOUT IT:

What are people called before they believe in Christ? (They are called enemies of God.)

Why are we called enemies of God? (The evil in our hearts and our sinful behavior alienates us from God.)

What does Paul tell us we need to do to be saved? (We need to have firm faith and hope in the gospel. Faith requires that we have repented [turned away] from our sin and placed our trust in the sacrifice of Jesus.)

What is the gospel? (The gospel is the good news that we can be reconciled to God by faith in the atoning sacrifice of Jesus Christ. Do not tire of asking your children to recall the gospel. If a person is to be saved, it will be through the truth of the message we have in the gospel of Jesus Christ. Every person who has grown up surrounded by the truth of Christ, yet finds no application of that truth to their life, has either misunderstood truth or rejected the gospel outright.)

PRAY:

Ask God to help each member of your family trust and hope in Christ their whole lives.

THURSDAY

THE STORY: COLOSSIANS 1:20

All things will be reconciled by the blood of the cross. The entire creation was affected by the fall, which came when Adam sinned. Romans 8:20-22 tells us that all of creation was frustrated and affected by the fall. Paul goes on in that passage to tell us that one day the creation will be liberated from this curse of sin and destruction and that the creation "groans" for this to happen. This does not mean the creation is actually making noise but that it needs to be fixed. Just like a crooked picture on the wall seems to say, "Straighten me up," so the creation is in need of restoration. Here in Colossians 1:20 we see just how this "fix" will come. Not only does Christ's sacrifice reverses the curse of sin in the lives of those who believe, but it also reverses the curse that the sin of Adam brought upon the world. This will happen at the end of the age, when Jesus returns.

TALK ABOUT IT:

What will change when God re-creates the world? (There will no longer be any sun or moon or stars for light, for Jesus the lamb will be the light [see Isaiah 24:23 and Revelation 22:5]. Another big change is that there will be no more death or pain [see Revelation 21:4]. The animals will no longer hunt one another but live together peacefully [see Isaiah 65:25].)

What should encourage us about this passage? (This passage helps us to see just how wonderful the sacrifice of Jesus is. Because of what Jesus did, the whole world will be changed! That is something to look forward to! We get excited when we see a shooting star or by our first visit to the Grand Canyon. Imagine just how exciting it will be to see the whole world made new!)

PRAY:

Thank the Lord for the amazing work of the cross, which is able to change every heart and reverse the curse of sin.

FRIDAY
ON THE ROAD TO EMMAUS

THE STORY: PSALM 22:14-16

Jesus' hands and feet were pierced when He was nailed to the cross. When Thomas doubted, he insisted on seeing and touching the nail marks in Jesus; feet and hands (see John 20:25). These verses in Psalm 22 are a picture of the crucifixion of our Lord.

TALK ABOUT IT:

What other references to the suffering of Christ do you see in this passage? (Jesus sweated terribly and lost a great amount of blood from His flogging. In that way He was poured out like water. Jesus certainly would have had little strength left and He would have been badly dehydrated. Jesus expressed His thirst on the cross [see John 19:28].)

How does reading this prophetic passage point to God's sovereign control over the sacrifice of Jesus on the cross? (By forecasting events through the prophets, we see God is really in control. Nothing happens by chance. God delivered Jesus up to be crucified according to His predetermined plan.)

PRAY:

Thank the Lord for suffering on the cross in our place.

CHOSEN BEFORE THE WORLD BEGAN

God's salvation was planned before the world began.

MONDAY

THE STORY: EPHESIANS 1:1-6

Our salvation in Christ was always God's plan. Following Paul's greeting, the first substantial paragraph (Ephesians 1:3-10) is actually one long continuous sentence of praise that celebrates the plan and accomplishment of God in redemption through Christ. We learn some mind-bending truths in Paul's praise of God. We learn that God knew us before we were born; that He chose us in Christ before we were born; that He chose us to be adopted as sons through Jesus Christ; and that all this was according to God's pleasure and will. God was not surprised by the fall of Adam; He knew Adam would fall. God always planned for man's redemption to be through Jesus.

This truth can be very confusing because it seems that when the gospel is presented to us, we must choose to believe. That is true. To be saved, all men must choose to believe in God's saving plan. And yet, in the mystery of God, before we were born, or able to do any choosing, God chose us. God did not choose us based on our works, or His anticipation that we would choose him. God chose us according to His pleasure; that is, God firmly decided, according to His delight, that He would save sinners by the work of Christ!

TALK ABOUT IT:

Did God know us before we were born? (Yes, God knew us before we were born.)

What did God plan to do before we were born? (God planned to save sinners through the death of His Son, Jesus, and adopt them as sons and daughters into His family.)

Why did God do this? (First, it was God's will. God decided on salvation and just how it would be accomplished. It was His plan. Second, Paul tells us that God did this according to His pleasure. The Bible tells us that God sent Jesus out of love for us.)

PRAY:

Praise God for His qualities – He knows all things, controls all things, and is able to accomplish His plan. He is holy, wonderful, full of mercy, and all-powerful. Take time to exalt God just as Paul did in the opening of his letter to the Ephesians.

TUESDAY

THE STORY: EPHESIANS 1: 7-12

Christ's sacrifice was always God's plan. God didn't scramble to come up with a plan after Adam and Eve sinned. He wasn't wondering what He would do next. God never said, "Oh, no! Adam and Eve disobeyed - now what am I going to do?" Even before the fall of Adam and Eve, God's plan to restore fallen man and bring all things together was to sacrifice His Son. Each of God's children was chosen in Christ as part of God's plan. God chose the exact time for Jesus' birth and arranged for it to be foretold by the prophets and even symbolized through the sacrifices He instituted.

TALK ABOUT IT:

How did God plan to save fallen men? (God planned to send His Son, Jesus, to die on the cross for the sins of His people. God's plan was that Jesus would suffer and die in our place. We in turn would be called to trust in Christ Jesus for our salvation. All who believe in Jesus will be saved. All those whom God called will believe.)

Why does God choose to save some to be His children? (God chooses to save sinners because He loves them and it is His pleasure to do so.)

PRAY:

Thank God for His kindness in saving sinners and for sending His Son, Jesus, to die on the cross for us. Ask God to open the eyes of every member of your family to the truth of the gospel that they might believe.

WEDNESDAY
WHERE IS THE GOSPEL?

THE STORY: EPHESIANS 1:13,14

We, who were chosen in Christ before the world began, were included in Christ when we heard the gospel and believed. Though we are chosen, we are yet sinners until the appointed time where we hear and believe. The gospel is the message of salvation and is the power of our salvation. We hear it and believe. At the moment of salvation, God places His Spirit in us as a deposit and a guarantee of our full redemption, which will be experienced when sin will be removed and our sinful bodies will be changed into glorified bodies.

In Ephesians 1:7 we read, "In him (Christ) we have redemption through His blood, the forgiveness of our trespasses, according to the riches of His grace." This is the heart of the gospel. It is Christ's shed blood on the cross is the foundation of the forgiveness of sins for all those who "heard the word of truth, of the gospel of your salvation and believed in Him" (Ephesians 1:13).

Paul's introduction to the Book of Ephesians is a repetition of the basic facts of the good news. To this he adds that God's plan for us individually was known in the mind of God even before the foundation of the world (Ephesians 1:4).

TALK ABOUT IT:

What part does the gospel play in our salvation? (The gospel message is what we believe and place our trust in to be saved.)

Who comes to dwell in us when we are saved? (God places His Holy Spirit in us.)

Can Christians feel or sense that the Holy Spirit is in them? (Yes, that is why the Holy Spirit is a deposit and guarantee. If we could not sense the presence of the Spirit in our lives, there would be no way to have a guarantee. The Holy Spirit is the one who assures us that we are his sons and daughters; He is the one who excites affections for God and enables us to say no to sin; He is the one who helps us remember the Word and works of Christ. The Holy Spirit is to be an experienced reality in the life of the true Christian.)

PRAY:

Pray that God would save each person in your family and that He would place His Spirit in your hearts that you might know with all certainty that you will one day go to heaven and be with God forever.

THURSDAY

THE STORY: EPHESIANS 1:15-23

God's plan of salvation evokes thanksgiving and prayer. Every time we hear that someone has believed in Jesus Christ, we should rejoice in the same way Paul rejoiced over the salvation of the Ephesians. Paul's prayer also helps us know what we can pray for in our own lives. We should ask God to help us know

Him better through the Spirit, that our hearts might be enlightened to see our great inheritance, and that we might know the great power made available to all believers.

TALK ABOUT IT:
What do Paul's prayers tell us about how we grow as Christians? (We don't understand all about God when we become Christians. We grow in our faith and in our understanding of Him. There is always more to learn. Since God's power and knowledge are infinite [never ending], we will spend all of eternity learning and experiencing more of God and we will never run out of more things to learn about and experience.)

PRAY:
Take time to pray for the same things Paul prayed for.

FRIDAY
ON THE ROAD TO EMMAUS

THE STORY: PSALM 45:1,2
Although this psalm, used at weddings, may have been used to describe earthly kings, Jesus is the only most excellent of men that God has blessed forever. Connecting Psalm 45:2 to Jesus, Luke records in his Gospel (Luke 4:22) that after Jesus spoke at the synagogue, the people "all spoke well of Him and were amazed at the gracious words that came from his lips." Later verses of this psalm are also attributed to Christ in the Book of Hebrews. (Psalm 45:6,7 is quoted in Hebrews 1:8,9.)

TALK ABOUT IT:
What words help us know that only Jesus could be the one described by these verses? (It is describing a king who is the most excellent of men that God has blessed forever. Only Jesus fits that description.)

The writer of this psalm introduces the psalm by saying that his heart is stirred by a noble theme and that this psalm is actually the work of a skillful writer. Why is this true? (The writer, though he may not have realized it, was not just writing a song – he was writing Scripture. He was not just writing about a king, but the King of Kings. The stirring to write was the activity of the Holy Spirit.)

PRAY:

Thank God for the wonderful way He used men to write Scripture and provide us with His words.

FROM DEATH TO LIFE

Salvation is all by God's grace.

MONDAY

THE STORY: EPHESIANS 2:1-3

Apart from grace, men are dead in their sins. Paul makes it perfectly clear that as sinners, we were not reaching out to God. We were dead in our sins. A dead man cannot help himself. Instead of reaching out to God, we satisfied our sinful cravings and desires. This is true of all men, Gentiles and Jews alike. As a result, we were by nature objects of God's wrath. Any thought that we were seeking after God is shattered by Paul's words. Apart from God breathing life into us, we were hopelessly dead in our sin, in rebellion against God.

TALK ABOUT IT:

Why does the picture of a dead man leave no room for us to think we contributed to our salvation? (A dead man can do nothing whatsoever. He can contribute nothing to his cause.)

What does Paul mean when he says we were objects of God's wrath? (We were all deserving God's anger and punishment for our sin.)

PRAY:

Have each person confess in prayer that he is a sinner in need of the grace of God. Then ask God to pour out His Spirit on every member of your family.

TUESDAY

THE STORY: EPHESIANS 2:4-11

Salvation is by grace. After establishing that all men are dead in their sins, Paul introduces the mercy of God, which can bring a dead man back to life. While we were dead in our sins, God made us alive in Christ. We bring nothing to our salvation; it is all by grace through faith alone. No one can boast that he or she sought after God. As Christians, we are Christ's workmanship, created in Christ Jesus to do good works that God prepared for us to do.

TALK ABOUT IT:

Can any man take credit for his salvation? (No, no one can take even the slightest credit for salvation.)

Who is at the center of all the good we do? (God is at the center of all the good we do. It is God who gives us faith while we are dead. It is God who re-creates us. And it is God who prepared the good works we walk in as Christians. Our only boast is in Jesus!)

PRAY:

Take time as a family to thank God for the grace you see in each member of your family.

WEDNESDAY
WHERE IS THE GOSPEL?

THE STORY: EPHESIANS 2:11-18

Once we were far away, but through the blood of Christ we have been brought near. That is the gospel! Paul also refers back to the gospel when he tells us in Ephesians 2:5 that God made us alive with Christ even when we were dead in our sins. Jesus died on the cross for sinners – His enemies.

We were objects of God's wrath, but Jesus received the wrath of the Father in order that we, who deserved death, might be made alive in Christ! It is the work of Christ that saves us. This removes all boasting. There is nothing we can do to make ourselves perfect. We can only accept the perfect work of Jesus on the cross. As a result, it is not right to boast in our salvation, except in what Christ has done.

TALK ABOUT IT:

What did God do to bring near to Himself those who were far off? (He sent His Son, Jesus, to die on the cross for our sins that we might be reconciled to God.)

Who are the two groups of people Paul tells us were both brought near through the cross? (Paul is talking about the circumcised [Jews] and the uncircumcised [Gentiles]. There is only one way of salvation through Jesus Christ for all men, both Jew and Gentile.)

PRAY:

Thank God for making a way for us to be brought near to God.

THURSDAY

THE STORY: EPHESIANS 2:19-22

Those who are saved are the temple of God. Since all men who are saved receive the Spirit of God, we are all members of the same family of God. We call that family the church. Christ is the cornerstone of the church, and all together we are the temple of the Holy Spirit. In the Old Testament, God dwelt in a temple made by human hands, where only the high priest had access to the presence of God. Now, all Christians, both Jew and Gentile, are filled with the Spirit of God like living stones built into a spiritual house (see 1 Peter 2:5).

TALK ABOUT IT:

What do all Christians together form? (We form God's holy temple, where the Holy Spirit lives. He lives in each believer and together as a whole all those who have been saved make up the temple of God.)

What do we call this temple? (We call it the church. We often refer to the building we meet in as the church. It would be more accurate to say that it is the church building, because the church itself is the people inside.)

Are all Christians related to one another? (Yes, we are all God's children. When we are saved, we become a part of God's household. That is why Christians call each other brothers and sisters in Christ.)

PRAY:

Pray that God would touch the lives of each member of your family that they might become members of God's family.

FRIDAY
ON THE ROAD TO EMMAUS

THE STORY: ISAIAH 53:6

Isaiah announces that we all have turned to our own way. All men are sinners, having rejected God and rebelled against Him. Isaiah doesn't say that some have turned away. Nor does he say that many have turned away. Isaiah tells us that each of us has turned to his own way. Paul says it like this: "All of us also lived among them at one time, gratifying the cravings of our sinful nature and following its desires and thoughts" (Ephesians 2:3). Isaiah doesn't leave us hopeless in our sin, though. In Isaiah 53:6b, we read the good news: "The Lord laid on Him the iniquity (the sin) of us all." Jesus took the punishment for all of us who turned away. that we might be "brought near through the blood of Christ" (Ephesians 2:13).

TALK ABOUT IT:

How does Isaiah's prophecy match what Paul is telling the Ephesians in Ephesians 2? (Isaiah is saying that all have turned away from God. Paul tells us that all are dead in their sins, following thier own desires. Isaiah tells us that we are saved by God's plan to punish Jesus in our place. Paul tells us that we were saved by the blood of Jesus.)

What does Scripture mean when it says the Lord has laid on Him the iniquity of us all? (Jesus took all our sins upon Himself and received the wrath of God, the punishment for our sins. 2 Corinthians 5:21 says, "God made Him who had no sin to be sin for us, so that in Him we might become the righteousness of God.")

PRAY:

Thank God that He did not judge us when we went our own way, instead sending Jesus to die in our place.

THE GIFT OF MEN

God gave men as gifts to help the church mature and grow.

MONDAY

THE STORY: EPHESIANS 4:1-6

As Christians we are called to live lives worthy of our calling. After spending the first three chapters of his letter teaching the Ephesians of the magnificence of Christ and the power of His grace, Paul turns to apply this teaching to their everyday lives. Paul tells them that as followers of Christ, they should make every effort to live in peace and kindness with one another. Sin divides, but Paul appeals for unity on the basis that all Christians share the same hope, the same faith, the same Spirit, the same baptism, and the same Lord.

TALK ABOUT IT:

Why should Christians, of all people, be unified and at peace? (We are brothers and sisters in Christ. We are from the same family.)

Do you remember the sin that caused arguments among the disciples? (They argued about who was the greatest.)

Where do you find arguments and division in your own family? (Parents, draw out your children. Then explain to them that the very same sins present in their lives can also affect people in the church. Ask them how Paul's encouragement to be humble, gentle, patient, and loving can help keep unity and avoid sinful division.)

PRAY:
Ask the Lord to help you all demonstrate humility, gentleness, patience, and love toward one another.

TUESDAY

THE STORY: EPHESIANS 4:7-14

God gave us men to help us grow and walk worthy of our calling. Paul was aware that the command to live in unity is not going to be easy. He announces that God has given each believer the grace needed to live in unity and that He has also given us gifts to help us. Paul goes on to explain that these gifts are actually leaders - specifically, apostles, prophets, evangelists, and pastor-teachers.

The men called to these roles are given to the church to prepare God's people for service until we all reach unity and become mature in Christ. Until this happens, when we are with the Lord in heaven, God has given these ministries to the church.

TALK ABOUT IT:

What are the four kinds of leaders God has given to help us? (The four kinds of leaders are apostles, prophets, evangelists, and pastor-teachers.)

How are you helped by these men in your local church? (Parents, review with your children how these ministries operate in your local church.)

PRAY:

Thank God for the good gifts of men He has given to help us until we are mature in Christ.

WEDNESDAY
WHERE IS THE GOSPEL?

THE STORY: EPHESIANS 4:15,16

In Ephesians 4, Paul turns to the practical issue of obedience, but the cross remains at the center. Although we need to obey and help one another obey, we do it for Christ. Our fellowship is designed to help us grow up into Christ, "reach unity in the faith and the knowledge of the Son of God, and become mature, attaining to the whole measure of the fullness of Christ" (Ephesians 4:13). We do not obey to become Christians; we obey to become more like Christ!

TALK ABOUT IT:

Why should we try to live holy lives? (We live holy lives so that we can be more like Jesus, who saved us.)

What does it mean to speak truth in love? (Even though our goal is to avoid sinning, we are still sinners and we will still sin. Often we need others to help us know when we are straying from the path because we can be blind to our own wandering. When individuals correct us in love, using God's Word, they are speaking the truth in love to us.)

Should you speak the truth in love to others in your family? (Yes, we should all welcome correction and be willing to offer loving correction, without anger, to each other.)

PRAY:

Ask God to help your family offer correction in love, without anger. And ask God to help you receive correction from members of your family.

THURSDAY

THE STORY: EPHESIANS 4:17-19

Live holy lives in the goodness of God's grace. After telling them of the grace of God and the gift ministries of men, Paul exhorts the Ephesians to live holy lives. When he tells them to no longer live like the Gentiles, he means the unbelieving Gentiles who have hardened their hearts and lost their sensitivity. They have become so familiar with sin that they are no longer bothered in their conscience and have been completely given over to sin.

TALK ABOUT IT:

Is living for Christ optional or does Paul insist that we live for Christ? (Paul is firm: All Christians must not live like unbelievers.)

What are the unbelieving Gentiles doing wrong? (They are separated from the life of God. They are hardening their hearts and becoming desensitized to sin.)

Could this happen to us as believers? (Yes. If we stop spending time in God's Word or with other Christians, and harden our hearts, little by little we will compromise. Before we know it we are willfully sinning against God.)

What helps protect us from falling into sin? (We need to say "no" to sin and stay connected to other believers in the church. We need to encourage and help one another, speaking the truth in love. Knowing God's Word teaches us right from wrong and provides the help we need to avoid sinning. Psalm 119:11 says, "I have hidden Your Word in my heart that I might not sin against You.")

PRAY:

Ask God to help each member of your family grow in love for Christ and His church.

FRIDAY
ON THE ROAD TO EMMAUS

THE STORY: PSALM 68:18

Paul quotes Psalm 68:18 in Ephesians 4:8 and then he relates it to Christ. Paul tells us in Ephesians 4:9 that if Jesus ascended, He must have descended. In Philippians 2:1-7, Paul tells us about Jesus descending to earth to become "nothing, taking the nature of a servant, being made in human likeness." We know, of course, that Jesus ascended after His resurrection.

When Jesus left, he left victorious, having accomplished what He set out to do. He was victorious over His captives: Satan, sin, and death. The result of His victory is that He is able to give gifts to men. In Ephesians Paul uses this passage from Psalm 68 to speak of the ministries of apostle, prophet, evangelist, and pastor-teacher.

TALK ABOUT IT:

How is Jesus' example of "descending" a good example for us to follow? (See Philippians 2:5-8, where Paul tells us that we should have the same attitude as Christ, who humbled Himself and became a servant.)

What are the gifts we receive from Jesus, who has ascended? (In addition to the list in Ephesians 4:11, we could also say that we are given the gift of the Holy Spirit and the gifts of the Spirit.)

PRAY:

Thank the Lord for the gifts He has given us.

PUTTING OFF THE OLD SELF

Christians should imitate Christ in all they do.

MONDAY

THE STORY: EPHESIANS 4:20-24

Put off your old self. Paul tells the Ephesians to put off their old self (their sin) and to put on their new self. Each person who has been re-created by God has been recreated to be like Him in true righteousness and holiness. The power of sin has been broken, so we should strive to say "no" to sin and "yes" to righteousness. As Christians, we are called to live for Christ and not for ourselves or the unbelieving world around us.

TALK ABOUT IT:

What is the old self? (The old self is a way to describe people before the Holy Spirit entered their lives and broke the power of sin over them. Before God changes our hearts, we have only a sinful nature; we are slaves to sin, bound to live sinful lives.)

What is the new self? (The new self is our changed, new life in Christ. Jesus conquered sin so that we could be freed from the slavery of sin. Now that we are free, we have the ability to live like we are free, saying "no" to sin and "yes" to God.)

PRAY:
Ask the Lord to change each member of your family and help you put off the old self and put on the new self and live for Christ.

TUESDAY

THE STORY: EPHESIANS 4:25-32
Paul lists the "put off"s and "put on"s. Paul doesn't leave any room for confusion for the Ephesians. After telling them to put off the old self and put on the new, Paul lists a number of areas so that they understand just what he is talking about. They need to put off falsehood and speak truth, and put off stealing and put on work. Paul is aware of the dangers of legalism, which is trying to earn favor with God, so he reminds them that their motivation is Christ. Each time Paul mentions Christ, he is reminding them and us of the cross and our salvation in Christ.

TALK ABOUT IT:
Where does Paul bring Christ into these two paragraphs? (Help your children see the connection to the cross but leave Ephesians 5:1 for tomorrow's lesson.)

Why is it important to remember that our reason for obedience is found in what Christ has already done? (It is important that we remember that Jesus lived a perfect life and that His righteousness has been given to us. We could never make ourselves righteous by our works. As we battle sin and strive to live in a manner pleasing to God, it is with gratitude for what Jesus did. We are trying to be like Him. We are not trying to be good enough so as to earn God's favor. We are trying to be good because we already have God's favor. If we are trying to earn God's favor, it is like saying that Christ's perfect life and sacrifice were not good enough for us. It is not necessary to add our obedience to Christ's obedience. His obedience satisfies God's holy requirement without any help from us.

PRAY:

Pray that each member of your family stays near the cross as you work to put off your old self and live for God.

WEDNESDAY
WHERE IS THE GOSPEL?

THE STORY: EPHESIANS 5:1

Even though Paul challenged the Ephesians to live holy lives, putting off the old self, he never forgot the gospel of grace. Paul continually reminds the Ephesians that they are following Christ's obedience, not striking out on their own path. Notice that Christ willingly gave up His life for us. The men who crucified Jesus did not force death upon Him. Jesus could have called down angels in his defense.

TALK ABOUT IT:

Why is it important to never forget the gospel when we talk about following God? (The gospel is how we are reconciled to God, not by our works. We obey out of the new life Jesus gave us; we do not obey to earn new life.)

What does it say was the reason Christ died for us? (Christ's love for us was His motivation.)

PRAY:

Thank Jesus for willingly dying on the cross for us.

THURSDAY

THE STORY: EPHESIANS 5:2-20

After repeating the gospel clearly in Ephesians 5:1, Paul goes after our remaining sin with a vengeance. There must not even be a hint of sin! Paul is aware of the way that sin works. It begins with a little compromise, then a little more, until the whole person is given over.

Paul tells us we should live as children of light. Again and again Paul reminds the Ephesians of the gospel as the foundation for good works that follow.

TALK ABOUT IT:

What does it mean to live as children of the light? (Living as children of the light simply means we should follow God. He has changed us and placed His Holy Spirit in us. God is light, and all Christians have been brought into the kingdom of light as a result of believing in the work of Jesus on the cross. In the Bible, sin is portrayed as darkness. When we trust Christ and are born again, we are taken out of the world of darkness and sin; we are placed in the kingdom of light. So we should strive to live a life following Jesus.)

In what ways do you struggle most to live as children of the light? (Parents, take the lead in confessing your own struggles. Point out to your children that it is not possible to live for God unless you first submit to God by placing your trust in what Jesus has done. Remember, we do not obey to qualify for salvation; we obey because Jesus qualified for us. We do not obey to earn God's favor; we obey because we already have God's favor. We obey because we are saved, not to earn our salvation.)

PRAY:

Pray that each member of your family would confess their sins and submit to God believing the gospel and living as children of the light.

FRIDAY
ON THE ROAD TO EMMAUS

THE STORY: PSALM 44:22

Paul quoted this passage in Psalms in Romans 8:36 to describe the persecution that comes to Christians as a result of following Christ. Jesus said, "If they persecuted me, they will persecute you also" (John 15:20). Our persecution will be like His. Jesus was the sheep that was led to the slaughter (see Acts 8:32-34). Jesus was like a lamb that went silently without objection. Ephesians 5:1 tells us that Jesus went to the cross willingly out of love for us.

TALK ABOUT IT:

Do all Christians face death? (No, many Christians live in countries where there is no serious persecution. Even so, we all face ridicule for living righteous lives and saying no to sin. We will all face ridicule for sharing the gospel.)

How can the fear of man hinder us from following Christ? (We can be afraid of what people will say about us and as a result shy away from living for God or sharing the message of salvation with others. If there are Christians in persecuted countries willing to die for their faith, we should at least be willing to be ridiculed for ours.)

PRAY:

Ask God for the Holy Spirit to give us courage to live for Christ and proclaim our faith boldly.

THE ARMOR OF GOD

The gospel that saves us also arms us for battle.

MONDAY

THE STORY: EPHESIANS 6:1-3

In writing to the Ephesians, Paul takes time to address the children directly. He does not say, "Parents, tell your children to obey you." Paul assumes that children will be reading this letter, so he speaks directly to them. He reminds all children of God's commandment to obey their parents and that if they do, they will be rewarded with a long, prosperous life. The illustration of the armor of God, which ends Paul's book, seems to be custom-tailored for children and is an easy illustration to understand.

Notice also that Paul tells the children to obey their parents in the Lord. Apart from the saving work of Christ, children, just like adults, are hopelessly bound in their sins. The phrase "in the Lord" tells children that they should obey not merely because their parents say so, but because God says so. But now that Christ has come, "in the Lord" means much more than the law. Those three words must now include grace through Christ as well!

TALK ABOUT IT:

Why is the Lord mentioned in this verse? (Children are to obey their parents not just because their parents tell them, but because the Lord tells them. And in their own strength, they cannot obey as they should. They need the Lord to help them.)

PRAY:

Parents, take time to lay your hands on each of your children one at a time and ask God to give them the grace to follow God and obey His Word.

TUESDAY

THE STORY: EPHESIANS 6:10-14

We need spiritual armor for a spiritual war. We are not fighting against men, we are fighting against a spiritual enemy. Our enemy is evil and powerful. But God has given us what we need to defend ourselves against the enemy's attack. We have the armor of God. A normal sword cannot save us against a spiritual enemy. We need spiritual armor! If we use the armor God gives, He promises that we will be able to withstand the attack. The first two pieces of armor are truth and righteousness. Since the enemy's attack relies often on lies, for he is the father of all lies, we must remember the truth of God. It alone can sustain us.

Our enemy also comes at us with partial truth. One of the enemy's greatest schemes is to point out weakness and suggest we are unworthy. This, of course, is true! We are weak and unworthy. But we must remember that it is not our own righteousness we wear. Christ's righteousness protects us like a breastplate. When the enemy tells us we are weak, we can say, "Yes, but my Lord is strong." When the enemy tells us we are unworthy, we reply, "Right, but Jesus is worthy." When the enemy tells us we have no righteousness, we reply that we have the perfect righteousness of Christ (2 Corinthians 5:21).

TALK ABOUT IT:

Why would a soldier wear a belt? (In addition to keeping his pants on and his uniform secure, the soldier's belt held his offensive weapons as well, such as his sword or knife. All that we have depends on the truth of God's Word. The soldier who goes to battle without a belt would not be able to run for fear of his pants falling down. That makes him a fairly easy target for the enemy!)

What does the breastplate protect? (The breastplate protects our most vital organs - our heart and lungs. One blow to the heart or lungs can kill a man in a minute.)

Why is this good picture of our righteousness? (If we don't have Christ's righteousness, we cannot live and are condemned in our sin. The enemy could condemn us by simply reminding us of all the sins we committed. If, however, we have the righteousness of Christ in place, no amount of accusations, whether true or false, can affect us as we carry the unassailable righteousness of our Lord.)

PRAY:

Ask God to save each member of your family so that they would be wearing God's righteousness, which comes to us by faith in Christ.

WEDNESDAY
WHERE IS THE GOSPEL?

THE STORY: EPHESIANS 6:15

All the armor, from the belt of truth to the sword of the Spirit, is connected to the gospel. Each piece takes us back to the cross. The belt of truth is our security because we know the truth of God's plan to send His Son, Jesus, to die on the cross for our sins. As a result we receive His righteousness as a breastplate along with salvation in Christ as our helmet. Faith in Christ and His sacrificial death is our shield. The Spirit that God pours into us at conversion helps us to use the Word of God against the schemes of the enemy.

So why do we have the gospel of peace in the midst of the battle? Well, we are to love our enemies, and there is no greater demonstration of love than to share the gospel of peace. In the midst of our battle against Satan and against our own sinful nature, we always need to be ready to give a reason for our hope.

TALK ABOUT IT:
Why is the gospel called the gospel of peace? (Romans 5:1 tells us that because of what Jesus did, we have peace with God. Hebrews tells us we should make every effort to live in peace with all men [Hebrews 12:14]. The gospel restores peace with God and also helps bring peace with our fellow man.)

Who has God placed near your life whom you might share the gospel of peace with? (Parents, consider whom the Lord might have your family reach out to in order to share the gospel of peace.)

PRAY:
Pray for those you would like to reach with the gospel.

THURSDAY

THE STORY: EPHESIANS 6:16-20
The shield, helmet, and sword protect us. Paul continues with the description of the defensive armor by describing our shield of faith and the helmet of salvation. The gospel is able to fully protect us from any attack. A fully equipped soldier can defend himself well. We are well defended as we stand upon the truth of God's salvation in Christ.

The sword is an offensive weapon with which we attack and defeat those who come against us. Our attack is not with human strength or skill. Our attack is mounted by using the Word of God, which is powerful beyond human strength. Paul concludes by encouraging the Ephesians to pray and by asking for their prayers for his own battle with sin. Sometimes we can think that the men who wrote Scripture were perfect and without sin. But Paul was tempted to give in to fear and not use his sword as he should. If Paul needed to pray, then we certainly need to pray also.

TALK ABOUT IT:

How is the sword different from the other parts of the armor? (The sword is a weapon that can be used to attack. The other items of armor are mostly used to defend.)

How can the fear of man hold us back from using our sword as we declare the gospel? (We can be concerned with what people will think of us if we tell them the good news about Jesus. We sometimes live to please those around us rather than honor the Lord. We should not be afraid to invite someone to church or tell them about Jesus, but often we are.)

PRAY:

Pray that God would give each member of your family courage to share the gospel with others. Pray that God would keep you aware of opportunities to make Him known to those you meet.

FRIDAY
ON THE ROAD TO EMMAUS

THE STORY: PSALM 69:17-29

When Jesus was crucified, He was offered wine mixed with gall to drink. Then He was offered wine vinegar to quench his thirst. These two items are mentioned in the account of suffering from Psalm 69 (Matthew 27:34 and Matthew 27:48). Jesus was also scorned, disgraced, and shamed. Jesus found no sympathy, for even His Father in heaven forsook Him on the cross. This psalm is quoted in the New Testament as a prophetic picture of the Lord's suffering.

TALK ABOUT IT:

When we read Psalm 69 should we think about the suffering of David who wrote the psalm or of Christ and His suffering? (We should consider David, but then quickly turn our attention to Christ. This psalm, like all the others, is designed to point to Jesus. Apart from Christ, all the stories of the scriptures are just stories.)

Why should the suffering of Christ increase our gratitude and thankfulness? (We can sometimes become too familiar with the cross and forget the genuine suffering that Christ endured for us. Thinking about every aspect of the suffering of Christ, even the small details like being offered vinegar when you are thirsty, can help us to appreciate what a great salvation we have.)

PRAY:

Praise the Lord for His willingness to suffer and die in our place.

THE HUMILITY OF CHRIST

Christ is our example and our motivation for godly living.

MONDAY

THE STORY: PHILIPPIANS 2:1-4

Consider others better than yourself. Paul's command that we live in humility, considering others better than ourselves, flows from the gospel. Good works need to flow out of our love for Christ and what He did for us on the cross. Paul makes that perfectly clear. Our obedience comes from the encouragement of being united with Christ. Our comfort comes from His love and our fellowship with the Spirit of God. When our obedience flows out of our love for Christ, obedience is not a hardship but a joy, and our obedience in considering others better than ourselves results spreads that joy to them as well.

TALK ABOUT IT:

How does thinking about what God did for us motivate us to live for God? (The Bible tells us in 1 John 4:19 that we love others because God first loved us. It is Christ's sacrifice that frees us from our sin, and Christ's example teaches us the path of righteousness.)

When we are selfish, what are we forgetting about God? (We can be sure that in the moment of our selfishness, we have forgotten the great sacrifice of Jesus on our behalf and are not enjoying His abundant grace.)

When are you most tempted to think of yourself and forget the sacrifice of Jesus? (Parents, lead with your own confession and then draw out your children.)

PRAY:
Ask God to help each member of your family remember the sacrifice of Christ as we work to live unselfish lives.

TUESDAY

THE STORY: PHILIPPIANS 2:5-7
Christ is our example in humility. This passage first confirms the deity of Christ and the harmony within the Godhead. There is no competition between the Father and the Son. Jesus willingly emptied Himself of glory and took on the nature of man. He never ceased to be God while laying aside His glory to take on the body of a man. In His high priestly prayer, Jesus confirmed the setting aside of His glory when He prays: "Glorify Me in Your presence with the glory I had with before the world began" (see John 17:5).

Paul tells us to look to Christ's example of humility and follow His willingness to make Himself nothing.

TALK ABOUT IT:
Why is the example of Christ's humility a good one? (When Jesus left his place of glory as God to become a man, it was a greater demonstration of humility than we could ever demonstrate.)

When are you most tempted to think of yourself over others? (Parents, lead with your own confession and then draw out your children.)

PRAY:
Ask the Lord to help you follow His example and live for Him.

WEDNESDAY
WHERE IS THE GOSPEL?

THE STORY: PHILIPPIANS 2:8

Jesus gave up the glory of heaven to come down to earth and become a servant. Philippians 2:8 tells us that He became obedient to death, even death on a cross. God, the creator of the universe, humbled Himself and took our punishment upon Himself. Jesus was fully God and fully man. Because of His deity, not being born in sin, He could remain utterly sinless and perfectly obedient. Because of His humanity, He could take our place upon the cross as a man and absorb the wrath our sin deserved.

TALK ABOUT IT:

Why was it important for our salvation that Jesus became a man? (It was man that deserved punishment and it was the sins of man that Jesus took upon Himself. When Jesus became a man, He became our representative. As our representative, He was able to stand in for us and receive our punishment. In Romans 5:19, Paul said "For just as through the disobedience of the one man [Adam] the many were made sinners, so also through the obedience of the one man [Jesus] the many will be made righteous.")

Why was the cross the greatest demonstration of the humility of Christ? (The Bible tells us that anyone who is hung on a tree is cursed of God. For Jesus to die on the cross would mean for Him to be cursed by his Father. The sinless Christ should never have been subjected to such humiliation. He did it out of love for us.)

PRAY:

Thank Jesus for His willingness to endure the suffering of the cross for our benefit.

THURSDAY

THE STORY: PHILIPPIANS 2:9-11

God exalted Christ over all. Because of Christ's unmatched humility and obedience in dying on the cross, God exalted Him to the highest place and made the name of Jesus unmatched in greatness. One day every knee will bow and recognize the kingship of Christ. On that day no one will stand in opposition before Him. Even those who denied Christ in this life will know and confess to their shame that Jesus Christ is Lord. We who have been saved will know Him as the author of our salvation. But those who rejected him will know Him as the eternal judge who sentences them to eternal fire. The gospel opens our eyes that we might worship Him freely without fear of judgment.

TALK ABOUT IT:

What did God do as a result of Jesus humbling Himself? (God exalted Jesus to the highest place.)

What does God promise to do for us when we humble ourselves? (God promises to give us grace and exalt us as well [see James 4:6 and Matthew 23:12].)

How can knowing this help us remain humble? (If we know God will take care of exalting us, we don't need to try and exalt ourselves. If we simply serve others and leave the exalting to God, we will one day be rewarded for our service. Living for a future reward is encouraged by God in the Bible, as long as we are willing for that reward to come to us in heaven and not on this earth. We are to live for heavenly treasure and reward.)

PRAY:

Pray that God would help each member of your family live a humble life in service to others.

FRIDAY
ON THE ROAD TO EMMAUS

THE STORY: PSALM 72:11-19

This passage in the book of Psalms is remarkably similar to the exaltation of Christ in Philippians 2:9-11. Both speak of knees bowing before the Lord and the exaltation of His name. Both end with the praise and glory of God being lifted up. Jesus is clearly the king mentioned in this psalm.

TALK ABOUT IT:

What other similarities to Jesus do you see in this psalm? (Parents, draw your children out. They should notice that Jesus took pity on the weak and the needy, that He saved us all from death, etc.)

How does this psalm affect your thoughts and heart? (Draw out your children. If they say they do not know, have them think about it in their own personal devotions. Tell them to place their name in the text to personalize it. For example, "He will deliver Marty who cries out," and "He will take pity on Emily who is weak and save her from death.")

PRAY:

Thank God for Jesus, who was willing to die on the cross for our sins so that we could be saved from death.

KEEP YOUR EYES ON THE PRIZE

All law keeping, accomplishments, and merit are rubbish compared to Christ.

MONDAY

THE STORY: PHILIPPIANS 3:4b - 7

All religious works are worthless apart from Christ. Paul had every reason to boast about his religious accomplishments. Not only was he born a Jew, but he also followed the law given by God almost perfectly. He was a man so full of zeal that he persecuted Christians, who he believed threatened to undermine the Jewish traditions given by God.

Once God opened his eyes to see how inadequate his works really were in comparison to the work of Christ, Paul gladly gave up everything he was counting on for salvation. He considered it a loss. He basically gave up his occupation as a Jewish religious leader on the spot. In its place he gained a much greater calling. Instead of being an instructor of legalism, Paul became an instructor of grace!

TALK ABOUT IT:

Why are religious works worthless apart from Christ? (Nothing we could ever do, no matter how good, could take away the evil we have already done. In addition, none of our works, no matter how good they appear, are free from the stain of sin. Our motives are mixed with sin apart from Christ because we are looking, in some measure, to glorify ourselves and not the Lord.)

What kinds of things might some people do to try to make themselves feel or look more holy? (Every religious work, whether praying, reading our Bibles, or even going to church, can all be done for the wrong reasons. We should do those things because we want to glorify God, not so that we can be religious or holy or feel better about ourselves.)

PRAY:

Pray that God would save every member of your family so that you can pursue Christ with the same kind of passion Paul had.

TUESDAY

THE STORY: PHILIPPIANS 3:8,9

All accomplishments are rubbish compared to gaining Christ. Paul didn't stop with his religious works. He went on to say that he considered everything a loss compared to knowing Jesus. Often we find our identity and motivation in our gifts, knowledge, or accomplishments in life. If a person is a good football player, for instance, he might be tempted to think he is something special because of his ability to play well. Paul realized, though that our boasting in anything but Christ is sinful. It is not that our gifts, talents or accomplishments are bad, but they should not define us. Compared to Christ, Paul tells us they are rubbish. The word for "rubbish" means the scraps thrown to the dogs at the end of a feast.

TALK ABOUT IT:

Does Paul say our accomplishments are worthless? (Yes, but only in comparison to Christ. Paul is not saying we should stop doing good things. We should do all things for the glory of God.)

What accomplishments, gifts, or talents in your life tempt you to think you are special? (Parents, take the opportunity to answer first. We all like to take pride in what we do. Recognizing where these temptations are strongest can help us fight them.)

PRAY:
Pray that God would help you find your identity in Christ and His accomplishments on the cross instead of what you have done yourself.

WEDNESDAY
WHERE IS THE GOSPEL?

THE STORY: PHILIPPIANS 3:10, 11

Paul speaks as one who has endured much suffering for the sake of Christ. Rather than complain at the end of his days, Paul sees his own struggle through the lens of the gospel. Jesus suffered and died, and then He rose again. Paul reverses this order, placing resurrection before suffering. This is the path of all believers. First, we experience the joy of being saved to newness of life before we share in the sufferings of our Lord. We, like Paul, should not be surprised at suffering. It is a part of the path of every Christian - some certainly greater than others. Christ is the focus of Paul's life, and we only need to read a few sentences of Paul's letter to the Philippians to see the message of the gospel woven in again and again.

TALK ABOUT IT:

Are all men called to suffer for Christ? (Yes. First we are called, like Christ, to deny ourselves the passing pleasures of sin. Then, like Christ, we are to proclaim truth to an unbelieving world. Some will reject us and our message. Some may also suffer physical persecution and even death for the sake of our Lord and the gospel.)

When will we experience the fullness of the power of Christ's resurrection? (We will experience the resurrection the moment we die and go to heaven to be with our Lord. In that moment we will know. We will see Him!)

PRAY:

Pray that God gives grace to every member of your family to live for Christ until the day you rise to be with Christ.

THURSDAY

THE STORY: PHILIPPIANS 3:12-14

All of our future is defined by pursuing Christ. Paul's greatest desire was to know more about Jesus. He left all his accomplishments behind and pressed forward toward Christ. Our prize is heaven with Jesus. So we should live in such a way that we keep our destination, heaven with Christ, in view. When we keep heaven in view, earthly accomplishments and treasures do not easily tempt us. Paul was quick to mention that he was not perfect. Like us, he still struggled with sin. Paul pressed on to know Christ, realizing that one day he would see Jesus.

TALK ABOUT IT:

Can you remember a time when you were excited about something that would happen in the future? (Help your children remember. Perhaps they looked forward to a vacation, getting their training wheels off their bikes, or finishing a school year.)

Why should we be just as excited about our future with Christ? (We have so much to look forward to in heaven. There will be no sickness, no sin, no pain, and no tears. We will see Jesus and will rejoice with all the Christians who have gone before us.)

PRAY:

Pray that God would give each member of your family an increasing eagerness to be with Christ.

FRIDAY
ON THE ROAD TO EMMAUS

THE STORY: PSALM 34:8

Peter quotes this verse (1 Peter 2:3) as a way to describe our conversion. Jesus is our refuge from sin, and when we place our trust and hope in Him, we find refuge from judgment and death. In Christ we have life, joy, peace, and hope everlasting. By trusting in Christ we have forgiveness. There could be no greater taste of goodness than being freed from the punishment we deserve.

TALK ABOUT IT:

What does it mean to take refuge in something? (When we take refuge, we are looking for protection or shelter from some pending danger. If a tornado were reported to be traveling in your direction, you might take refuge in your basement or a secure room in the middle of your home.)

How do we take refuge in Christ? (Jesus saves us from the wrath of God we deserve for our sin. In Christ we have refuge from that judgment and from eternal death and hell.)

PRAY:

Thank the Father for sending His Son to be our refuge.

CHARACTER COUNTS

Leaders in the church lead by example.

MONDAY

THE STORY: 1 TIMOTHY 3:1-7

Pastors must be above reproach. Some of the instructions that Paul gave Timothy were given to help him watch over the local churches under his care. Timothy, helped Paul care for the local churches that sprung up from Paul's gospel preaching. One of Timothy's responsibilities was to establish leaders in those local churches. Paul wanted Timothy to be certain that any man desiring to lead the church be qualified to do so. Nearly all of the qualifications Paul mentioned relate to a man's character. The only qualification that has to do with a man's gifting is that he be "able to teach." Pastors must have very godly character to qualify to lead the church!

TALK ABOUT IT:

Why must a pastor have godly character? (All the people in the church should follow the pastor's example. If he doesn't have godly character, he should not try to lead others in godliness.)

Why does a pastor need to manage his own family well? (If he cannot lead his family, a small group of people, how can he lead the church, a larger group of people? To use an analogy, if a man finds it difficult to juggle three balls, he certainly won't be able to juggle five balls well at all!)

PRAY:

Take time to pray for your pastor. Pray that God would pour out grace on him and his family to live godly lives in service to Christ and the church.

TUESDAY

THE STORY: 1 TIMOTHY 3:8-13

Other leaders (in addition to pastors) and their wives must be worthy of respect. Not only must the pastors in the church live godly lives, but the other leaders and the wives of leaders must lead godly lives as well. Just as the pastors are examples to the leaders they train, the other leaders are an example to the congregation. Paul understood that we grow, in part, by imitating other godly people. He said, "Follow my example, as I follow the example of Christ." All leaders must live lives worthy of emulating, and if they fail, they should be willing to yield leadership to others better qualified. Paul also connects godly living with faith in Christ. Although we don't do good works to earn our salvation, good works are a product of our salvation. If a person claims to have faith, but has no works, James says that such faith is worthless and dead (James 1:26 and 2:17).

TALK ABOUT IT:

Why is following by example a good way to learn? (It is a lot easier to watch someone do something and then do it than it is to read about it in a book. Imagine reading in a book how to hold a baseball bat. It is much easier to watch someone hold a bat and imitate him.)

Why does Paul hold a leader responsible for his children's behavior? (Parents are responsible to teach their children. Their children's behavior is a reflection on the way leaders and their wives have led in their home.)

PRAY:

Pray for the pastor and the other leaders in your church. Ask God to pour out His grace on them, their wives, and their children.

WEDNESDAY
WHERE IS THE GOSPEL?

THE STORY: 1 TIMOTHY 3:16

At the conclusion of Paul's exhortation to leaders and the church, Paul lists a confession of the mystery, or revealed secret, of godliness. Living godly lives can be a challenge. So Paul gives us the one key piece of information we need: Jesus.

Jesus, who took on human flesh, was proven true by the working of the power of the Spirit of God. He accomplished the salvation of all men, which is now preached and believed among the nations. When His mission was completed, He was taken up in glory. Though the presentation was poetic, it was the gospel nonetheless.

Jesus said in Matthew 16:18, "I will build My church and the gates of hell will not prevail against it." He loves the church, gaving His life to save the lost and bring them into His church family. He is the chief shepherd, and all the leaders under Him must be able to lead by example so that those for whom He died will be well cared for. If it were not for Christ's death on the cross, which brings us redemption, there would be no church and no need for godly leaders.

TALK ABOUT IT:

What did Paul say that helps us know He is talking about Jesus? (Paul says that He was preached among the nations and believed and taken up in glory. Jesus fits that description better than anyone.)

Why is Jesus the mystery of godliness? (Prior to Christ, men would have thought the way to holiness was following the law. In the Bible a mystery is a truth that was hidden, but is now revealed or known. Our righteousness comes from Jesus, and our strength to obey comes from His grace, not the law. Jesus revealed the mystery, or the secret, of a righteousness that is by faith and of obedience empowered by grace.)

PRAY:
Thank God that we don't have to rely on our own strength to obey or on our own works to be righteous.

THURSDAY

THE STORY: 1 TIMOTHY 3:14,15

The congregation must follow the example of its leaders. When we read through the qualifications for leadership in 1 Timothy 3, we should not use this to judge our leaders, but to judge ourselves. When Paul summarizes these instructions, he tells Timothy that he is giving them to Timothy so that "people" will know how to behave. He does not gave them just to leaders. Paul's goal is that we all would live godly lives. We are to all set a worthy example for others to follow. It is much easier to lead a godly life if everyone around you is leading a godly life.

TALK ABOUT IT:

How many of the qualifications for leaders apply to our lives? (All of them apply to everyone. We should all desire to live godly lives, and just about everyone is going to be called to teach someone. Even a small child will grow up to teach his younger brothers and sisters.)

Which of the qualifications on the list do you most struggle with? (Parents, lead by confessing your weaknesses first and then draw out your children.)

PRAY:

Pray for your leaders, their wives, and their children.

FRIDAY
ON THE ROAD TO EMMAUS

THE STORY: PSALM 144:1-4

The words in verse three are almost identical to the words of Psalm 8:4 and are quoted in Hebrews 2:6. Jesus is the Son of Man spoken of here. Jesus is also our Rock and our Deliverer. Jesus used the title Son of Man to describe Himself on multiple occasions. See Matthew 12:32 and Matthew 26:64.

TALK ABOUT IT:

Where do you see Jesus in Psalm 144:2? (Have your children look at the verse, encouraging them to reason for themselves.)

What does Jesus deliver us from? (Jesus died on the cross for our sin to deliver us from evil, the bondage of sin, and the punishment of sin.)

PRAY:

Thank God for sending the Son of Man to deliver us from our sin and eternal punishment.

GOD BREATHED THE SCRIPTURES

The Scriptures are able to carry us through times of evil and trial.

MONDAY

THE STORY: 2 TIMOTHY 3:1-9

There will be terrible times in the last days. Paul wrote this letter to Timothy from prison in Rome believing that his execution was close at hand (see 4:6). Paul warned Timothy, who was in Ephesus, about the evil that he is sure to confront in his ministry. As Timothy continued caring for the young churches, Paul wanted him to be aware of the evil around him, that he might guard against it and protect the church.

TALK ABOUT IT:

Are we in the last days? (Yes, we are in the last days and will be until Jesus returns.)

Is there evil today like the evil Paul describes? (Yes we have the same evil around us, but children are often protected from knowing much about it by their parents.)

Why is disobedience to parents on the list with these other sins? (Children sometimes falsely assume that disobedience to their parents is not serious. In fact, disobedience by children toward their parents is wicked in the sight of God. That is why children need to repent of their sin and turn to Jesus. They are just as much in need of a Savior as adults.)

PRAY:
Pray that we would see the evil in our own hearts and cry out to God for forgiveness through Jesus Christ.

TUESDAY

THE STORY: 2 TIMOTHY 3:10-15

God's word is an anchor in terrible times. After painting a pretty dark picture of sin, Paul contrasted the wickedness of the world with the righteousness that comes to God's people. Paul offered his own life as a testimony of God's grace and then encouraged Timothy. In the midst of great evil and persecution, God's grace would be available through Scripture which is God-breathed.

Although men wrote scripture, God spoke through men so that they wrote the words God wanted them to write. God breathed the scriptures by his Holy Spirit. Peter spoke of it this way: "Above all, you must understand that no prophecy of Scripture came about by the prophet's own interpretation. For prophecy never had its origin in the will of man, but men spoke from God as they were carried along by the Holy Spirit," 2 Peter 1:20,21.

As a result of God directing the process, scripture is not the mere words of men. It is the actual words of God to us. That is why reading the scriptures sustains us and serves as an anchor in terrible times.

TALK ABOUT IT:

What does Paul mean when he tells us scripture is God-breathed? (Draw your children out about how it could be that, even though men wrote scripture, God is the author. Use the analogy of a pen. Write something with a pen and ask them if the pen wrote the lines. Of course, the pen did make the marks, but you used the pen as an instrument to write your words. Men, in a manner of speaking, were the "pens" of God.)

How do the scriptures help us in terrible times? (The scriptures can fill us with hope; correct us if we start to follow and evil path and strengthen us so that we are equipped to do good works even in the worst of times.)

PRAY:
Thank God for giving us His Word.

WEDNESDAY
WHERE IS THE GOSPEL?

THE STORY: 2 TIMOTHY 3:15
The scripture is God-breathed and is able to lead us into righteousness. It is able to "make you wise for salvation through faith in Christ Jesus." The purpose of the scripture, all of the Old Testament and New Testament, is to point to the salvation available through Christ's death on the cross. Jesus told His disciples on the road to Emmaus how the Old Testament pointed to him (see Luke 24:27). The Bible is not first a book of rules, but a book of faith. Salvation does not come by works, but by faith (see Ephesians 2:9).

TALK ABOUT IT:
When did Timothy first begin to hear the scriptures? (Timothy first heard the scriptures as a very small child.)

What does Paul say the scripture is able to do in the midst of difficult times? (The scripture is able to make us wise for salvation through faith in Jesus Christ.)

Will the scripture do the same for us today? (Yes, that is why it is so important for us to train our children from an early age in the scripture. The only hope anyone has, is to be convinced of the Gospel and place their trust in Jesus Christ.)

PRAY:
Pray that God would use the scripture to touch the lives of all the children of your family.

THURSDAY

THE STORY: 2 TIMOTHY 3:16,17

The ministry of the Word sustains the church in terrible times. Paul finishes his exhortation to Timothy by charging him to preach the Word. Paul opened his letter to Timothy charging him to guard the good deposit of sound doctrine (2 Timothy 1:14) and that theme continues here. If we believe that the Bible is God's Word, able to sustain us in terrible times, then the only logical thing to do is to proclaim it!

Paul first encouraged Timothy personally and here instructs Timothy to care for the church and to do the work of an evangelist, preaching to unbelievers. Clearly Paul has in mind the time he spent proclaiming the word of God to combat false doctrines that threatened to corrupt the church.

TALK ABOUT IT:

What is sound doctrine? (Sound doctrine is the accurate teaching of the Bible. Doctrines are the truths the Bible teaches. Doctrine includes truths like the fact that Jesus was both God and man; that he lived a sinless life and that he rose from the dead. The word "sound" means true or trustworthy and accurate.)

Why do men reject sound doctrine? (Sin would love to convince us that we can do what we want. If we preach sound doctrine it tells us that our sin is wrong. If we change what we preach to allow us to continue in our sin, we don't feel as bad. People want their teachers to encourage them. Take giving for example. The Bible teaches us that we should give money to God and others. That is not good news to the sin of greed in our hearts. Wouldn't it be easier for a rich man if His pastor taught that God wanted all men to be rich in money, instead of teaching them that God wants all men to be rich toward God? If we maintain sound doctrine we cannot change what the Bible says.)

PRAY:
Lift up your pastors in prayer and ask God to help them preserve and proclaim sound doctrine in your church.

FRIDAY
ON THE ROAD TO EMMAUS

THE STORY: ISAIAH 59:20,21
Paul refers to this passage in Romans 11:26-27. Jesus is the Redeemer who will come to Zion. The covenant spoken of is the New Covenant in Jesus blood that he introduced at the last supper. "In the same way, after the supper he took the cup, saying, "This cup is the new covenant in my blood, which is poured out for you." (Luke 22:20).

Notice also the promise God makes to sustain His Word. The words of Isaiah and the words of Christ have been written down for us to read and embrace. We are some of the descendants God is speaking about. His Word will carry on forever!

TALK ABOUT IT:
When will God's Word depart and no longer be needed? (God's Word is eternal and carries on forever.)

Did you know the Bible talks about you? (Yes, we are included when the Bible mentions "the mouths of their descendants". Each time we proclaim God's word we are helping to keep God's word alive forever.)

PRAY:
Ask God to help you believe His Word and then proclaim His Word.

THE HEART'S DESIRES

Sinful desires lead us away from God.

MONDAY

THE STORY: JAMES 4:1-2

Sinful desires lie at the root of conflict. James gives us a wonderful look into the heart of every man. He tells us that our quarrels and fights spring from sinful desires. We want something but we don't get it. We like to blame sin on our situation, but James places responsibility for our behavior in our hearts.

We might say, for example, "I needed to get a good grade, so that's why I cheated." Or we like to blame others as if they are responsible for our sin: "You make me so angry!" Sometimes we excuse our sin because of hardship or suffering: "I spoke harshly because I was tired."

James cuts through our excuses and goes right for the heart. We sin because we don't get what we want. In our hearts we want money, we want control, or we crave comfort and ease. The Bible says that these kinds of desires, though not always bad in themselves, can rise to sinful heights and lead to sinful behaviors. When that happens, inordinate desires wrestle for control against God's Spirit within us.

TALK ABOUT IT:

Do you have quarrels and fights? (Everybody does, but it is good to admit that we do and see our own lives in this text.)

What sinful desires do you have within you? (Parents, help your children look for the root causes that lead to their arguments and quarrels. For example, an inordinate desire for candy can lead to fights between siblings. Remember, if they have quarrels and fights, there are sinful "wants" at work in their lives.)

PRAY:

Pray that God would help you not to blame your circumstances for your sin.

TUESDAY

THE STORY: JAMES 4:3

Sinful desires lead to selfish prayers. If we don't check our sinful desires, soon we will be asking God to bless them and give us what we sinfully long for. We treat God as though He were a servant to our desires instead of the other way around. God wants us to pray according to His will, not for what we want for our own pleasure.

God is not required to answer our prayers. He will always hear our prayers, but He will not always answer our prayers. When God doesn't grant our selfish requests He is actually loving us. Think of it this way: We tend to love worldly things instead of God. For example, the Bible says we cannot love both God and money. If God were to grant a request for a lot of money, He may be helping us on a path away from the love of God.

TALK ABOUT IT:

What kinds of things do men desire sinfully? (The desire for just about anything, even good things. can become sinful. Money is not evil; wanting money more than God is evil. Football or other sports are not evil, but loving them more than God is.)

What kinds of things have you desired sinfully? (Parents, help your children here. You are probably more aware of what sinfully drives them than they are. If you can't think of anything, just go back to James' key verse. What have they quarreled after?)

PRAY:

Have each person in your family confess their sinful desires and then ask the Lord to help your family want Him, his kingdom, and his righteousness above all else.

WEDNESDAY
WHERE IS THE GOSPEL?

THE STORY: JAMES 4:4

In James 4:4, James gives this rebuke: "You adulterous people." This is not because the people were struggling in the area of physical adultery (stealing someone else's wife or husband) but because they had turned to other loves. Scripture compares our relationship with the Lord to a marriage. When we turn to idols, it is like turning to another husband or wife. It is adultery against God.

This is a serious sin because God has demonstrated His love in the most profound way — by sending his own Son to take the punishment for our sins. When we covet something in the world, we are rejecting God's love and the relationship He extends to us in Christ. God wants our pleasures, our desires, and our love to be focused upon Christ.

TALK ABOUT IT:

Why is loving other things instead of loving God such a serious sin? (God sent Jesus to die for us. If we turn to worldly things, we are rejecting Jesus.)

Are the things we turn to bad? (Sometimes they are bad, such as taking illegal drugs to feel good, but often they are not bad in themselves. It is not wrong, for instance, to play a computer game. But it is wrong to love computer games so much that if someone says we are not allowed to play, we get angry and say unkind things.)

PRAY:

Ask God to help you recognize when you are loving other things more than Him.

THURSDAY

THE STORY: JAMES 4:6-12

God's grace comes to those who repent. What a joy to know that if we humble ourselves, God will pour grace into our lives. Paul told Titus, "For the grace of God that brings salvation has appeared to all men. It teaches us to say 'No' to ungodliness and worldly passions, and to live self-controlled, upright and godly lives in this present age, while we wait for the blessed hope — the glorious appearing of our great God and Savior, Jesus Christ" (Titus 2:12-14).

When we humble ourselves, we receive God's grace. We need His grace to resist the devil and our own sinful desires. James tells us to repent and draw near to God. Then he promises that God will respond by drawing near to us.

TALK ABOUT IT:

What stands in our way of receiving God's grace? (Pride stands in our way. It can make us refuse to admit that the object of our desire has become an idol.)

What does James say we should do? (We should humble ourselves, demonstrate godly sorrow and draw near to God.)

How does pride keep you from admitting your weakness? (Parents, help your children recall their sinful responses to your correction. Help them to see pride at work in their lives. Keep the category of pride alive in your home this week. Point it out when you see it at work in their lives.)

PRAY:

Ask God to give you the grace you need to repent of your pride and humble yourself before the Lord.

FRIDAY
ON THE ROAD TO EMMAUS

THE STORY: PSALM 22:7,8

Psalm 22 details the suffering and crucifixion of our Lord with amazing accuracy. It is astonishing to consider that this psalm was written hundreds of years before the birth of Christ. In this passage we see that it even predicts what the mockers would say to our Lord when He was crucified.

TALK ABOUT IT:

Read Matthew 27:39-43. How are the two passages similar? (Draw out your children regarding obvious similarities.)

What does seeing this kind of detail prophesied hundreds of years before the event tell us about the sovereignty of God? (God does not simply know about what is going to happen. He knows exactly what is going to happen and is in control of all things, down to the last word!)

PRAY:

Thank God for His amazing, sovereign control over all things.

BORN AGAIN!

Salvation in Christ is the sovereign plan of God to save His own.

MONDAY

THE STORY: 1 PETER 1:1,2

God's People have been chosen. Peter opens his letter with a blessing to the Gentile believers scattered throughout Asia and the surrounding lands. In these first two verses, he summarizes the whole of his letter. God's people are not primarily identified by nationality, or by their works. They are chosen people — chosen according to the knowledge of God.

From eternity past, God knew His people and His saving work through which they would become His people. God's choice of His family was not based on a future view of their good works. He chose His own out of love. The Gentiles were not an afterthought to a plan for the nation of Israel gone bad. All of God's people, whether Jews like Peter, or Gentiles like Cornelius, were known to God in Christ from eternity past.

Knowing God's sovereign choice in election should cause us to repent of our sins. Those who falsely think they control their own salvation may think they can sin for a while now and choose to follow God later. But the Bible warns against this. Today is the day of salvation; if you hear His voice, do not harden your heart but repent and believe for the salvation of your souls. Those who repent and place their trust in Christ are believers saved by God's grace through their faith. Those who reject God are lost.

TALK ABOUT IT:

When did Peter first realize that God's eternal plan included the Gentiles? (Peter first learned this when God gave him the vision of a large sheet coming down with both clean and unclean animals; God told him to take and eat. Read through the account in Acts 10 and focus on verses 34 and 35.)

Did God always know His chosen people? (Yes, Being all-knowing, God always knew those He chose to be His people.)

How can we be sure that God chose us? (Our only hope is to repent of our sin and believe in Jesus Christ. If we place our trust in Christ, we will be saved. If we reject Christ, we are lost.)

PRAY:

Pray that every member of your family will repent of their sin and trust in Christ.

TUESDAY

THE STORY: 1 PETER 1:3-5

God's people have been born again. Peter is writing to Christians who will soon suffer persecution under Nero of Rome. To encourage them, Peter reminds them that their salvation is in Jesus Christ, who gave them new birth through His death, the "sprinkling of blood," and His resurrection. Peter then moves on to remind them of their inheritance in Christ, which can never be lost. No matter what earthly trials we endure, we have the hope of heaven with Christ. An inheritance that will never spoil or fade awaits us.

TALK ABOUT IT:

Can you think of another verse that talks about being born again? (In John 3:3, Jesus said to Nicodemus, "I tell you the truth, no one can see the kingdom of God unless he is born again.")

How did Peter encourage the Christians he was writing to? (Peter lifted their eyes to their heavenly hope and their inheritance. He also told them that until that day, they were being shielded by God's power.)

Why is placing our hope in heaven more encouraging than placing our hope in this world? (Heaven will never pass away. All our earthly possessions will one day be lost. Why put your hope in what is being destroyed when you can place your hope in something that will last forever? Think of children riding bikes with training wheels. They enjoy riding, but long for the day when the training wheels will be taken off and they can ride wherever they want to go. They endure the hardship that comes with learning to ride — the falls and the scrapes — but they long for the day when there will be no more falls. That is how we should see our lives here.)

PRAY:
Ask God to help you look forward to being with Him in heaven.

WEDNESDAY
WHERE IS THE GOSPEL?

THE STORY: 1 PETER 1:10-12

This is a wonderful window into the Old Testament prophets and their lives. Peter tells us that the prophets had a sense that the things they were writing were not for themselves but for a future generation. As a result they searched intently into the very words they themselves proclaimed. They knew salvation was hidden in God's prophetic words. Imagine Isaiah when God gave him the fifty-third chapter of his book. Isaiah knew those words did not concern the immediate situation in Israel, and he longed to understand just how God would bring salvation.

Even the angels long to look into the mystery of God's plan revealed. The amazing thing is that we know — and can believe. That plan, that mystery, is the gospel!

TALK ABOUT IT:

What does Peter tell us God revealed to the Old Testament prophets? (God revealed to them that their writing was serving generations to come.)

Why should knowing this help us to be grateful? (When we consider how many people longed to understand God's plan, it can help us realize just how special it is.)

PRAY:

Thank God for revealing His gospel to your family.

THURSDAY

THE STORY: 1 PETER 1:6-9

God's people are refined through trials. Peter uses the example of gold being refined as an illustration of what God does in the lives of believers. When gold ore is mined, it contains other minerals and impurities. When the ore is melted, the impurities are separated from the gold and can be skimmed off the surface of the molten metal as dross.

God uses this kind of testing in two ways. First, persecution removes those with insincere faith. Only those with sincere faith are willing to endure persecution. Those without genuine faith recant their beliefs. Secondly, God sends all kinds of trials to expose weaknesses and idolatries so that we might repent and grow in our faith (see James 1:2-4).

TALK ABOUT IT:

What do men do to refine gold? (They melt it to get out the impurities.)

What does God do to refine our faith? (He brings trials that both expose our sin and force us to trust in Him.)

Can you think of a trial that forced you to trust in God? (Most children have had nights when they were afraid and needed to trust in God. You might share a time when your bills exceeded your income and how that forced you to trust in God.)

PRAY:
Thank the Lord for the trials He brings to refine our faith.

FRIDAY
ON THE ROAD TO EMMAUS

THE STORY: ZECHARIAH 13:7
Jesus quoted Zechariah in Matthew 26:31. He told the disciples that on that very same evening they would all fall away on account of Jesus. Peter objected, saying that even if all fell away, he would never fall away. Of course, we know that Peter did fall away, denying Christ three times. When Zechariah wrote and possibly spoke these words, he likely wondered what they meant. Like all the prophets, Zechariah knew he was not writing these words for the Israel of his day, but for another day (see 1 Peter 1:10-12).

TALK ABOUT IT:
Who is the shepherd in Zechariah's word? (Jesus is the shepherd.)

How was the shepherd struck? (Jesus was arrested, mocked, and beaten, and then crucified for our sins.)

How did this scatter the sheep? (The sheep were those who followed the shepherd — that is, His disciples. When Jesus was arrested, they were scattered, fearing for their own lives.)

PRAY:
Thank the Lord for suffering on our behalf.

GOD'S WORD IS LIVING!

The Word of God is active.

MONDAY

THE STORY: HEBREWS 4:12

The living Word of God judges our hearts. It is true that the words of Scripture never change and that no one can add or take away from them. But that does not mean they do not speak today. The Word of God is active. When we hear it, something wonderful happens. The Word of God probes us. Its truth judges our hearts. Even our attitudes, hidden in the depths within, are uncovered.

TALK ABOUT IT:

What does the writer compare the active work of the word of God to? (He compares it to a sword penetrating to our very souls.)

Have you ever been convicted by the Word of God actively working in your heart? (Parents, take time to lead in confession of your sin and speak of how God has used His Word to affect your life. Your younger children may not have had this experience. If you have younger children, encourage them to aspire to read and listen to the preached Word of God as well.)

PRAY:

Thank God for His Word.

TUESDAY

THE STORY: HEBREWS 4:13

Nothing is hidden from God's sight. His Word reveals what is hidden to us or to those around us, but nothing is hidden from God. We might fool ourselves into thinking a sin we committed is hidden, but God knows everything we have done. His word will expose it. If a person has stolen something and hidden it away, he might think he has gotten away with his crime. But every time he reads the words "Thou shall not steal," he becomes freshly aware that God knows he is a thief. One day we will all need to give an account before God for all we have done.

TALK ABOUT IT:

How can this Scripture help us live godly lives? (When we realize that none of our sins can be hidden from God, we are more likely to fear the Lord and not commit sin. For example, no one speeds on the highway when they see a policeman holding a radar gun at the traffic. They don't speed because they fear the consequences.)

What is a good thing to do when we do sin? (It is a good thing to confess the sin, bringing it out into the open, and ask for forgiveness. Doing that honors God, who sees all we do.)

PRAY:

Ask God to help you be quick to confess when you sin.

WEDNESDAY
WHERE IS THE GOSPEL?

THE STORY: HEBREWS 4:13

Immediately following the description of the probing work of God's Word, the writer of Hebrews turns our attention to Jesus our great high priest. This is not an accidental transition. Verse 14 begins with "therefore," connecting it to the verses before. In other words, God's Word exposes our sin, making us aware of our need for forgiveness. Therefore we should run to the throne of grace.

TALK ABOUT IT:

Why do we need a high priest? (We need someone to stand before God and appeal for our forgiveness. That is what a priest does. Jesus continually pleads our case before the Father. His wounds settle our case. God judged Jesus in our place.)

What sinful things have you done in your life that indicate a need for a high priest? (Take time as a family to confess your sins, thus admitting you are sinners. This is a humbling exercise that positions us to more greatly appreciate grace. Parents, lead your children in confession and then help them by drawing them out.)

PRAY:

Thank God for our great high priest Jesus, for His work on the cross, and that he is now in heaven praying for us.

THURSDAY

THE STORY: HEBREWS 4:15,16

Jesus sympathizes with our struggles. We can run to the throne of grace in our time of need because we have a faithful high priest. Jesus was tempted like us in every way, so He can sympathize with our struggles. Unlike us, He did not sin.

His sinlessness made him the perfect sacrifice for our sin. Now, in heaven, the sacrificial lamb of God stands as our high priest before God. His sacrifice pleads for us before the throne of God night and day forever. Later, in Hebrews 7:23-25, we read:

"Now there have been many of those priests, since death prevented them from continuing in office; but because Jesus lives forever, he has a permanent priesthood. Therefore he is able to save completely those who come to God through him, because he always lives to intercede for them. Such a high priest meets our need — one who is holy, blameless, pure, set apart from sinners, exalted above the heavens. Unlike the other high priests, he does not need to offer sacrifices day after day, first for his own sins, and then for the sins of the people. He sacrificed for their sins once for all when he offered himself."

TALK ABOUT IT:

How is Jesus' priesthood different from that of all the other priests in the Old Testament? (The sacrifice Jesus offered was able to take away our sins. Their sacrifices were not. Each of those high priests died and could not carry on their ministry. Jesus rose again and is alive. He is the eternal high priest interceding on our behalf forever.)

How can remembering that Jesus was tempted like us help us approach God when we are struggling with sin? (Jesus experienced the same temptations we did. He is aware of the power of temptation. He chose us and saved us with full knowledge of all our sin. We never need fear that any sin confessed to the Lord will be too evil to be forgiven.)

PRAY:

Pray that God would give you the grace to confess your sin and trust the Lord's grace to change you.

FRIDAY
ON THE ROAD TO EMMAUS

THE STORY: PSALM 45:6,7

The writer of Hebrews quotes this passage in Hebrews 1:8,9 and attributes it to the Son of God. Jesus is God, whose throne will last for ever and ever. Jesus died on the cross so that we sinners might receive the righteousness of God. Because of Christ's humility, taking on human flesh and offering Himself up as a sacrifice, God exalted Him above all.

TALK ABOUT IT:

What do we learn about Jesus from the writer of this passage from Hebrews? (We learn that Jesus is God. He tells us that when the writer of Psalm 45 says, "Your throne, O God," he is referring to Jesus.)

In what way did Jesus extend righteousness to His entire kingdom? (By dying on the cross, Jesus extended righteous to the many sinners whom He died for.)

PRAY:

Thank Jesus for dying on the cross that we might receive the righteousness of God.

BY FAITH

Without faith it is impossible to please God

MONDAY

THE STORY: HEBREWS 11:1-4

Faith is believing what we do not see. Faith is trusting God's Word. Unbelievers do not lack truth; they lack faith. They refuse to believe what they cannot see. People of faith believe what God says even if they cannot see it. We cannot always see but we can always read God's Word and believe it.

The writer of Hebrews turns to Creation for his first example. The Bible begins with these words: "In the beginning God created the heavens and the earth" (Genesis 1:1). From the very opening of Scripture, we are called to believe something we cannot see. It takes faith to accept that everything around us was made by God from nothing. Our finite minds cannot comprehend it. Even though it is rational, science cannot confirm it. But if the Spirit of God has made us alive, we will believe it is true. We believe not only because it is reasonable to do so, but also because God says it in His Word.

TALK ABOUT IT:

What does it mean to have faith? (Faith is belief in something you cannot see yet regard to be true.)

What do we believe as Christians? (We believe God's Word to be true in all it contains.)

PRAY:
Ask God to give every member of your family faith to believe the Word of God.

TUESDAY

THE STORY: HEBREWS 11:5-12

Without faith it is impossible to please God. Faith is the basic fundamental of Christianity. If a person has no faith, then he must conclude that God, who cannot be seen, does not exist. If someone denies God's existence, then he doesn't care to please Him.

But there is more to saving faith than believing that God exists. Those who believe in God but do not trust in God's Word are compared to demons, who know that God exists (see James 2:19) but who are not saved. Faith cannot save a person if what he or she trusts in is not Jesus and His gospel. Our faith must be in Christ. We must believe in God's plan as revealed in the Bible; we must believe the gospel. We must also trust God's Word. Believers demonstrate trust in God's Word by obeying it and agreeing with it.

TALK ABOUT IT:

Why is it not good enough to simply believe that God is real? (The demons know that God is real, but they do not please God. We need to trust in God's plan in Jesus Christ.)

How did Abraham believe in God's plan? (Abraham didn't know where he was going, but he was willing to go because God sent him.)

PRAY:

Pray that every member of your family would place their trust in God's plan for their lives and trust in Jesus as their Savior.

WEDNESDAY
WHERE IS THE GOSPEL?

THE STORY: HEBREWS 11:13,39,40

Abraham was "looking forward" to a future city whose builder and maker was God (see Hebrews 11:10). Moses regarded disgrace "for the sake of Christ" as greater value than the treasures of Egypt, because he was looking ahead to his reward (see Hebrews 11:26). How was it that they looked ahead to a heavenly city and to the coming of the Savior when neither of these things yet existed? God granted them faith in a future hope. All those who died in faith prior to Christ were saved, for they were looking forward to Christ. The same gospel hope we possess saved those who had faith in God's promise of redemption. Together with us who know Christ by name, they are made perfect.

TALK ABOUT IT:

How were the Old Testament heroes saved? (They were saved by faith, trusting in God's plan for their redemption. They did not trust in their own works.)

What kind of faith must we demonstrate to be saved? (We must confess that Jesus is our Lord and believe in our hearts that God raised him from the dead [see Romans 10:9].)

PRAY:

Ask God to help each family member come to saving faith in Jesus.

THURSDAY

THE STORY: HEBREWS 11:14-38

The writer of Hebrews continues listing the men and women of faith pointing out their vision for a better country, a heavenly one. What an amazing thought to consider that God opened their eyes to understand that their earthly home was temporary. They looked forward longing for a place where God would live with them. The earth was a temporary country for them. They saw themselves as aliens – that is, not even a part of the earth. The people of God witnessed a taste of the power and majesty of God in the miracles they observed. The leading of the Israelites out of Egypt, the crossing of the Red Sea, the collapse of Jericho all served to build their faith in a mighty God. As a result, they were strengthened to follow God and their faith lead them even though at the end of their lives they did not receive the promise.

TALK ABOUT IT:

How should our lives be the same as these great men of faith? (We too should live like strangers in this present world and look forward to the coming of the Messiah. Only this time it is not the first coming but the second when the curse of sin will be finally defeated.)

How can the pleasures, the things we like in this world, keep us looking downward at the world instead of looking forward to a better country? (We can love the things of this world more than the things of God. We are called to live in the world but not love it more than God and His kingdom. Although the pleasant treasures of this world are fine to enjoy, we can not allow them to distract us from our first love, Jesus.)

What things in the world are most likely to distract you? (Parents, help your children here see the temptations they face in this area. You might want to start by answering this question yourself first.)

PRAY:

Ask God to help each of you keep your eyes and your love toward God and heaven, a better country.

FRIDAY
ON THE ROAD TO EMMAUS

THE STORY: PSALM 25:1-7

David prayed to God in the midst of his suffering. But he prayed for more than just relief from his temporal enemies. David looked forward to a Savior who, out of God's great mercy and love, would not remember the sins of his youth or his rebellious ways. Jesus is God's answer to David's prayer. When we look back at this Scripture, we see Jesus.

Paul wrote to Titus, saying, "But when the kindness and love of God our Savior appeared, he saved us, not because of righteous things we had done, but because of his mercy. He saved us through the washing of rebirth and renewal by the Holy Spirit, whom he poured out on us generously through Jesus Christ our Savior, so that, having been justified by his grace, we might become heirs having the hope of eternal life" (Titus 3:4-7).

TALK ABOUT IT:

Where do you see Jesus in this psalm? (Have your children look at the entire psalm and point out where they see Jesus or the plan of salvation by grace.)

Where do you see yourself in this psalm? (We can all see ourselves as sinners like David in need of a Savior. This psalm is particularly relevant for young people because David realized that even the sins of his youth needed forgiveness.)

PRAY:

Pray that God would pour out His gift of faith and save every member of your family.

LOVING ONE ANOTHER

The Gospel is our motive to love.

MONDAY

THE STORY: 1 JOHN 3:9-12

True love flows from the gospel. Love in our culture is motivated by selfish gain. We tend to love in order to get love. When our love is selfishly motivated, we withdraw it the moment we stop getting what we want. Love in God's kingdom is inspired and motivated by the example of unselfish love we see in the gospel. John is moving in his discussion on love to this point: "This is love: not that we loved God, but that He loved us and sent His Son as an atoning sacrifice for our sins. Dear friends, since God so loved us, we also ought to love one another" (1 John 3:10).

When our love flows from grace and is motivated by a desire to glorify God by following Christ's example, we will continue to love no matter what people do to us. Husbands love their wives as Christ loved, whether their wives respect them or not. Wives persevere in love and respect for their husbands in obedience to God regardless of whether their husbands return the love and care. The same is true for every relationship, even with our enemies!

TALK ABOUT IT:

What kinds of things do we say we love? (In our society, we say we "love" anything good. Help your children see this by drawing them out extensively. We say we love pizza and popcorn, love sunny days and rainy nights, or love a good movie and a good nap.)

How is this different from the kind of love John speaks of? (None of those demonstrations of love are motivated by the gospel; they are motivated by our emotions.)

If we love someone based on how they make us feel, what will we do when they hurt us? (We will withhold our love, or worse we will try to hurt them in some way.)

PRAY:
Ask God to pour His Spirit into the lives of each member of your family that they might believe and then demonstrate gospel-motivated love.

TUESDAY

THE STORY: 1 JOHN 3:13-15
True love marks our conversion. Love motivated by the example of Christ's love in the gospel should mark every Christian. This kind of love is a product of our conversion. We know we have passed from death into life if we have this love; it is a key evidence of our conversion. That does not mean gospel-motivated love is automatic. If it were automatic, John would have no need to encourage his hearers toward it.

Unbelievers are incapable of this love; they are slaves to sin. But we who know "the love the Father has lavished on us" should live and must live gospel-inspired, love-filled lives. The person who consistently demonstrates God's kind of love has confidence in his salvation. The person who won't forgive, or who can't find motivation in the cross to love others, should doubt the sincerity of his or her conversion.

TALK ABOUT IT:

Why is gospel-motivated love a good evidence of our conversion? (Any time the cross of Jesus is at the center of our motive, it is evidence that the cross of Jesus is at the center of our lives. In other words, gospel motivation is what it means to follow Christ!)

Do Christians love perfectly? (No, we continue to sin and often love for selfish reasons. We must, however, always remember that we don't have to be selfish. We have been freed from the slavery of sin to do good works.)

PRAY:

Ask God to help each member of your family demonstrate gospel-centered love.

WEDNESDAY
WHERE IS THE GOSPEL?

THE STORY: 1 JOHN 3:16

We obey in faith not in works. We obey because we have salvation in Christ; we do not obey in order to earn salvation in Christ. We love others because He first loved us. Once again we see the gospel clearly outlined in Scripture. Verse 16 tells us that the ultimate example of love is Jesus laying down His life for us. Jesus did just what John is exhorting us to do. He saw that we were "in need" (verse 17) and gave up His life for us. Jesus' sacrifice motivates us to love one another. Our motivation for loving someone is grounded upon what Jesus did for us, not upon what others have done for us. This is how we can find the grace to love even our enemies.

TALK ABOUT IT:

This passage tells us to love one another because of the example of Christ. Do we always live that way? (No, we don't always live that way.)

What are some examples of how you struggle to love your brother or sister? (Parents help the children see the times when they get angry etc.)

Jesus loved us by giving up His life for us on the cross. What kinds of things might we give up for our brothers and sisters? (Most of us are not going to follow Jesus' example and actually die for others. Instead, we will be called to sacrifice our preferences and wants for the good of others. We can love others by giving up of ourselves in service to them as well.)

Can you think of how others have sacrificed for you? (Mom and dad help the children see how the service and sacrifice of others has helped your children. Do not be afraid to use your own example of providing food and shelter for your children. Just as we are to love others because of Christ's example, so we can help encourage others to follow along by our own example of love by sacrificing for others. The apostle Paul put it this way, "follow my example as I follow the example of Christ," [1 Corinthians 11:1].)

PRAY:
As God to help each person in your family follow Christ's example of giving up of themselves for the benefit of others.

THURSDAY

THE STORY: 1 JOHN 3:17-24
True love demands action. Gospel-motivated love is practical. Because our example is Christ, who laid down his life for us, we know love is about giving, sacrifice, and action. James said it this way: "Suppose a brother or sister is without clothes and daily food. If one of you says to him, 'Go, I wish you well; keep warm and well fed,' but does nothing about his physical needs, what good is it? In the same way, faith by itself, if it is not accompanied by action, is dead" (James 2:15-17). John tells us not to love with words but with deeds.

TALK ABOUT IT:
What does it mean to love with deeds? (We should not just tell people we love them; we should serve them.)

What kinds of things could you do to demonstrate love by actions in your family? (Parents, draw your children out. Make sure they see that all our love should be primarily motivated from a desire to glorify God by following Christ's example and not merely to please their parents.)

PRAY:
Ask God to help your family members remember what Jesus did for us that they might be motivated to serve one another in love.

FRIDAY
ON THE ROAD TO EMMAUS

THE STORY: PSALM 35:19,20
Jesus connects this passage to himself in John 15:24,25 when he informed His disciples that they would be persecuted just as He was. The enemies of Jesus hated Him for no reason. Jesus told his disciples that they would be persecuted because they follow Him. John echoes this in his letter when he tells us, "Do not be surprised, my brothers, if the world hates you" (1 John 3:13).

TALK ABOUT IT:
What was Jesus' response to those who were His enemies? (Jesus did not defend Himself on the road to the cross, where He willingly gave up His life for us.)

What should our response be to those who hate and persecute us? (Jesus said, "Love your enemies and pray for those who persecute you, that you may be sons of your Father in heaven.")

How is this like what John is saying in 1 John? (John tells us that gospel-motivated love is evidence of our conversion. Jesus knows that only a true follower of Christ will have this kind of love.)

PRAY:

Thank God for sending Jesus to die on the cross and rise again victoriously so that one day we, too, might go to be with our Father in heaven.

WORTHY IS THE LAMB

Jesus, the Lamb of God, is worthy.

MONDAY

THE STORY: REVELATION 5:1-5

The Lion of the tribe of Judah is worthy. On his deathbed, Jacob, who was called Israel, gathered his twelve sons to tell them what would happen to them in the future. To Judah he said, "You are a lion's cub, O Judah; you return from the prey, my son. Like a lion he crouches and lies down, like a lioness — who dares to rouse him? The scepter will not depart from Judah, nor the ruler's staff from between his feet, until he comes to whom it belongs and the obedience of the nations is his." (see Genesis 49:9,10)

Jesus is the lion of the tribe of Judah. Jesus is also the Root of David who has triumphed. The lion has triumphed and is worthy to open the scroll! The scroll is symbolic for the final plan of God. The final plan of God to dwell with His people in heaven forever is about to be opened!

TALK ABOUT IT:

Who was the Root of David and why is that name given to Him? (Jesus is the Root of David because He came from the stump of David, or in the line of David.)

Why is the Lion of the tribe of Judah worthy? (The lion has triumphed. Jesus died on the cross for our sin and rose again victoriously. This scene is like a victory parade!)

PRAY:
Thank the Lord for dying on the cross for us and rising again in victory so that we, too, one day will rise.

TUESDAY

THE STORY: REVELATION 5:6-8

The Lion is the Lamb. When the imagery of Revelation changes, it does not mean a new character or event is being introduced. Here the switch to talking about the lamb provides a further description of the Lion. Imagine that one of the elders said, "Look, the lion has triumphed!" but when John looked, he saw a Lamb who was slain. In reality, all these pictures are talking about the same person, Jesus Christ.

The Book of Revelation was written with the symbolic number seven, which is the number of completion. The Lamb did not have seven literal horns and eyes. Horns were used to designate power, so this passage is telling us that the Lamb seen here had supreme or complete authority and power. When the Lamb removed the scroll, without resistance from God, all heaven worshipped. The Lamb was worthy!

TALK ABOUT IT:

What does it mean when it says the Lamb looked as if it had been slain? (Although Jesus rose from the dead, the scars of His wounds remain visible as a testimony of His sacrifice.)

Should this passage cause us to worship? (Yes, when we consider that God's Son died for us so that we could live with Him, we should respond with worship.)

PRAY:
Praise and thank the Lord for His sacrifice on our behalf.

WEDNESDAY
WHERE IS THE GOSPEL?

THE STORY: REVELATION 5:9-11

Worthy is the Lamb who was slain. The Lamb who was slain is Jesus. The hundreds of thousands of lambs sacrificed in Old Testament times could not take away sin. But Jesus, the Lamb of God, was a worthy sacrifice for sin. His worth is sufficient to atone for our sins, and His worth commands our worship and praise. We join all of heaven when we sing, "Worthy is the Lamb."

There is only one Lamb who sits on the throne — Christ, who conquered death. Here in the book of Revelation we see the culmination of the gospel. The books are opened, and the heavens praise the Redeemer, who has brought salvation by his death. By His blood He ransomed people for God from every tribe and language and people and nation. The gospel promise given to Abraham is finally fulfilled by the Lamb.

TALK ABOUT IT:

Where do you see God's promise to Abraham fulfilled? (People are in heaven from every tribe and language and nation.)

How can knowing what will happen at the end of the age motivate our praise today? (When we worship, we can pray with the enthusiasm described in this passage. We can sing, "Worthy is the Lamb" now!)

PRAY:
Take time to pray using the song of the angels in Revelation 5.

THURSDAY

THE STORY: REVELATION 5:12-14

All of creation will worship the Lamb. Here we see that everyone joins in the worship of the Lamb in heaven. No one is sleepy or distracted. Everyone has one purpose: to worship the Lamb. Each Sunday when we gather, we come with the same purpose —worship. We worship the Lamb, we worship the Father who sent the lamb, and we worship with the help of the Holy Spirit dwelling within us.

TALK ABOUT IT:

Who is singing to Jesus? (Angels by the millions sing to him. Ten thousand times ten thousand is one hundred million! Every creature on earth and in heaven eventually joins the singing.)

How is this picture a fulfillment of God's promise to exalt the name of Jesus above every name and that every knee will bow before Him? (See Philippians 2:9,10.)

Why do we have greater reason to worship the Lamb than do the angels? (Unlike the angels, who saw God's salvation to men and rejoiced, we are the actual recipients of the gift of salvation. Because we are the ones who are given the gift, we have greater reason to be thankful.)

PRAY:

Thank and praise the Lord for our salvation in Christ.

FRIDAY
ON THE ROAD TO EMMAUS

THE STORY: PSALM 89:26-29

Jesus called God His Father, and it is Jesus whose throne will last forever. The covenant that Jesus introduced — the covenant in His blood — will never fail. John called Jesus "the firstborn" in Revelation when he wrote:

"Jesus Christ, who is the faithful witness, the firstborn from the dead, and the ruler of the kings of the earth; To him who loves us and has freed us from our sins by his blood, and has made us to be a kingdom and priests to serve his God and Father — to him be glory and power for ever and ever! Amen" (Revelation 1:5,6).

TALK ABOUT IT:

How are Revelation 1:5,6 and Psalm 89:26-29 similar in talking about Jesus? (Have your children look up both passages and compare them.)

Could the passage in Psalm 89 be referring to anyone other than Jesus? (No, no other king's throne would last forever. Even when God promises to David that his throne will last forever, it endures forever through Jesus, the son of David.)

PRAY:

Thank God for sending Jesus to die on the cross and rise again victoriously so that one day we, too, might go to be with our Father in heaven.

AT THE THRONE WORSHIPPING

God keeps His promises.

MONDAY

THE STORY: REVELATION 7:9

God's promise is fulfilled in heaven. The scene in heaven of a multitude of people from every nation, tribe, people, and language signals the fulfillment of God's promise. God promised by His own initiative to multiply Abraham's descendants that they would be more numerous than the stars (see Genesis 15:5) and that all nations would be blessed through him (see Genesis 12:3). These promises will one day be completely fulfilled!

TALK ABOUT IT:

What do the white robes represent? (The white robes represent the purity of the saints. The stain of sin has been removed. See Isaiah 1:18.)

Where else do you remember a celebration with palm branches? (When Jesus entered Jerusalem on a colt, they waved palm branches in celebration [see John 12:13].)

What must we do to qualify to be one of those who stand before the throne in white robes? (We must place faith in Jesus and believe that His death and resurrection paid for our sins and guaranteed our place in heaven. He did the work; we need to trust in Him.)

PRAY:
Ask God to pour out His grace so that all your family members might put their faith in Christ.

TUESDAY

THE STORY: REVELATION 7:10-12
God is exalted in heaven. When Jesus entered into Jerusalem prior to His death, the crowd shouted, "Hosanna!" and waved palm branches. Days later, many of the very same people were shouting, "Crucify Him!" Jesus rode through that first celebration toward the cross. He knew of another celebration. And it was for the joy of that later celebration that He endured the cross, scorning its shame. Here in Revelation we catch a glimpse of that other celebration. God is exalted because of the sacrifice of His Son. One day we who trust in Christ will join their heavenly chorus.

TALK ABOUT IT:
What is the great multitude celebrating? (They are celebrating God's salvation through Jesus.)

Can we celebrate this same way today? (Yes, every Sunday we celebrate the resurrection of our Lord.)

Notice that worship marks every believer. Do you think a person can be a Christian and yet not want to worship? (No, if a person is a Christian he will love to worship God. That doesn't mean he won't have days where he is distracted or doesn't feel like worshipping. But if a person consistently has no desire to worship, they don't appreciate the gospel personally and should not assume they have been born again.)

PRAY:
Pray that God would place in your heart a growing desire to worship Him.

WEDNESDAY
WHERE IS THE GOSPEL?

THE STORY: REVELATION 7:14
This passage of Scripture, and the entire chapter, is full of the gospel. The Lamb is Christ, who sits on the throne and has made the robes white by His blood. The blood of the Lamb is the blood of Jesus shed upon the cross for the forgiveness of the sins of all His people. The multitude worships the Lamb in heaven, and He continues to be their shepherd, guiding them to springs of living water. In John 4:10 Jesus said to the woman at the well, "If you knew the gift of God and who it is that asks you for a drink, you would have asked Him and He would have given you living water."

TALK ABOUT IT:
What does it mean that the robes were made white in the blood of the lamb? (The death of Jesus made a way for sins to be forgiven.)

What is the great tribulation? (The great tribulation is the time of suffering prior to the return of Jesus. Many consider it the worst and the last of the last days.)

Will we one day have white robes? (Everyone who trusts Jesus will be made sparkling clean; all of sin's stains will be removed. Only those who trust in Jesus will be blessed this way.)

PRAY:
Pray that God would save each member of your family by His Spirit with the gospel.

475

THURSDAY

THE STORY: REVELATION 7:15-17

Our suffering ends in heaven. Imagine for a moment that we will not hunger; Jesus will be our eternal bread. We will not thirst; Jesus will be our living water. We will not tire; we will have lasting strength. We will not experience sorrow; in Christ we will have everlasting, indescribable joy. Every tear will be wiped from our eyes!

TALK ABOUT IT:

Who will be at the center of heaven? (Jesus will be at the center.)

What do you look forward to most when you think of heaven? (Parents, draw out your children and answer this question yourselves.)

PRAY:

Thank God for the promise of heaven and thank Him for all the blessings we will receive in heaven.

FRIDAY
ON THE ROAD TO EMMAUS

THE STORY: PSALM 96:9-13

Jesus is the one who is going to come to judge the earth in righteousness and truth. In Revelation 19:11 we get a picture of the Lord coming down to judge the earth. In Revelation 7:9,10 we get a picture of the final rejoicing the Psalmist points toward. The whole earth will sing on the day of God's judgment, for in that day He will put an end to the curse.

TALK ABOUT IT:

When will Jesus come to judge the nations? (Jesus will one day return to earth, but no one knows when. That is why Paul warned that we should be ready at all times because he said the day of the Lord would come like a thief in the night, when we least expect Him (see 1 Thessalonians 5:2).

What can we do to be prepared for when Jesus returns? (We need to place faith in Him and live for Christ. We really only have two things to do. John said it well: "We need to believe in the name of His Son Jesus and to love one another as he commanded us" [1 John 3:23].)

PRAY:

Pray that God would extend grace to every member of your family to believe and place their trust in Him, as well as love one another.

NEW TESTAMENT · SPECIAL LESSON

EASTER

Jesus rose from the dead just as He said he would.

MONDAY

THE STORY: JOHN 20:1-10

Jesus rose from the dead but the disciples didn't understand. Mary along with a small group of women came to the tomb Sunday morning bringing spices for the body, (Luke 24:1). There they found the stone rolled away and the body of Jesus gone. Stunned that the body of Jesus is missing, she ran back to Simon Peter and John (the other disciple) to report the body of Jesus had been taken. Peter and John returned to the tomb to see for themselves. Once they observed for themselves that Jesus body was missing they believed the woman's story yet they did not understand that Jesus must rise from the dead. Jesus had told the Jews, "Destroy this temple and in three days I will rise it up," John 2:19 but they did not understand he was referring to His own body. Jesus even very accurately predicted His death, (Mark 8:31,9:31) but the disciples just didn't understand. Although the angels had told the women Jesus had risen, (Luke 24:6) the disciples did not believe, (Luke 24:11). It wasn't until Peter and John saw for themselves the body was missing that they dared to believe Jesus might yet be alive.

TALK ABOUT IT:

What did Peter and John find inside the tomb? (The linen cloths and the face cloth folded up, but the body of Jesus was not there.)

479

Did Peter and John rejoice and start celebrating that Jesus was risen? (No they did not.)

Why didn't Peter and John celebrate Jesus' resurrection? (They didn't understand the scripture that Jesus must rise from the dead.)

Is it possible to know the story about Jesus but not believe today? (Yes, people know the story of Jesus but do not believe and trust in what He did.)

PRAY:
Pray that God would help every member of your family believe and put their faith in the death and resurrection of Jesus.

TUESDAY

THE STORY: JOHN 20:11-18
Jesus appeared to Mary risen in body. Mary remained at the tomb though the disciples left to go back home. The sadness of the missing body, still not realizing that Jesus was alive but instead thinking the body of Jesus was stolen. Jesus, standing nearby, asked her, "Woman, why are you crying?" Mary, thinking the man must be the gardener asked if he had carried Jesus away. Then, Jesus calls Mary by name. Instantly she recognizes Jesus turns to him and embraces Jesus. What a wonderful picture of the call of Christ to the sheep. Jesus said in John 10, that He is the good shepherd and His sheep know who he is and listen to His voice. Jesus rose with a real body that Mary could grab hold of. Jesus was not a ghost or spirit He was a real man, His body had been risen from the dead!

TALK ABOUT IT:
Who did Mary think Jesus was? (Mary thought he was the gardener.)

When did Mary finally recognize Jesus? (Mary recognized Jesus when He called her by name.)

Does Jesus call us today? (Yes, there are many places in the New Testament that refer to Christians being called by God. Look up and read 2 Thessalonians 2:13-14.)

PRAY:
Thank God for the call of the Holy Spirit through the Gospel and ask God to call each member of your family.

WEDNESDAY
WHERE IS THE GOSPEL?

THE STORY: 1 CORINTHIANS 15:13-19
The Resurrection is the proof that Jesus was God and not just a man. The Resurrection is the promise that death could not hold Jesus and that Jesus' sacrifice on the cross was worked to take away our sins. In explaining just how critical the resurrection is to the Gospel Paul said in 1 Corinthians 15:13-19:

"But if there is no resurrection of the dead, then not even Christ has been raised. And if Christ has not been raised, then our preaching is in vain and your faith is in vain. We are even found to be misrepresenting God, because we testified about God that he raised Christ, whom he did not raise if it is true that the dead are not raised. For if the dead are not raised, not even Christ has been raised. And if Christ has not been raised, your faith is futile and you are still in your sins. Then those also who have fallen asleep in Christ have perished. If in this life only we have hoped in Christ, we are of all people most to be pitied."

TALK ABOUT IT:
Why is the resurrection important? (If Jesus didn't rise from the dead he would be a liar and a fake with no power over death. Jesus' resurrection proves His words were true, that He is truth and that He conquered death!)

Why is Jesus' resurrection important for us? (Jesus died as our substitute taking the punishment for our sins. Jesus also rose as our substitute and with His new life we also get new life!)

PRAY:

Take turn praising Jesus for his power over death and for dying on the cross so we could be forgiven.

THURSDAY

THE STORY: JOHN 20:19-23

Jesus appeared to His disciples risen in power. That same evening, after the women reported to the disciples all they had heard and seen, the disciples were afraid and locked their doors for fear of the Jews. Somehow, in spite of the locked doors, Jesus stood among them. Jesus showed them His hands and His side. Then, the men believed. Jesus, could not be stopped by death nor locked doors, for He had risen with power.

TALK ABOUT IT:

How did Jesus get into a locked room without a key? (The Bible does not tell us how, but you can be sure it had to do with his power not an ability to pick a lock.)

What did Jesus show the disciples? (Jesus showed them his hands and side.)

Why were Jesus' hands and side important? (The hands and side of Jesus bear the wounds of His crucifixion. It is in the death of Jesus that we place our trust. We will all look upon those same wounds in heaven and remember the work of Jesus on the cross.)

PRAY:

Thank Jesus in your prayers for dying on the cross to take our sins upon himself.

FRIDAY
ON THE ROAD TO EMMAUS

THE STORY: MARK 10:32-34

God used the Old Testament prophets point to Jesus. Jesus, however, was the greatest prophet of all. In a demonstration of Jesus prophetic office and the sovereignty of God over the coming suffering of Christ, Jesus predicts his death and resurrection. With amazing clarity Jesus taught His disciples he would be mocked, flogged, spit upon and that three days later He would rise from the dead. Every part of Jesus' prophetic teaching came true.

TALK ABOUT IT:

Why do you think, given the accurate detail, the disciples didn't understand the prophetic teaching Jesus gave them about His death and resurrection? (The disciples were looking for an earthly kingdom and believed the Messiah would bring an end to the dominion of Rome. Suffering and death just would not have made sense to them.)

Jesus told the disciples exactly what would happen, yet they did not believe. What does that tell us about our need for God to move upon our hearts with His Holy Spirit before we can believe? (It is clear that without God touching our sinful hearts, we just won't turn to the Lord. We need God to awaken us from our death in sin before we will ever believe in Jesus.)

Are there people today that are similar in their unbelief to the disciples Jesus taught? (Yes. Many people know all the facts of the Gospel yet do not believe or truly understand the great miracle of Jesus death and resurrection for the sins of those who would believe. Though they know the story they just don't believe.)

PRAY:

Thank Jesus for the ressurection.

APPENDIX A - SCRIPTURE REFERENCES

This appendix contains the Old Testament (OT) and New Testament (NT) scripture references from Get Into the Story Volume I (OT Lessons) and Get Into the Story Volume II (NT Lessons). Scriptures are listed in biblical index order.

GENESIS

Gen. 1 .... OT 1 M, T, H
Gen. 14:7-15:1 ...... OT 9 M
Gen. 1:3-26 .... OT 1 T
Gen. 2:1-5 .... OT 2 M
Gen. 2:15-18 ..... OT 2 T, H
OT 3T
Gen. 3:1-7 .... OT 3 M
Gen. 3:8-19 .... OT 3 T
Gen. 3:15 .... OT 25 F
Gen. 3:20-24 .... OT 3 H
Gen. 3:28,29 .... OT 9 W
Gen. 4:1-5 .... OT 4 M, T
Gen. 4:6-12 .... OT 4 T, H
Gen. 4:13-26 .... OT 4 H
OT 5 M
Gen. 6:1-12 .... OT 5 M
OT 6 T
Gen. 6:13-7:5 .... OT 5 T
OT 6 T
Gen. 7:6-10 .... OT 5 H
Gen. 7:11-24 .... OT 6 M
Gen. 8:1-19 .... OT 6 T

Gen. 8:20,21 .... OT 6 W
Gen. 9:1-17 .... OT 6 H
OT 22 M
Gen. 10:1-32 .... OT 7 M
Gen. 11:1-9 .... OT 7 T
Gen. 11:27-12:2 OT 8 M, T
Gen. 12:1-7 .... OT 8 T
Gen. 12:3 .... NT 51 F
NT 78 M
Gen. 12:8-20 .... OT 8 H
OT 13 M
Gen. 14:17-15:1 ....OT 9 M
Gen. 15 .... OT 9 T
Gen. 15:4 .... NT 59 M
Gen. 15:15 .... NT 78 M
Gen. 16 .... OT 10M
Gen. 17:1 ....OT 10 T, H
Gen. 17:2-8 .... OT 10 T
Gen. 17:5 .... OT 45 F
Gen. 17:6 .... OT 54 H
Gen. 17:9-27 .... OT 10 H
Gen. 17:12 ....NT 3 M
Gen. 17:16 .... OT 54 H
Gen. 17:19 ....OT 13 T, F
Gen. 18:1-8 ....OT 11 M

Gen. 18:9-15 .... OT 11 T
Gen. 18:16-23 ..... OT 11 H
Gen. 18:18 .... OT 45 F
Gen. 19:1-14 ....OT 12 M
Gen. 19:15-22 ...... OT 12 T
Gen. 19:23-29 ..... OT 12 H
Gen. 19:36,37 ......OT 50 M
Gen. 20 ....OT 13 M
Gen. 21:1-7 ....OT 13 M
Gen. 21:8-21 .... OT 13 H
Gen. 22:1-8 ....OT 14 M
Gen. 22:2 .... OT 13 H
Gen. 22:9-14 ....OT 14 T, H
Gen. 22:15-19 ..... OT 14 H
Gen. 22:18 .... NT 42 T
Gen. 24:1-9 .... OT 15 H
Gen. 24:10-21 ...... OT 15 T
Gen. 24:15-67 ..... OT 15 H
Gen. 25:1-23 ....OT 16 M
Gen. 25:24-28 ...... OT 16 T
OT 17 M, T
Gen. 25:29-34 ..... OT 16 H
Gen. 26 ....OT 17 M
Gen. 26:4 .... NT 42 T
Gen. 27:1-4 ....OT 17 M

Gen. 27:5-17 .... OT 17 T
Gen. 27:18-38 ..... OT 17 H
Gen. 27:42-28:5 ..OT 18 M
Gen. 28:10-17 ...... OT 18 T
Gen. 28:18-22 ..... OT 18 H
Gen. 28:20,21 .... OT 20 T
Gen. 29:1-14 ....OT 19 M
Gen. 29:15-20 ...... OT 19 T
Gen. 29:21-35 ..... OT 19 H
Gen. 30:25-31:9 ..OT 20 M
Gen. 31:10-21 ...... OT 20 T
Gen. 31:13 .... OT 19 H
Gen. 31:22-25 ..... OT 20 H
OT 21 M
Gen. 32:1-21 .... OT 21 T
Gen. 32:22-32 ..... OT 21 H
Gen. 35:1-14 ....OT 22 M
Gen. 35:23-27 .....OT 22 M
Gen. 37:1-4 .... OT 22 T
Gen. 37:12-20 .....OT 23 M
Gen. 37:31-36 ..... OT 23 H
Gen. 39 ....OT 24 M
Gen. 40:1-41:4 ..... OT 24 T
Gen. 40:15-39 ..... OT 24 H
Gen. 41:41-57 .....OT 25 M
Gen. 42:1-38 ....OT 25T
Gen. 42:21 .... OT 23 T
Gen. 44:1-34 .... OT 25 T
Gen. 45:1-11 ....OT 26 M
Gen. 45:12-15 ...... OT 26 T
Gen. 45:16-45:4 .. OT 26 H
Gen. 48:22 ....OT 22 M
Gen. 49:1-10 .... OT 13 F
Gen. 49:9,10 ....NT 77 M
Gen. 50:15-21 ...... OT 26 T
Gen. 50:22-26 .....OT 27 M

EXODUS

Ex. 1 .... OT 27 T
Ex 2:1-10............. OT 27 H
Ex. 2:24 ....OT 28M
Ex. 2:11-25 ....OT 28 M
Ex. 3 ....OT 28 T
OT 44 T
Ex. 3:8 ....OT 40 M
Ex. 3:14 ....OT 40 M
Ex. 3:17 ....OT 40 M
Ex. 4:1-17 .... OT 28 H
Ex. 4:18-23 ....OT 29 M
Ex. 5:1-21 ....OT 29 M
Ex. 5:22-6:9 .... OT 29 T
Ex. 6:1 ....OT 30 M
Ex. 6:26-7:13 ...... OT 29 H
Ex. 7:14-24 ....OT 30 M
Ex. 8:2 .... OT 30 H
Ex. 8:15 .... OT 30 T
Ex. 8:23 .... OT 30 T
Ex. 9 .... OT 30 T
Ex. 9:12 .... OT 30 T
Ex. 10 .... OT 30 H
Ex. 10:1 .... OT 30 T
Ex. 10:20............... OT 30 T
Ex. 10:22............... OT 30 H
Ex. 10:27............... OT 30 T
Ex. 11 ....OT 31 M
Ex. 11:10..............OT 30 M
Ex. 12:1-28 ....OT 31 T
Ex. 12:31-42 ....OT 21 T
Ex. 12:38...............OT 38 T
Ex. 13:5 ....OT 40 M

Ex. 13:1-16 ....OT 32 M
Ex. 13:17-22 ....OT 32 T
Ex. 16:9-35 ....OT 32 T
Ex. 17:1-17 .... OT 33 H
Ex. 17:7 .... OT 57 F
Ex. 17:9-13 .... OT 45 H
Ex. 19 ....OT 34 M
Ex. 20:1-21 ....OT 34 T
Ex. 20:23...............OT 36 T
Ex. 20:22-26 .... OT 34 H
Ex. 20:3-6 ....NT 3 T
Ex. 22:6 .... OT 48 H
Ex. 23:16..............NT 44 W
Ex. 24:3 ....OT 36 T
Ex. 25:1-8 ....OT 35 M
Ex. 26 ....OT 36 T
Ex. 27:1-8 .... OT 35 H
Ex. 28:1 ....OT 26 M
Ex. 29 ....OT 36 M
Ex. 30:6-10 ....OT 58 W
Ex. 31:1-14 ....OT 26 T
Ex. 32:1-11 ....OT 37 M
Ex. 32:4 .... OT 61 H
Ex. 33:12-21 ....OT 37 T
Ex. 34:1-16 .... OT 37 H

LEVITICUS

Lv. 9 ....OT 63 T
Lv. 16:2 ....OT 58 W
Lv. 18:3 ....NT 13 M
Lv. 19:18 ....NT 14 T

NUMBERS

Nm. 4:15 .... OT 58 M
Nm. 8:7 .... NT 58 F
Nm. 10:11-28 ...... OT 38 M
Nm. 11:1-3 .... OT 38 M
Nm. 11:4-17 .... OT 38 T
Nm. 11:11 .... OT 38 H
Nm. 11:18-35 ...... OT 38 H
Nm. 11:24-29 ...... OT 39 M
Nm. 12:1 .... OT 39 M
Nm. 12:1-9 .... OT 39 T
Nm. 12:3 .... OT 39 W
Nm. 12:9-16 .... OT 39 H
Nm. 13 .... OT 40 M
Nm. 14:1-10 .... OT 40 T
Nm. 14:10-44 ...... OT 40 H
Nm. 14:20 .... OT 40 W
Nm. 14:45 .... OT 42 M
Nm. 19:18,19 .... NT 58 F
Nm. 20:1-5 .... OT 41 M
Nm. 20:6-9 .... OT 41 T
Nm. 20:10-13 ...... OT 41 H
Nm. 21:1-3 .... OT 42 M
Nm. 21:4-6 .... OT 42 T
Nm. 21:7-9 .... OT 42 H
Nm. 24:15-19 ...... OT 15 F
Nm. 28:26-31 ..... NT 44 W

DEUTERONOMY

Dt. 5:16 .... OT 43 M
Dt. 6:13 .... NT 6 T
Dt. 7:1-5 .... OT 46 M
Dt. 8:3 .... NT 6 M
NT 13 F
Dt. 14:4-20 .... NT 51 M
Dt. 15:15 .... OT 32 W
Dt. 16:6 .... NT 3 M
Dt. 18:15 .... NT 47 W
Dt. 15:15-19 .... OT 24 F
Dt. 21:23 .... NT 37 W
Dt. 28:63-68 .... OT 7 H
Dt. 30:1-5 .... OT 76 H

JOSHUA

Jos. 1:10-2:1 .... OT 43 M
Jos. 2 .... OT 44 H
Jos. 2:23,24 .... OT 43 M
Jos. 2:1-7 .... OT 43 T
Jos. 2:8-21 .... OT 43 H
Jos. 2:21 .... OT 43 W
Jos. 3:15 .... OT 44 M
Jos. 4:15-5:1 .... OT 44 M
Jos. 5 .... OT 44 T
Jos. 5:1 .... OT 45 M
Jos. 5:14 .... OT 44 F
Jos. 6 .... OT 44 H
Jos. 6:23 .... OT 43 W
Jos. 7:1-9 .... OT 45 M
Jos. 7:10-26 .... OT 45 T
Jos. 8:1-29 .... OT 45 H
Jos. 8:30-35 .... OT 45 W

JUDGES

Jgs. 1:1-33 .... OT 46 M
Jgs. 3:9 .... OT 48 M
Jgs. 3:15 .... OT 48 M
Jgs. 6:1-10 .... OT 46 M
Jgs. 6:6 .... OT 48 M
Jgs. 6:11-24 .... OT 46T
OT 46 W
OT 47 W
Jgs. 6:16 .... OT 46 W
Jgs. 6:25-40 .... OT 46 H
Jgs. 7:1-8 .... OT 47 M
Jgs. 7:2 .... OT 47M
Jgs. 7:9-15 .... OT 47 T
Jgs. 16-25 .... OT 47 H
Jgs. 8:22 .... OT 47 H
Jgs. 8:22-35 .... OT 47 W
Jgs. 10:10 .... OT 48 M
Jgs. 13:1-5 .... OT 48 M
Jgs. 13:8-20 .... OT 48 T
Jgs. 13:21-25 .... OT 48 W
Jgs. 13:22 .... OT 48 T
Jgs. 14:1-9 .... OT 48 H
Jgs. 15:15 .... OT 48 H
Jgs. 16:2 .... OT 49 M
Jgs. 16:4-14 .... OT 49 M
Jgs. 16:5 .... OT 49 M
Jgs. 16:15-22 .... OT 49 T
Jgs. 16:17 .... OT 49 M
Jgs. 16:23-31 .... OT 49 H
Jgs. 16:26 .... OT 49 T

RUTH

Ru. 1 ....OT 50 M
Ru. 2 ....OT 50 T
Ru. 3 ....OT 50 T
Ru. 4 ....OT 50 H

1 SAMUEL

1 Sm. 1:1-11 ....OT 51 M
1 Sm. 1:13-23 ....OT 51 T
1 Sm. 1:24-2:11 ... OT 51 H
1 Sm. 1:28............. OT 52 T
1 Sm. 2:9,10.......... NT 21 F
1 Sm. 2:10............. OT 51 F
1 Sm. 2:11............. OT 52 T
1 Sm. 2:12............OT 52 M
1 Sm. 2:18-21 ...... OT 51 H
1 Sm. 2:26............OT 52 W
1 Sm. 2:27-34 ......OT 52 M
1 Sm. 2:35,36.......OT 52 W
1 Sm. 3:1..............OT 52 M
1 Sm. 3:1-14......... OT 52 T
1 Sm. 3:11-21 ...... OT 52 H
1 Sm. 4 ....OT 53 M
1 Sm. 5 ....OT 53 T
1 Sm. 6:1-16 .... OT 53 H
1 Sm. 7:3-11 ....OT 53 W
1 Sm. 8 ....OT 54 M
1 Sm. 8:5..............OT 54 W
1 Sm. 8:8.............. OT 59 F
1 Sm. 8:19............. NT 13 T
1 Sm. 8:20............. OT 57 T

1 Sm. 9:15,16........ OT 54 T
1 Sm. 10................ OT 54 T
1 Sm. 10:1............. OT 54 H
1 Sm. 10:9............ OT 54 H
1 Sm. 10:23........... OT 57 T
1 Sm. 11................ OT 54 H
1 Sm. 12:19-25 .... OT 54 H
1 Sm. 13:1-12......OT 44 M
1 Sm. 13:8-12 ...... OT 58 H
1 Sm. 13:13-15 .....OT 55 T
1 Sm. 14:47,48...... OT 55 T
1 Sm. 15:1-23 ...... OT 55 H
1 Sm. 15:24-28 ....OT 56 M
1 Sm. 16:1-5 .... OT 56 T
1 Sm. 16:6-13 ...... OT 56 H
1 Sm. 16:7............NT 17 M
           NT 31 T
1 Sm. 16:10.......... OT 56 H
1 Sm. 16:14-23 ....OT 57 M
1 Sm. 17:56..........OT 57 M
1 Sm. 17:1-30 ....OT 57 T
1 Sm. 17:31-39 ....OT 57 W
1 Sm. 17:37.......... OT 57 H
1 Sm. 17:40-58 .... OT 57 H
1 Sm. 23:15-29 ..... OT 59 T

2 SAMUEL

2 Sm. 6:1-11 ....OT 58 M
2 Sm. 6:12-15 ....OT 58 T
2 Sm. 6:16-23 ...... OT 58 H
2 Sm. 7:1-17 ....OT 59 M
2 Sm. 12:25..........OT 61 M
2 Sm. 15:10-14 ..... NT 40 F

1 KINGS

1 Kg. 11:1-10.......OT 61 M
1 Kg. 11:14-43......OT 61 T
1 Kg. 11:43-12:30 OT 61 H
1 Kg. 16:29-17:7..OT 62 M
1 Kg. 17:8-16........OT 62 T
1 Kg. 17:17-24..... OT 62 H
1 Kg. 18:1 .... OT 63 H
1 Kg. 18:1-19.......OT 63 M
1 Kg. 18:20-39......OT 63 T
1 Kg. 18:37,38 .....OT 63 W
1 Kg. 18:40-46..... OT 63 H

2 KINGS

2 Kg. 2:1-5...........OT 64 M
2 Kg. 2:6-14.......... OT 64 T
2 Kg. 2:9 .... OT 64 W
2 Kg. 2:13-15 .... OT 64 H
2 Kg. 4:1-7...........OT 65 M
2 Kg. 4:8-17.......... OT 65 T
2 Kg. 4:18-37....... OT 65 H
2 Kg. 5:1-8...........OT 66 M
2 Kg. 5:8-18.......... OT 66 T
2 Kg. 5:19-27....... OT 66 H
2 Kg. 14:24-27.....OT 69 M
2 Kg. 17:1-5.........OT 67 M
2 Kg. 17:7-12........ OT 67 T
2 Kg. 17:13,14 .....OT 67 W
2 Kg. 17:16-20..... OT 67 H
2 Kg. 23:28-24:17 OT 71 M
2 Kg. 24:1-7.........OT 71 M

2 Kg. 25:1 .... OT 71 H
2 Kg. 25:9,10 .... OT 71 H
2 Kg. 25:13-15 ..... OT 71 H

1 CHRONICLES

1 Chr. 15:212-15 .OT 58 M
OT 58 T
1 Chr. 16:1 .... OT 58 H
1 Chr. 22:7-10 ..... OT 60 M
1 Chr. 22:9,10 ...... OT 60 W
1 Chr. 28:1-13 ..... OT 60 M
1 Chr. 28:19 .... OT 60 M
1 Chr. 29:1-22 ...... OT 60 T
1 Chr. 29:14-16 .... OT 60 T

2 CHRONICLES

2 Chr. 7:1 ....OT 06 W
2 Chr. 7:1-6 .... OT 60 H
2 Chr. 22:7 .... OT 68 T
2 Chr. 28:2 ....OT 68 M
2 Chr. 29:1-30 ..... OT 68 M
2 Chr. 30:1-22 ..... OT 68 W
2 Chr. 32:24-31 ...OT 68 M
2 Chr. 33:1-11 ...... OT 68 T
2 Chr. 33:10-25 ... OT 68 H
2 Chr. 34:1-7 ....OT 70 M
2 Chr. 34:8-28 ...... OT 70 T
2 Chr. 35:1-19 ..... OT 70 H
2 Chr. 36:1-16 ...... OT 71 T
2 Chr. 27:17-23 ... OT 71 H

2 Chr. 36:13 .... OT 71 H

EZRA

Ezr. 1 ....OT 76 M
Ezr. 2:64,65 ....OT 76 M
Ezr. 3:1-7 .... OT 76 T
Ezr. 3:8-13 .... OT 76 H
Ezr. 3:12,13 ....OT 76 W
Ezr. 6:13-15 ....OT 77 M
Ezr. 6:16-18 ....OT 77 W
Ezr. 6:19-22 .... OT 77 T
Ezr. 6:22 .... OT 77 M
Ezr. 7 .... OT 77 H

NEHMIAH

Neh. 1 ....OT 78 M
Neh. 1:8 .... OT 78 T
Neh. 1:8,9 .... OT 7 H
Neh. 2 .... OT 78 T
Neh. 3 ....OT 78 W
Neh. 4 .... OT 78 H
Neh. 4:7-9 .... OT 78 T
Neh. 6:16 .... OT 78 H

JOB

Jb. 19:23-27 .... OT 50 F

PSALM

Ps. 1 .... OT 1 F
Ps. 2:1,2 .... OT 4 F
OT 20 F
Ps. 2:2 .... OT 41 F
Ps. 2:6,7 .... OT 5 F
Ps. 2:10-12 .... OT 6 F
Ps. 4:4,5 .... OT 8 F
Ps. 5:11 .... OT 14 F
Ps. 6:1-4 .... OT 9 F
Ps. 7:1-8 .... OT 21 F
Ps. 7:9-11 .... OT 10 F
Ps. 8 .... OT 11 F
Ps. 8:4 .... NT 70 F
Ps. 14:1-7 .... NT 18 F
Ps. 16:8-10 .... OT 37 F
Ps. 18:30 .... OT 33 F
Ps. 19:7-14 .... OT 16 F
Ps. 22:7,8 .... NT 72 F
Ps. 22:14-16 .... NT 62 H
Ps. 22:17,18 .... NT 37 F
Ps. 22:22-31 .... NT 61 F
Ps. 23 .... NT 20 F
Ps. 23:1-3 ....OT 59 M
Ps. 23:4,5 ....OT 59 T
Ps. 23:6 .... OT 59 H
Ps. 25:1-7 .... NT 75 F
Ps. 27:1-4 .... OT 59 H
Ps. 31:5 .... NT 55 F
NT 56 F
Ps. 31:9-6 .... NT 56 F
Ps. 34:8 .... NT 68 F
Ps. 34:19,20 .... NT 39 F
Ps. 35:19,20 .... NT 76 F

𝕯
PROVERBS

𝕴
ISAIAH

Is. 53:3,4 .... NT 38 F
Is. 53:4 .... NT 22 F
Is. 53:5 .... NT 38 F
Is. 53:6 .... NT 64 F
Is. 53:8 .... NT 15 F
Is. 53:9 .... NT 57 F
Is. 53:10 .... NT 59 F
Is. 53:11 .... NT 27 F
　　　　　　　　　NT 35 W
Is. 53:23 ....OT 56 W
Is. 53:7 .... NT 6 H
　　　　　　　　　NT 36 F
Is. 53:12 .... OT 36 F
　　　　　　　　　NT 37 M
Is. 55:1-13.............. NT 13 F
Is. 56:7 .... NT 47 F
Is. 59: 20,21 .... NT 56 F
Is. 60:16 .... NT 60 F
Is. 60:16-20........... OT 60 F
Is. 61:1-3 .... NT 6 F
Is. 62:11,12 .... NT 7 F
Is. 64:6 .... NT 17 T
Is. 65:1,2 .... NT 60 F
Is. 65:25 .... NT 62 H

JEREMIAH

Jer. 7:3 .... OT 71 T
Jer. 9:24-26 .... NT 52 F
Jer. 11:7 .... OT 71 T
Jer. 22:24-26 .... OT 39 F
Jer. 23:5,6 .... OT 17 F

　　　　　　　　　OT 71 T
　　　　　　　　　NT 1 F
Jer. 23:5 .... OT 78 F
Jer. 25:8-12 ....OT 76 M
Jer. 31:31-34 .... OT 34 F
Jer. 32:37-41 .... OT 71 F
Jer. 33:14,15 .... OT 45 F
Jer. 33:15,16 .... OT 78 F
Jer. 33:16 .... OT 46 F
Jer. 33:17 .... OT 74 F
Jer. 33:18 .... OT 48 F
Jer. 34:18 ....OT 9 T

EZEKIEL

Ez. 34:20-24 .... OT 49 F
Ex. 36:23-27 ....OT 56 W
Ex. 27:25-29 .... NT 10F

DANIEL

Dn. 1:1-3 ....OT 71 M
Dn. 1:17-20 ....OT 73 M
Dn. 2:1-16 ....OT 72 M
Dn. 2:17-30 ....OT 72 T
Dn. 2:31-49 .... OT 72 H
Dn. 2:49...............OT 73 M
Dn. 3:1-12 ....OT 73 M
Dn. 3:13-18 .... OT 73 T
Dn. 3:19-30 .... OT 73 H
Dn. 4:3-27 ....OT 74 M
Dn. 4:28-33 .... OT 74 T

Dn. 4:34-37 .... OT 74 H
Dn. 6:1-9 ....OT 75 M
Dn. 6:10-18 .... OT 75 T
Dn. 6:19-28 .... OT 75 H
Dn. 7:9,10............. OT 58 F
Dn. 7:13,14.......... NT 35 H
Dn. 9:24-26 .... OT 41 F

HOSEA

Hos. 2:18-20......... NT 54 F
Hos. 11:1 .... NT 2 H
Hos. 11:1,2 .... NT 2 F
Hos. 13:11 ....OT 54 M
Hos. 13:14 .... NT 28 F

AMOS

Am. 9:11-15 .... NT 19 F

JONAH

Jon. 1:1-6 ....OT 96 M
Jon. 1:7-2:10 .... OT 69 T
Jon. 3:1-4:11 .... OT 69H
Jon. 4:1................OT 69 M
Jon. 4:2................OT 69 M

MICAH

Mi. 5:1,2 .... OT 19 F
Mi. 5:2 .... NT 2 M

NAHUM

Na. 1:6,7 .... OT 12 H

HABAKKUK

Hb.1:5-12 .... OT 65 F

ZEPHANIAH

Zep. 3:14-20 .... OT 44 F
Zep. 12:10 .... NT 43 F

HAGGAI

Hg. 2:2-9 .... OT 76 W
Hg. 2:6-9 .... OT 38 F
Hg. 2:20-23 .... OT 39 F

ZECHARIAH

Zec. 2:10,11 .... OT 40 F
Zec. 3:1-5 .... OT 77 F
Zec. 3:6-10 .... OT 78 F
Zec. 6:12 .... OT 78 F
Zec. 9:9 .... OT 23 F
Zec. 9:10,11 .... NT 44 F
Zec. 11:12,13 .... NT 32 F
Zec. 12:10,11 .... NT 43 F
Zec. 13:1 .... NT 25 F
Zec. 13:7 .... NT 35 F
NT 73 F

MALACHI

Mal. 3:1 .... OT 54 F
Mal. 3:1-4 .... OT 61 F
Mal 3:2-5 .... OT 55 F
Mal. 3:6 .... OT 63 W
Mal. 4:1-4 .... OT 76 F
Mal. 4:4-6 .... OT 64 F
Mal 4:5,6 .... NT 4 T

MATTHEW

Mt. 1: 1-17 .... OT 43 W
Mt. 1: 1,2 .... NT 1 M
Mt. 1: 1-6 .... OT 43 W
Mt. 1: 5,6 .... OT 50 W
Mt. 1: 15-18 .... OT 22 W
Mt. 2: 1-6 .... NT 2 M
Mt. 2: 7-21 .... NT 2 H
Mt. 2: 1-6 .... OT 19 W

Mt. 2: 6 .... OT 19 F
Mt. 2:10,11 .... OT 70 F
Mt. 2: 13-16 .... OT 20 W
Mt. 2: 15 .... NT 2 F
Mt. 3: 1-3 .... NT 4 M
Mt. 3: 4-11 .... NT 4 T
Mt. 3: 17 .... OT 5 F
Mt. 4: 4 .... NT 13 F
Mt. 5: 1-12 .... NT 13 M
Mt. 5: 13-16 .... NT 13 T
Mt. 5: 16 .... NT 15 M
Mt. 5: 17-20 .... OT 70 W
NT 13 W
NT 14 W
Mt. 5: 21-22 .... OT 6 H
Mt. 5: 21-26 .... NT 13 H
.... NT 14 H
Mt. 5: 38-42 .... NT 14 M
Mt. 5: 39 .... NT 14 F
Mt. 5: 43-47 .... NT 14 T
Mt. 5: 44 .... NT 14 W
Mt. 6: 12-14 .... NT 15 W
Mt. 6: 16-18 .... NT 15 H
Mt. 6: 19-24 .... NT 16 M
Mt. 6: 25-32 .... NT 16 T
Mt. 6: 25-34 .... OT 13 M
Mt. 6: 33,34 .... NT 16 H
Mt. 6: 1-4 .... NT 15 M
Mt. 6: 5-13 .... NT 15 T
Mt. 6: 8 .... OT 41 T
Mt. 7: 11 .... NT 15 T
Mt. 7: 15-20 .... NT 17 M
Mt. 7: 21-23 .... NT 17 T
Mt. 7: 24-27 .... NT 17 H
Mt. 8: 14-17 .... NT 22 F
Mt. 8:23-29 .... NT 20 W

Mt. 8:28 .... NT 20 T	Mt. 18:21,22 .... NT 37 W	Mt. 28:16,17 .... NT 42 M
Mt. 9:1-8 .... NT 12 W	Mt. 19:21 .... NT 19 H	Mt. 28:18 .... OT 70 F
Mt. 9:26 .... OT 10 M	Mt. 21:2-6 .... OT 23 F	NT 20 M
Mt. 10:30 .... NT 32 F	Mt. 21:5 .... NT 44 F	Mt. 28:18-20 .... OT 28 H
Mt. 11 .... OT 30 F	Mt. 21:9 .... OT 75 F	Mt. 28:16-20 .... NT 42 W
Mt. 11:7-12 .... NT 4 M	Mt. 21:13 .... NT 48 H	Mt. 28:18 .... OT 70 F
Mt. 11:9-13 .... NT 24 H	Mt. 21:8-32 .... OT 55 W	Mt. 28:19 .... NT 42 T
Mt. 11:13,14 .... OT 64 F	Mt. 21:42 .... OT 72 F	Mt. 28:20 .... NT 42 H
Mt. 11:14 .... OT 64 H	OT 74 F	
NT 4 T	Mt. 23:12 .... NT 68 H	
Mt. 11:28 .... NT 20 H	Mt. 25:31-34 .... OT 52 F	
Mt. 12:18-21 .... OT 12 F	Mt. 26:31 .... NT 73 F	**MARK**
Mt. 12:32 .... NT 70 F	Mt. 26:35 .... NT 39 H	
Mt. 12:39 - 41 ..... OT 69 W	Mt. 26:53 .... NT 6 H	Mk. 1:1-3 .... OT 54 F
Mt. 13:1-3 .... NT 18 M	Mt. 26:56 .... NT 35 W	Mk. 1:23,24 .... NT 17 T
Mt. 13:1-17 .... NT 18 T	Mt. 26:64 .... NT 70 F	Mk. 2:10 .... OT 70 F
Mt. 13:18-23 .... NT 18 H	Mt. 26:69-75 .... NT 21 F	Mk. 3:11 .... NT 8 T
Mt. 13:31-33 .... NT 19 M	NT 36 W	Mk. 6:34 .... NT 21 M
Mt. 13:35 .... NT 19 W	Mt. 27:11 .... OT 47 F	Mk. 6:56 .... NT 22 W
Mt. 13:44 .... NT 19 T	Mt. 27:17-26 .... OT 23 W	Mk. 8:11 .... NT 8 T
Mt. 13:45,46 .... NT 19 H	Mt. 27:27-31 .... NT 38 W	Mk. 9:1-4 .... NT 24 M
Mt. 14:14 .... NT 21 M	Mt. 27:32-44 .... NT 38 T	Mk. 9:-8 .... NT 24 T
Mt. 14:22,23 .... NT 22 M	MT. 27:34 .... NT 67 F	Mk. 9:9,10 .... NT 24 W
Mt. 14:24-31 .... NT 22 T	Mt. 27:35 .... NT 37 W	Mk. 9:9-13 .... NT 24 H
Mt. 14:3 .... NT 22 W	Mt. 27:29-43 .... NT 71 F	Mk. 9:11 .... OT 64 H
Mt. 14:34-36 .... NT 22 H	Mt. 27:39-43 .... NT 8 W	Mk. 9:35 .... NT 33 T
Mt. 15:8,9 .... NT 31 F	Mt. 27:45-61 .... NT 38 H	Mk. 12:10 .... OT 72 F
Mt. 16:8 .... OT 72 W	Mt. 27:48 .... NT 67 F	OT 74 F
Mt. 16:13,14 .... OT 70 F	Mt. 27:49-54 .... OT 63 W	Mk. 12:41-44 .... NT 31 W
Mt. 16:7-19 .... NT 23 M	Mt. 27:50-54 .... OT 35 W	Mk. 14:29 .... NT 36 M
Mt. 16:13 .... OT 70 F	Mt. 27:51 .... NT 39 M	Mk. 14:32-42 .... NT 35 M
Mt. 16:18 .... NT 70 W	Mt. 27:55 .... NT 40 F	Mk. 14:43-50 .... NT 35 T
Mt. 16:21 .... OT 24 F	Mt. 27:57 .... NT 57 F	Mk. 14:53-65 .... NT 35 H
Mt. 17:5 .... NT 24 T	Mt. 27:62-66 .... NT 39 M	Mk. 14:71 .... NT 41 H
Mt. 17:0 .... OT 64 F	Mt. 28:1-10 .... NT 39 T	Mk. 15:24 .... NT 37 F
Mt. 18:20 .... OT 53 W	Mt. 28:11-15 .... NT 39 H	Mk. 15:25-32 .... OT 24 W

JOHN

Jn. 1:8 .... NT 62 M
Jn. 1:14.................. OT 40 F
                          OT 70 W
                          NT 30 F
Jn. 1:21.................. OT 24 F
Jn. 1:29.................. NT 59 F
Jn. 1:35-42 .... NT 11 M
Jn. 1:40-51 .... NT 11 W
Jn. 1:43-51 .... OT 18 W
Jn. 2:1-5 .... NT 7 M
Jn. 2:6-11 .... NT 7 T
Jn. 2:11.................. NT 30 F
Jn. 2:12.................. NT 7 H
Jn. 2:13-17 .... NT 8 M
Jn. 2:17.................. NT 8 F
Jn. 2:18-22 .... NT 8 T
Jn. 2:18-25 .... OT 76 W
Jn. 2:21.................. NT 8 W
Jn. 2:22.................. NT 8 W
Jn. 2:23-25 .... NT 8 H
Jn. 3:1-15 .... NT 9 M
Jn. 3:3 .... NT 73 T
Jn. 3:9-15 .... OT 42 W
Jn. 3:14.................. NT 9 F
Jn. 3:16.................. OT 8 T
                          OT 9 F
                          OT 43 M
                          OT 50 H
                          OT 67 F
                          NT 9 W
                          NT 59 F
Jn. 3:16-18 .... NT 9 T
Jn. 3:18.................. NT 9 W

Jn. 3:19-21 .... NT 9 H
Jn. 3:17.................. OT 9 F
Jn. 3:19.................. NT 9 M
Jn. 4:5 .... OT 22 T
Jn. 4:10.................. NT 78 W
Jn. 4:16.................. NT 50 T
Jn. 4:35.................. OT 18 F
Jn. 5:18.................. OT 37 F
                          NT 31 T
Jn. 5:19.................. NT 2 F
Jn. 6:1-4 .... NT 21 M
Jn. 6:5-13 .... NT 21 T
Jn. 6:14,15............. NT 21 H
Jn. 6:15.................. NT 23 T
Jn. 6:25-40 .... NT 21 W
Jn. 6:15.................. NT 14 M
Jn. 6:31-40 .... OT 33 W
Jn. 6:35.................. NT 13 F
Jn. 6:35-40 .... OT 62 W
Jn. 6:37.................. NT 8 M
Jn. 6:38.................. OT 37 F
Jn. 7:19.................. NT 31 T
Jn. 7:25.................. NT 31 T
Jn. 7:41,42............. OT 19 F
Jn. 8:12.................. OT 29 F
                          NT 9 H
Jn. 8:19.................. OT 39 F
Jn. 8:36.................. OT 30 F
Jn. 8:40.................. NT 31 T
Jn. 9:1-11 .... OT 65 W
Jn. 10:1-3 .... OT 52 F
Jn. 10:1-6 .... NT 26 M
Jn. 10:7-10 .... NT 26 T
Jn. 10:9.................. OT 57 F
Jn. 10:11,12........... NT 26 W
Jn. 10:14,15........... OT 49 F

                          OT 59 W
Jn. 10:17............... NT 28 W
Jn. 10:22-42 .... NT 26 H
Jn. 10:28............... NT 26 F
Jn. 10:30............... OT 39 F
Jn. 11:1-16 .... NT 28 M
Jn. 11:17-24 .... NT 28 T
Jn. 11:25............... NT 28 F
Jn. 11:28-53 .... NT 28 H
Jn. 12:10............... NT 30 T
Jn. 12:12-16 .... NT 30 M
Jn. 12:13............... NT 78 M
Jn. 12:17-19 .... NT 30 T
Jn. 12:20-33 .... NT 30 W
Jn. 12:23-32 .... NT 7 W
Jn. 12:37............... NT 30 F
Jn. 12:37-50 .... NT 30 H
Jn. 12:44-50 .... NT 33 M
Jn. 12:46............... OT 29 F
Jn. 13:1-5 .... NT 33 T
Jn. 13:6-11 .... NT 33 W
Jn. 13:12-17 .... NT 33 H
Jn. 13:18............... NT 35 F
Jn. 14:1-4 .... NT 34 M
Jn. 14:5-27 .... NT 37 T
Jn. 14:6.................. OT 18 W
                          OT 28 F
                          NT 11 F
                          NT 34 W
                          NT 53 F
Jn. 14:12............... NT 46 T
Jn. 14:16............... NT 46 F
Jn. 14:26............... NT 54 W
Jn. 14:27............... NT 42 F
                          NT 44 F
Jn. 14:31............... OT 52 W

Acts 17:31.............. OT 52 F	Rom. 4:11 .... OT 10 H	Rom. 10:5-13........ NT 60 T
Acts 18:24-19:8 ...NT 53 M	Rom. 4:18-25....... NT 59 H	Rom. 10:9 ....OT 32 W
Acts 19:9,10.......... NT 53 T	Rom. 4:18-25......... OT 9 H	OT 77 W
Acts 20:1-6 .... NT 53 H	NT 59 H	NT 75 W
Acts 20:17.............. NT 53 T	Rom. 4: 22 ....NT 59 W	Rom. 10:9,11 ....NT 60 W
Acts 20:17-24......NT 53 W	Rom. 4:22-25......... OT 9 H	Rom. 10:12-23......OT 7 W
Acts 21:27-36 ......NT 61 M	Rom. 4: 23-25......NT 59 W	Rom. 10:13 ....OT 78 M
Acts 22:4-20........NT 50 W	Rom. 5:1 ....OT 63 M	Rom. 10:14-18..... NT 60 H
Acts 23:11.............. NT 61 T	NT 67 W	Rom. 10:17 ..... NT 40 W, H
Acts 23:12,13.......NT 61 M	Rom. 5:8 ....OT 63 M	Rom 10:20............ NT 60 F
Acts 26:28.............. NT 46 F	NT 35 M	Rom. 11:5 .... OT 68 F
Acts 28:11-20......NT 61 M	Rom. 5:8,9 ....NT 38 W	Rom. 11:26 .... NT 51 F
Acts 28:17-23 .... NT 61 T	Rom. 5:10 ....NT 14 W	Rom. 11:26,27 ...... NT 71 F
Acts 28:24-31 ...... NT 61 H	Rom. 5:19 ....NT 68 W	Rom. 15:12 .... NT 29 F
Acts 28:31...........NT 61 W	Rom. 6:3,4 ....NT 42 W	Rom. 21:1 ....OT 4 M
	Rom. 6:4 ....NT 8 W	
	Rom. 6:6 .... OT 25 H	

ⓡ

ROMANS

	Rom. 6:17,18 .... NT 6 F	
	Rom. 8:6-9 .... OT 56 H	ⓒ
	Rom. 8:11 ....NT 8 W	**1 CORINTHIANS**
Rom. 1:1-6 ....OT 8 M	Rom. 8:18-25........ NT 62 T	1 Cor. 1:18 .... OT 28 F
Rom. 1:16 .... NT 40 H	Rom. 8:20-22....... NT 62 H	1 Cor. 1:11,12......NT 54 M
Rom. 1:16,17 ....OT 51 W	Rom. 8:28 .... NT 32 F	1 Cor. 1:27-31 ......MT 52 F
Rom 1:20,21 .... NT 60 T	Rom. 8:34 .... OT 36 H	1 Cor.1:31-31 .... OT 45 F
Rom. 2:29 .... OT 44 T	Rom. 8:35-39........ OT 73 T	1 Cor.1:28-31 ......OT 13 W
Rom. 3: 9-20........NT 58 M	Rom. 8:36 .... NT 66 F	OT 24 H
Rom. 3:10-12........ NT 19 F	Rom. 8:38,39 ....OT 53 W	1 Cor.1:30............. OT 46 F
Rom. 3: 21-24....... NT 58 T	Rom. 9:6-8 .... NT 26 F	1 Cor. 3:1-4 ....NT 54 M
Rom. 3: 25,26 ......NT 58 W	Rom. 9: 7,8 .... NT 59 T	1 Cor.3:10............NT 17 W
Rom. 3: 21,22 ......NT 58 W	Rom. 9:8-15 ....OT 16 W	1 Cor.3:16,17.......OT 60 W
Rom. 3: 27-31...... NT 58 H	OT 21 W	OT 76 W
Rom. 3:24 .... OT 66 F	Rom. 9:15-18.......OT 29 W	1 Cor.3:16-19 ......OT 35 W
Rom. 3:25 .... NT 59 F	Rom. 9:25 ....OT 21 W	1 Cor. 5:1 ....NT 54 M
Rom. 4: 1-8..........NT 59 M	Rom. 9:30-33.......OT 72 W	1 Cor.5:7...............OT 68 W
Rom. 4:3 .... OT 8 H	Rom. 9:33 .... OT 28 F	1 Cor.5:7,8...........OT 31 W
Rom. 4: 9-17......... NT 59 T	Rom. 10:1-4 ....NT 60 M	1 Cor.5:21............. OT 73 F

1 Cor. 6:1-11 .... NT 54 M
1 Cor.6:19,20 .... OT 77 W
1 Cor.10:4 .... OT 33 W
           OT 41 H
1 Cor.10:31 .... OT 4 M
1 Cor. 11:1 .... NT 76 W
1 Cor. 12:1-11 ..... NT 54 H
1 Cor. 12:12-26 .... NT 54 T
1 Cor. 12:27 .... NT 54 W
1 Cor. 12:27-31 ... NT 54 H
1 Cor. 13:1-3 .... NT 50 H
1 Cor. 13:4-7 .... NT 55 T
1 Cor. 13:8-14 ..... NT 55 H
1 Cor. 13:10 .... NT 55 W
1 Cor. 14:1 .... NT 44 H
           NT 54 H
           NT 55 W
1 Cor.14:5 .... NT 44 H
           NT 51 H
1 Cor. 14:26-28 ... NT 54 H
1 Cor.15:3 .... NT 15 F
1 Cor.15:17 .... NT 39 W
1 Cor.15:13,14 ..... NT 39 W
1 Cor.15:20-22 ..... OT 3 W
1 Cor.15:20-23 .... NT 39 W
1 Cor. 15:22-26 .... OT 15 F
1 Cor.15:33 .... OT 12 M
1 Cor.15:45-49 ..... OT 2 W
1 Cor.15:50-56 .... OT 57 W
1 Cor.15:54-56 .... OT 31 W
1 Cor.15:55-58 ..... NT 28 F

2 CORINTHIANS

2 Cor. 1:3-5 .... OT 50 M
2 Cor.1:21,22 .... NT 9 M
2 Cor. 4:4-7 .... NT 16 W
2 Cor. 5:11-15 ..... NT 56 M
2 Cor. 5:16,17 ...... NT 56 T
2 Cor. 5:17-21 ..... NT 56 W
2 Cor. 5:20-6:2 .... NT 56 H
2 Cor.5:21 .... OT 45 W
           NT 64 F
           NT 67 T
2 Cor.6:14 .... OT 61 M
2 Cor.6:16 .... OT 35 W
2 Cor. 9: 1-9 .... NT 57 M
2 Cor.9:8 .... NT 32 F
2 Cor. 9: 10-12 ...... NT 57 T
2 Cor. 9: 13 .... NT 57 W
2 Cor. 9: 8 .... NT 57 W
2 Cor. 9: 14,15 ..... NT 57 H
2 Cor. 16: 1-3 ...... NT 57 M

GALATIANS

Gal.2:3-5 .... NT 52 M
Gal. 3:13 .... OT 32 M
           NT 37 W
Gal. 3:13,14 .... OT 50 W
Gal. 3:16 .... NT 51 F
Gal. 3:19-24 .... OT 34 W
Gal. 3:26-4:7 .... OT 8 W
           OT 9 W
           NT 2 M
Gal. 4:4 .... NT 2 M
Gal. 4:21-31 .... OT 10 M
           OT 13 H

Gal.5:1-15 .... NT 52 M
Gal.5:16-23 .... NT 52 T
Gal. 5:19-26 .... OT 5 M
           OT 22 T
Gal.5:24 .... NT 52 W
Gal.5:25-6:1 .... NT 52 H
Gal. 6:7 .... OT 19 H
Gal. 6:7,8 .... OT 4 T
           OT 30 H
           OT 61 T
Gal. 6:14 .... OT 24 H
           NT 58 H

EPHESIANS

Eph.1:1-6 .... NT 63 M
Eph. 1:3-10 .... NT 63 M
Eph. 1:3-12 .... OT 15 W
Eph. 1:4 .... NT 63 W
Eph. 1:7 .... NT 63 W
Eph. 1:7-11 .... OT 74 W
Eph. 1:7-12 .... NT 63 T
Eph.1:11 .... OT 23 F
Eph.1:11-14 .... OT 53 W
Eph.1:11,12 .... OT 74 W
Eph. 1:13,14 .... NT 63 W
Eph. 1:15-23 .... NT 63 H
Eph. 2:1-3 .... NT 64 M
Eph. 2:3 .... NT 64 F
Eph. 2:4-11 .... NT 64 H
Eph. 2:5 .... NT 64 W
Eph.2:8 .... OT 9 H
Eph.2:8,9 .... NT 9 M
Eph. 2:9 .... NT 71 W
Eph. 2:11-18 .... NT 64 W

Eph. 2:13 .... NT 64 F
Eph.2:19-22 ....OT 77 W
.... NT 27 W
.... NT 64 H
Eph.2:21,22 .... NT 31 H
Eph. 4:1-6 ....NT 65 M
Eph. 4:7-14........... NT 65 T
Eph. 4:8,9 .... NT 65 F
Eph. 4:11 .... NT 65 F
Eph. 4:13 ....NT 65 W
Eph. 4:15,16 ....NT 65 W
Eph. 4:17-19........ NT 65 H
Eph. 4:20-24........NT 66 M
Eph. 4:25-32......... NT 66 T
Eph.4:26................. OT 8 F
Eph. 5:1 ......NT 66 W, H, F
Eph. 5:2-20.......... NT 66 H
Eph.5:18............... NT 44 H
Eph. 6:1-3 ....NT 67 M
Eph. 6:2,3 ....OT 30 M
Eph. 6:10-14......... NT 67 T
Eph. 6:15 ....NT 67 W
Eph. 6:16-20........ NT 67 H

PHILIPPIANS

Phil. 1:12-18........NT 61 W
Phil. 2:1-4............NT 68 M
Phil. 2:1-7............. NT 65 F
Phil. 2:1-11..........OT 39 W
Phil. 2:5-7............. NT 68 T
Phil.2:5-11 ....OT 10 W
.... OT 11 F
Phil.2:6,7 .... NT 20 H

Phil.2:7-10 ....NT 9 M
Phil.2:7,8.............NT 33 W
Phil. 2:8 ....NT 68 W
Phil.2:8-10 ....OT 55 W
Phil. 2:9,10 .... NT 77 H
Phil.2:9-11 ....OT 72 W
.... NT 33 F
.... NT 68 H, F
Phil.2:10 .... NT 24 F
Phil. 3:4b-7..........NT 69 M
Phil. 3:8,9 .... NT 69 T
Phil. 3:10,11 ....NT 69 W
Phil. 3:12-14........ NT 69 H
Phil.4:6 ....NT 7 M

COLOSSIANS

Col. 1:3 ....NT 62 M
Col. 1:6 .... OT 18 F
Col.1:10-14 ....OT 38 W
Col. 1:15 ....NT 34 M
Col. 1:15,16 ....OT 1 W1:16
Col. 1:15-17 ....NT 62 M
Col. 1:16 .... OT 57 F
.... NT 7 T
Col. 1:16,17............ OT 3 F
.... NT 20 M
Col. 1:18,19 .... NT 62 T
Col. 1:19,20...........OT 3 W
.... OT 4 T
Col. 1:20 .... NT 62 H

Col. 1:21-23 ....NT 62 W
Col. 2:15 .... OT 44 F
Col. 3:21................. OT 4 T

2 THESSALONIANS

2 Thes. 1:5-7 .... OT 44 F

1 TIMOTHY

1 Tm. 1: 15........... NT 58 H
1 Tim. 1:15-17.....OT 54 W
1 Tim. 1:17 ....OT 47 W
1 Tim. 2:1-6 ....OT 40 W
1 Tim. 2:5,6 .... NT 47 F
1 Tim. 3:1-7 ....NT 70 M
1 Tim. 3:8-13 ....NT 70 T
1 Tim. 3:14,15 ..... NT 70 H
1 Tim. 3:16 ....NT 70 W
1 Tim. 4:1 .... OT 55 F
1 Tim.6:15.............. OT 6 F

2 TIMOTHY

2 Tim.1:8-10 ....OT 11 W
2 Tim. 1:14.......... NT 71 H
2 Tim. 2:7-10 ......NT 18 W
2 Tim. 3:1-9 ....NT 71 M
2 Tim. 3:10-15...... NT 72 T

1 Pt. 1:10-12.... NT 73 W, F
1 Pt. 1:24,25 ....OT 74 W
1 Pt. 2:3 .... NT 69 F
1 Pt. 2:4 .... NT 23 F
1 Pt. 2:4-9............ OT 74 F
1 Pt. 2:5 .... NT 64 H
1 Pt. 2:5-9............ OT 42 F
1 Pt. 2:6-9............ OT 56 F
1 Pt. 2:7 .... OT 72 F
1 Pt. 2:21-25.......OT 66 W
1 Pt. 2:23,24 ....NT 38 M
1 Pt. 3:20-22.........OT 5 W
1 Pt. 4:16 .... NT 46 F
1 Pt. 5:5 .... OT 74 H
1 Pt. 5:7 ....NT 7 M

ⓓ

2 PETER

2 Pt. 1:20,21 .... NT 71 T
2 Pt. 2:7-9............OT 12 W
2 Pt. 3:10-12......... OT 55 F

ⓙ

1 JOHN

1 Jn. 2:1,2.............NT 49 W
1 Jn. 1:8,9.............. NT 12 T
1 Jn. 1:9.................. NT 9 H
1 Jn. 3:9-12..........NT 76 M
1 Jn. 3:13.............. NT 76 F
1 Jn. 3:13-15 .... NT 76 T
1 Jn. 3:16..............NT 76 W
1 Jn. 3:17-24........ NT 76 H

1 Jn. 4:8-11 ....NT 55 W
1 Jn. 4:10............... OT 67 F
              NT 55 T
1 Jn. 4:19.............NT 68 M
1 Jn. 5:1-5 ....NT 9 W

ⓡ

REVELATION

Rv. 1:5,6................. NT 77 F
Rv. 1:12-14 .... OT 58 F
Rv. 1:16.................OT 31 R
Rb. 5:1-5...............NT 77 M
Rv. 5:5................... OT 13 F
Rv. 5:6-8 .... NT 77 T
Rv. 5:6-14 ....OT 14 W
Rv. 5:9................... OT 40 F
Rv. 5:9-11 ....NT 77 W
Rv. 5:12,13............ NT 49 F
Rv. 5:12-14 .... NT 77 H
Rv. 6:10................. OT 51 F
Rv. 7:9...................NT 78 M
Rv. 7:9,10..............OT 7 W
              NT 78 F
Rv. 7:10-12 .... NT 78 T
Rv. 7:14................... OT 7 F
              NT 78 W
Rv. 7:15-17 .... NT 78 H
Rv. 7:17................. NT 20 F
Rv. 17:14................. OT 6 F
Rv. 13:8................OT 13 W
Rv. 14:6................. OT 53 F
Rv. 17:14................ NT 24 F
Rv. 19:7................. NT 54 F
Rv. 19:11................ NT 45 F

              NT 78 F
Rv. 19:11-16 .... OT 31 F
              OT 44 W
Rv. 19:16................. OT 6 F
Rv. 20:21............... OT 38 F
Rv. 21:3................. OT 40 F
Rv. 21:4................OT 66 W
Rv. 21:4................ OT 62 H
Rv. 21:9-27 .... OT 60 F
Rv. 21:14..............NT 44 M
Rv. 21:16..............OT 35 T
Rv. 21:22..............OT 77 W
              NT 8 T
Rv. 21:23..............NT 24 M
Rv: 21:23,24 .... OT 60 F
Rv: 22:5 .... NT 62 H

About the author...

Marty Machowski currently serves as one of the family life pastors at Covenant Fellowship Church in Glen Mills, Pa. He has been a staff member at the church since 1988. In addition to caring for married couples, Marty oversees Promise Kingdom, Covenant Fellowship's ministry to children, as well as Compass, the church's home-school program. In addition to being the author of *Get Into the Story*, Marty is the author of *God's Story*, a gospel-focused children's ministry curriculum. He resides in West Chester, Pa., with his wife, Lois, and their six children.

Inquires may be directed to
Covenant Fellowship Church
1 Fellowship Drive
Glen Mills, PA 19342
www.covfel.org
www.godsstory.net